120 Seats in a Boiler Room

THE CREATION OF A COURAGEOUS PROFESSIONAL THEATER

Text Copyright © 2022 by Lewis Kempfer

All rights reserved.

No part of this book may be reproduced, scanned, or distributed in any printed or electronic form without permission. Please do not participate in encouraging piracy of copyrighted materials in violations of the author's rights. Purchase only authorized editions.

Published by Vecta Books

This is a work of nonfiction and everything that happened is true. Certain names, locations, and identifying details have been altered for sake of clarity and to honor the privacy of individuals.

ISBN: 979-8-218-04418-3 (paperback)
ISBN: 979-8-218-04419-0 (e-book)

Library of Congress Control Number: 2022913813

www.LewisKempfer.com

Cover Design by Lewis Kempfer
Author Photo by Martin Bentsen, New York City

Printed in the United States of America

First Edition

120 Seats in a Boiler Room

THE CREATION OF A COURAGEOUS PROFESSIONAL THEATER

LEWIS KEMPFER
WITH A FOREWORD BY JAKE CANNON

DEDICATED TO THE MEMORY OF

Dan McGeachy

June 1, 1953–November 6, 2019

May your star be shining as brightly in Heaven
As it did on so many stages on Earth.

ALSO BY THE AUTHOR

Don't Mind Me, I'm Just Having a Bad Life: A Memoir

RECIPIENT OF 7 AWARDS INCLUDING

— 2022 First Place LGBTQ Biography from The BookFest Awards
— 2021 Independent Author Network Book of the Year Award for LGBTQ
— 2021 IndieReader Discovery Award for LGBTQ Non-Fiction
— 2021 Gold Medal from Literary Titan
— 2020 and 2021 Silver Medals from Readers' Favorite International Book Awards

"The writing is fluid and filled with humor, the descriptions allow for clear and powerful images, and the author does an incredible job of exploring the dark despair that stole into his soul many times… Lewis Kempfer's writing is filled with wisdom and insight, a story that is shared with unusual honesty and a voice that is irresistible. There is a bit of every one of us in this memoir and that's what makes it so appealing and enjoyable." — *Readers' Favorite*

"The author shares his storied rough-and-tumble life, and smartly invites the reader into his world via sensory experiences... a fine dramatic opening with feelings of dread. Author handles a time jump to earlier days well, seamlessly carrying continuity to the earlier stage. Well done. All realism is intact... I enjoyed the author's instinct to not over-describe... the author writes such good descriptions concisely that often dialogue is not necessary. Well done. Overall, lots of realism and connection to the author throughout." — *Writer's Digest*

"A brutally honest redemption story about a man's journey from abused and isolated gay boy to highly destructive... addict, *Don't Mind Me, I'm Just Having a Bad Life* is fascinating, disturbing, and ultimately delivers just a touch of hope."— *Indie Reader*

"Such a joy to read Lewis's fluid writing! Wonderful vibrant dialogue and images. His is a vivid and very honest voice. Bravo!"
— Martin Moran, author of *The Tricky Part* and *All the Rage*

"Loved it, Lewis. Gritty, powerful, in-your-face writing. Takes courage to write like this. Well done."
— *Fellow Author, 2021 Page Turner Awards*

"This book drew me in right from the start. First of all, the book cover made me curious, then the title made me intrigued, and lastly, the prologue hooked me to continue reading until there were no pages left. Lewis Kempfer's writing style is simply stunning. It is one of those rare writing styles where even the darkest of moments have a witty undertone and a beautiful simplicity that makes the reading comfortable and fast-paced. I was constantly in suspense after every new scene about how this would contribute to the 'bad life' and it made for a quick read." — *Amazon Reviewer*

CONTENTS

FOREWORD: Jake Cannon - Possibility   1
INTRODUCTION: What If?   9
OVERTURE: The Last Night of the World   17
CHAPTER 1: The Euphoric Catalyst   21
CHAPTER 2: Birds and Biohazards   27
CHAPTER 3: The Infamous LLC   33
CHAPTER 4: Seats and Schedules   41
CHAPTER 5: Five, Six, Seven, Eight   49
CHAPTER 6: Flip This Mess   53

THE INAUGURAL 2001 SEASON—One Sensational Season   59
CHAPTER 7: Opening Day   61
   Hot Tips - Be Prepared   70
CHAPTER 8: Ruthlessly Challenging   73
   Hot Tips - Understanding Understudies   81
BOILER ROOM VOICES: Lauri Dismuke - Forever Grateful   82
CHAPTER 9: What We Did for Love   93
   Hot Tips - Go Big or Go Home   102
BOILER ROOM VOICES: Renée Hatfull Brooks - Added to the Circle   104
CHAPTER 10: Total Chaos   111
   Hot Tips - Know Thy Audience   117

2002 SEASON—Around the World in Seven Plays — 119

CHAPTER 11: Miscarriage — 121

Hot Tips - What's in a Name? — 127

CHAPTER 12: Sometimes You Get Lucky — 129

Hot Tips - Unknown vs Overdone — 137

More Hot Tips - Fun with Accounting — 139

BOILER ROOM VOICES: Patrick Kramer - Worth Fighting For — 141

BOILER ROOM VOICES: Sondra Morton - Once in a Lifetime — 143

CHAPTER 13: Six Degrees of WTF — 147

Hot Tips - Mind Your Media Manners — 151

BOILER ROOM VOICES: Brandy Austin - Bitten — 153

CHAPTER 14: Where the Wind Comes Blowing Up Your Kilt — 157

Hot Tips - Try Something New — 162

CHAPTER 15: Winches and Wenches — 165

Hot Tips - No Unauthorized Gender-Bending — 171

BOILER ROOM VOICES: Pat Street - Bravo, My Friends — 173

CHAPTER 16: Length Matters — 179

Hot Tips - Don't Alienate Subscribers — 182

2003 SEASON—Sentimental Journey — 183

CHAPTER 17: Gamblers and Drunks — 185

CHAPTER 18: And All That Spray Paint — 193

Hot Tips - Stick to the Script, Not The Floor — 202

CHAPTER 19 - Dogs and Cats — 203

Hot Tips - Right Show, Wrong Time — 211

CHAPTER 20: Something Witchy This Way Comes — 213

BOILER ROOM VOICES: Steve Boysen - The End of Innocence — 219

2004 SEASON—Ignite Your Imagination — 225

CHAPTER 21: Let Us Try to Entertain You — 227

CHAPTER 22: A Miracle Should Have Happened — 233
   Hot Tips - Don't Change a Word — 237
BOILER ROOM VOICES: Mark Beall - A Very Bright Light — 238
CHAPTER 23: Just Too Damn Melancholy — 245
CHAPTER 24: So, A Dog and Five Nuns Walk Into a Bar… — 251
CHAPTER 25: Saving the Boiler Room — 257
   Hot Tips - Keep Your Customers — 263
CHAPTER 26: The Best Audition Ever — 265
   Hot Tips - The Occasional Joys of Auditions — 272
CHAPTER 27: The Haunted Lobby — 273
CHAPTER 28: Cutting Edge — 279
BOILER ROOM VOICES: Alan Lee - Lightning in a Bottle — 289
CHAPTER 29: The Most Wonderful Gift of the Year — 293
   Hot Tips - The Christmas Dilemma — 304

2005 SEASON—Classic Tales — 305
CHAPTER 30: The One That They Wanted — 307
   Hot Tips - Not So Magic Changes — 316
CHAPTER 31: Rocket Man — 319
CHAPTER 32: Something Gold, Something New — 323
CHAPTER 33: A Glorious Success and a Well-Kept Secret — 327
   Hot Tips - All Hail the Costumer — 333
CHAPTER 34: Wrangling the Beast — 335
   Hot Tips - Production Budgets — 346
BOILER ROOM VOICES: Lane Wright - Upon a Strong Foundation — 347

2006 SEASON—Your Ticket to Adventure — 353
CHAPTER 35: What Goes? — 355
CHAPTER 36: Dying Swan Song — 359
BOWS: I'm Leaving—I'm Gone — 365

2007 SEASON—Unlock the Magic	**369**
CHAPTER 37: The Last Hurrah	371
EXIT MUSIC: Because We Knew You	379
BOILER ROOM VOICES: David Warfle - Where I Grew Up	386
ENCORE: There's Only This	389
APPENDIX A: Bibliography	391
APPENDIX B: Season Schedules, Benefits, Grants, Awards	397
APPENDIX C: Acknowledgements	407
APPENDIX D: All the BRT People Ever	409
APPENDIX E: Corporate Sponsors and Advertisers	419
ABOUT THE AUTHOR	423

FOREWORD

Possibility

BY JAKE CANNON, AUGUST 2022

I was 5 years old when the Boiler Room Theatre (BRT) opened its doors. It was a professional theater devoted to fresh-from-New-York musicals, original works, and less frequently produced classics. That doesn't sound like the typical after-school hangout, but this place became just that thanks to the youth theater-and-music school known as the Act Too Players. In its early years, Act Too performed at the Boiler Room and was closely linked to the theater's Mainstage season, with young Act Too performers frequently playing the roles of children and teenagers in Boiler Room shows. It was through this connection that I made my professional theater debut.

But first, how did I become interested in theater? And how did I discover the Boiler Room? When I was likely 6 or 7 years old, I experienced my first "local" show one December evening at the Boiler Room. I cannot for the life of me remember the title of the show, but I know it had to do with Christmas and was set in the 1960s. After a little digging, I found out that the show was called *That '60s Christmas Show*, written by co-founders Lewis Kempfer and Jamey Green. I was there to see my parents' friend Melodie Madden Adams perform. Melodie was (and is) married to Matty Adams, one of my Dad's colleagues. My parents have always been casual fans of theater, they always make a point of seeing a play or musical when they are in one of the big "theater towns" such as New York, London, Chicago, D.C., etc., and occasionally attend their local theater. They were happy to have a night out at the theater, and I was eager to tag along. I enjoyed the show and felt proud of myself for getting most of the jokes, which were usually intended for audience members over the age of 7. A few months after that first Boiler Room outing, my family took a trip to New York City to celebrate my cousin's 16th birthday. It was on this trip, sitting in row J of the Majestic Theatre on West 44th Street, that I caught the theater bug, and a spark was ignited inside me that continues to burn brightly to this day.

As the following summer rolled around, I needed something to do. I was a gregarious and energetic elementary schooler with no real talent for sports. A perfect combination. One Sunday morning at church, my friend Tyler Bond mentioned something to me about a "fun and energetic" acting camp in Brentwood. I didn't think much of it at the time; I enjoyed watching other people tell stories on stage, but I had never seriously considered it as something that I could do. I think my Mom was more excited than I was on the first day of the week-long camp. I walked into Act Too's rehearsal studio (located at that time in Brentwood, about 20 minutes from where I lived in Franklin), and found "my tribe." That energy and creativity I had been channeling by distracting other kids in school finally had a place to belong. I finally had a place to belong. Act Too, founded in 2002 by teacher/performer Sondra Morton, has served as a creative and professional springboard for a host of young performers. Many have gone onto careers in performing, writing, directing, technical theater, and teaching.

That first week of summer, theater camp was a whirlwind with 20-some of us kids learning a number of songs and dances as an ensemble, as well as performing scenes in small groups. I learned the basics of acting, learned real choreography for the first time, and sang in a group where I could actually hear my own voice. I was amazed by the talent of the performers around me, many of them my age or younger, who could sing and dance circles around me (sometimes literally).

I was also completely mesmerized by Sondra—our teacher, director, sometimes-choreographer, and music director. Her skills at the piano, as a teacher, and as a performer were an inspiration to me the moment I heard her speak. She continues to inspire me today. The end of the week culminated in an hour-long performance at the Boiler Room Theatre. It felt like a high-pressure situation to me. We were going to speak lines and sing solos completely by ourselves. "Ms. Sondra" wasn't going to be up there to help us to remember our lines, music, or choreography, something she had had to remind us of many times.

While some of the kids around me turned white as a sheet when they were told this, my smile only widened. I couldn't believe it. They were encouraging me to explode with energy on that stage! I could hardly sleep the night before the performance. It was my first time on a "real stage" (not in a church pageant), and I had a tangible responsibility to Sondra and to my fellow campers. I appreciated the trust and the sense of closeness that responsibility brought with it. The performance was magical, a rush of adrenaline mixed with a flurry of emotions. I was definitely hooked.

After two summers spent doing theater and music camps, I enrolled in my first full-length show at Act Too, *101 Dalmatians*. That experience and those that followed proved to be exhilarating, tiresome, effortful, and rewarding. There was nowhere else I wanted to be other than in rehearsals and on stage. More specifically, on the stage of the Boiler Room Theatre.

It was a Saturday morning in the spring of 2007 when Sondra called my house. I was petrified. Had I said something mean about another performer? Did I leave my script at the rehearsal studio? Did I leave my underwear backstage? Was I in serious trouble? Thankfully, she was calling to offer me a role in the upcoming Boiler Room Mainstage professional production of *Assassins*, a dark and edgy musical by Stephen Sondheim and John Weidman. Before my Dad could even finish telling me about the show, I blurted out, "Yes, I want to do it!" Rehearsals began soon after, and I found myself, at 10 years old, surrounded by theater professionals who had been perfecting their craft for 20, 30, or 40 years. I had a lot to learn and not a lot of time to learn it. I came face-to-face with a new breed of performers, directors, music directors, and stage managers for the first time. I soaked it up like an eager sponge.

As a fifth grader, I was overjoyed to be in an "adult" show. While *Assassins* brought many wonderful learning experiences, it also brought challenges. I had to miss birthday parties, church events, neighborhood celebrations, and family gatherings to do the show. We performed Tuesday, Thursday, Friday, Saturday, and Sunday afternoons for five weeks. Not to mention four or five weeks of rehearsal (five nights a week) before opening night. That was a lot of time! I began to realize the commitment and passion that was truly required to work in the theater (or any facet of the entertainment industry). It was not for the faint of heart. I learned more in those two months than I eventually would in several years of college. It was a life-altering experience made possible by Sondra Morton and the Boiler Room Theatre.

After *Assassins*, I appeared in a few more BRT shows over the following years, including *Nuncrackers* and *Fiddler on the Roof*. Whenever I wasn't onstage in a BRT or Act Too show, I was in the audience. I couldn't get enough. No matter the show, I would find a way to see it, multiple times if possible. This duality of my theatrical life, as a frequent performer and an avid audience member, gave me a rare vantage point. I worked alongside Boiler Room professionals regularly, either in a Mainstage show or in their capacity as an instructor or guest artist with

Act Too. I saw how they worked, what they did well, what they didn't do well, and how the collaborative forces behind the Boiler Room continually produced high-quality theater. I also saw many final products. In seeing the same show multiple times, I saw my friends and colleagues triumph and falter on stage. I saw standing ovations, tear-jerking monologues, missed cues, light-board malfunctions, and nights when I was one of ten people watching the show. As an audience member, I adored these performers and creative people. As a performer, I was able to watch their process up close and personal, year after year. This environment taught me more through example than I could ever learn from one instructor or book. I learned the essence of professionalism by growing up at the Boiler Room Theatre.

As the years progressed, so did my interests. At a charity concert held at the Boiler Room, I saw Jamey Green, Boiler Room co-founder and theatrical jack-of-all-trades, play the piano with more energy and joy than I had ever seen in my life. I wanted to do that. I began piano lessons again after a few years off (I had grown tired of playing Baby Mozart arrangements). My passion for music was reignited. I dove into piano lessons with a fervor I never had before. I joined band and choir and made music an important element of my life. Again, the Boiler Room provided opportunities. With my background in performing and love of music, it made sense that I would find my way into music directing. The opportunity first presented itself in the fall of 2012, my sophomore year of high school. My friend Tayler asked me to direct the music at a charity concert at the Boiler Room, not unlike the one that had inspired me to begin seriously studying the piano three years prior. I had almost no clue what I was doing, but there I was: teaching harmony parts and coaching solos to a room of my peers. Once again, kismet. I was hooked. As high school rolled on, performing became less and less of my focus as music directing and playing the piano became more enjoyable and fulfilling. In

Possibility

my junior year of high school, I was generously afforded the opportunity to play piano for my first full-length musical, the school's production of *Footloose*. There is no way I would have been given that chance had it not been for my experiences as a musician and a performer at the Boiler Room.

In my senior year, things came full circle. The Boiler Room was producing *Legally Blonde*, which unfortunately became their final show. Sondra, the person who first put me on the stage of the Boiler Room, was directing, and Jamey, my long-time piano teacher and musical mentor, was music directing. I was asked to play "Keyboard 2" (encompassing all of the synthesizer and non-piano keyboard sounds), an important and exciting task. To play that show, directed by the person who introduced me to musical theater, and conducted by the person who made me love music, still stands as one of the most meaningful moments of my life. I didn't know it then, but that would be the last time I ever worked on a show at the Boiler Room Theatre. As Lewis details later in this book, the Boiler Room met an untimely and unfortunate end at the hands of businesspeople not the tiniest bit concerned with live theater—at least not the Boiler Room Theatre.

For a little over a decade, that small brick building at the edge of The Factory at Franklin was a safe haven for me. That stage, and the people who inhabited it, kept its lights on, built its sets, scooped the popcorn, scrubbed its toilets, and turned on the old heater in the winter, were the ultimate mentors and teachers for me. I looked up to them in every possible way; they represented the culmination of years of study, hard work, determination, and grit. Their talent pushed me to work harder in my theater, dance, and music classes. Their work ethic inspired me to rise above mediocrity and constantly reminded me that I could and should be better tomorrow than I am today. Through all of it: The triumphs on stage, the hours spent practicing a piano piece only to have it fall apart in front of Jamey, the tears when an adult cast member would get angry with "the kids," the countless nights I spent in tech rehearsals and performances, and the magical nights when the Boiler Room whisked me away in a story with heart and humor, that "postage-stamp-sized stage" represented possibility. I felt like every opportunity imaginable was available through the Boiler Room Theatre. To me, that sense of hope and freedom I so badly craved is the ultimate legacy of the Boiler Room and its founders. As I've gone to pursue an undergraduate degree in music and a graduate degree in musical theater music directing, I can say that the one thing that inspired me from the very beginning was the Boiler Room Theatre and the people who provided opportunity there. Regardless of what my future holds, I will always cherish the memory of the Boiler Room, the memory of possibility.

INTRODUCTION

What If?

AUGUST 2022

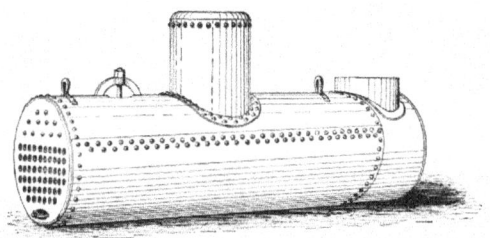

It's been 21 years since the Boiler Room Theatre (BRT) exploded onto the scene, and eight years since it closed forever. This is not a grand, sweeping saga, but it's a good story and one that needs to be told. A story filled with humor and heartbreak, gratitude and grit, and delight and disappointment.

There were infamous moments that some of us will never forget, but a lot of my business partners' memories during the theater's 14-year run have started to fade, are already gone, or have been blocked out. People move on. Other projects and business ventures took over and BRT became a distant memory. For others, it's just too bittersweet and emotional to dig into the memories.

As the theater's archivist and historian, I knew I was the one to tell this story, at least the tale of the first five years or so before I left to work for Disney in California. After all, I'm the guy who's lugged around for two decades six fire safes full of press clippings, photos, blueprints, backup CDs, show DVDs, programs, promotional brochures, and even a few t-shirts.

I moved on from the Boiler Room 11 years ago, and since then, I have hardly been able to bring myself to see a live show or listen to a new Broadway cast album, with the one exception being *Wicked* because I had a couple of dates with the Los Angeles "sit-down" production's company manager and then fell in love with the show. Although my career had jumped to hyperdrive working as an entertainment production manager and occasional producer (and eventually occasional show writer) at Disneyland in Southern California, I had little opportunity to work on the creative or performance side of things, and watching and listening to others doing what deep down I still wanted to do was very painful. You might ask: If it hurt so much to leave the theater I helped create, the theater where I got to play (most of) the roles I wanted, where I directed and produced and designed sets, and made popcorn and cleaned restrooms and created elaborate lobby displays, then why the hell did I leave? It's a difficult question with a complicated answer.

The first musical I immersed myself in when starting this book was *If/Then*. Written by Tom Kitt and Brian Yorkey and starring the legendary Idina Menzel, the show has a gorgeous score, but a plot that's hard to follow, which is probably why it didn't achieve greater success on Broadway. It's the type of show I would have fought hard to stage at BRT, but which ultimately may have only played to 12 people per night. Basically, the main character Elizabeth is shown living two different lives upon moving back to New York City—as Liz, who finds romance; and as Beth, who enjoys a successful career—each based on seemingly small, yet life-altering decisions. Just as the main character sings in the opening number, I've spent most of my adult life asking, "What if?"

I had two windows of opportunity to take the grand plunge and move to New York City to pursue my dream of singing on Broadway. The first time was in 1986 when I was 20. I had just met my now-mentor of 36 years, Martin Moran, a boy-next-door kind of guy from Denver who had just landed his first role—a starring role—on Broadway in *Big River*. We had one magical hour of conversation in the parking lot of a long-since-gone gay dance club in Denver. He encouraged me to come to NYC and said he would help open doors where and if he could. He even offered a patch of floor to sleep on in the large SoHo warehouse loft where he lived with several other up-and-coming actors. But I had no money, frequently tripped over my uncoordinated feet in dance auditions, and had zero confidence. His opening night closely coincided with one of mine. I was playing the leading role of Prince Charming in Rodgers and Hammerstein's *Cinderella* in east Denver, which seemed to underscore that I should have gone to New York, but at the time I was a no-self-esteem chicken.

In 1987, after a disappointing year of performing local dinner theater, on a whim, I moved to Phoenix, with no plans, no job, and no real clue why I was moving. I had a friend who'd moved to Phoenix, and I fell in love with the palm trees and the therapeutic heat on a quick visit between shows at Ye Olde Wayside Inn Dinner Theatre (YOWIDT) in Berthoud, Colorado. After a sour parting of the ways with YOWIDT, I swore off ever doing theater again. I would instead pursue a steady, and as my Dad said, honorable career as a fast-food restaurant manager. Hell, I wasn't qualified to do anything else. But that didn't last. When the theater bug came back to bite (as that particular bug always does), I started doing as many shows as my work schedule as a glorious second assistant manager at McDonald's would allow.

I've always believed that one simple, small decision can change the entire course of a person's life. It could be answering the phone, or talking to a stranger, having a date with the wrong person, or buying a vintage cookie jar off eBay that's been accidentally stuffed with cash. OK, OK, so the latter has never happened to me. Dang it.

But my life did change one night in 1992. I had gone alone to Marshall's, the largest country dance club at that time in the Phoenix area. I knew the band's lead singer, Julie, and she publicly goaded me to get onstage and sing. A couple of Garth Brooks songs later, I was forming my own country group and taking over Julie's former spot as the house band at a tiny country dive bar.

Had I not got onstage that night, I probably wouldn't have had the dream of becoming a country singer nor the opportunity to move to Nashville which arose when I spoke to Marty Roe of Diamond Rio in between sets after opening for his then-chart-topping group. He referred me to a development person at a record label, and three months later I was living in Music City. Had those events not occurred, I wouldn't have been a founding partner of the Boiler Room Theatre and would never have amassed the vast body of theatrical design work I needed to grab Disney's attention.

The point of *If/Then* is that once a person makes a particular choice, all other choices disappear. And *then*, they ask themselves that infuriating question: *What if?*

The next opportunity to move to NYC came in 1997. I was still living in Nashville, doing shows after my never-was-meant-to-be-a-country-singer career hit the skids. Then a production team of auditioners from the Broadway show *Rent* came to town to cast one of the national touring companies. They were ready to offer me the understudy for leads Mark and Roger (while playing ensemble roles). But I didn't know the show, only that it was a rock opera, and it had something to do with AIDS and intravenous drug use. Rock operas weren't my thing. I felt I was too squeaky clean (at that time anyway) to be in such an edgy show. But

Mark would have been an ideal role for me. Fortunately, I did have money from a long-term consulting gig as a graphic designer. I could have taken the tour and made a new home in the city I've loved since the first moment I ever set foot there. But I was still a no-guts chicken. It flabbergasts me that I moved to Phoenix without the slightest goal, but couldn't do the same with New York. *What if I can't get work after touring? What if I can't find a place to live? What if…*

So, the chicken that I was stayed in Nashville and went on to play a slew of great roles in numerous shows. Soon, I met the man who would become my close friend, vocal coach, co-writer of shows, and business partner. One of our first collaborations was recording a five-song studio demo of musical-theater material. With this calling card, I put feelers out to regional theaters, and to my great surprise, received some amazing offers. But still, I was afraid. By then I had a house and a mortgage. I had bills. And a lot of excuses.

Now, I can't claim that if I'd left Nashville that that man, Jamey Green, wouldn't have started his third theater company without me. But he's not sure he would have. If he had, we both agree it would have been quite different without me. The decision I made to join him in the venture was probably the single biggest decision that changed my life.

This book began purely as a memoir, the second in a trilogy of memoirs. But unlike my first memoir, *Don't Mind Me, I'm Just Having a Bad Life,* which covered at least 40 years of my life, this book is a close look, a deep dive into a little more than five years of the most important and most intense years of my life. It occurs during those 40 years, but in the first book I barely touched on it. This period was marked by the triumphs and challenges of following a pipe dream with some folks for whom I care deeply, and the sobering realities of entrepreneurship in a difficult industry. It's not a business-school how-to manual, nor is it a how-to-open-a-regional-theater guide, although some good information might certainly be gleaned from it.

And it's no longer just a memoir. I don't even know how to classify it. Quasi-memoir? Semi-memoir? *Memoiresque* history of a theater company?

As I was posting on Facebook about this project, people who had worked at the Boiler Room started to come forward with their own stories about their time there. Stories of what the theater meant to them or how it had changed the entire trajectory of their lives and careers. I knew those stories needed to be told. And I knew the book had become bigger than my own memories. I asked those same people, folks who had served as actors, choreographers, and technicians, if they'd be willing to write a guest chapter. Happily, they obliged.

The main thing I need to be clear about is that the main narrative of the book—how the theater was founded and the events that occurred—are from my perspective. They're my memories. My former business partners may have different memories of certain things, or as I've mentioned, no memories at all. With some exceptions, most dialogue is approximate. Some lines are infamous and known by many. But most of the dialogue was private and is how I remember things being said. I've run a lot of those conversations by my founding partners and their response was basically, "Your guess is as good as mine, but yeah, we said those things, maybe just in other words." It's just part of how a memoir is written.

This book tells the story of how the "scrappy little theater that could" was born and stumbled and survived through its first five years and the many triumphs, tragedies, and lessons learned. It's the story of how an intimate professional theater changed my life, and just so happened to touch the lives of hundreds of others: From people who'd never been on stage, to old pros who had performed on Broadway and television; from young adults in the children's program growing into fine, seasoned performers, to cast members who would go on to star on Broadway and television.

Although BRT lost its namesake performance space in 2014, the Boiler Room Theatre still, in 2022, has a fiercely loyal fan base, and remains cherished by the legion of actors, singers, and dancers who graced its stage, the pros who ran its lights and sound, built its sets, played in its bands, served as directors, producers, costumers, choreographers, stage managers, house managers, and box office staff, and the many thousands of guests who made it all possible.

But more than anything, this book tells a story that has been aching to be told. It's not the complete history of the Boiler Room, nor does it attempt to be. This is my story of chasing my passion and pouring heart, soul, and savings into a little brick building in Franklin, Tennessee.

It's the story of what happened when four founding partners dared to ask the question, "What if?"

"I'm always so incredibly proud of what we did.
It lives in many who we touched, trained, and empowered.
It won't soon be forgotten."
Jamey Green, Founding Partner and Artistic Director

"It was the craziest, most messed up, tiring,
exasperating, magical, and wonderful time I can remember."
Corbin Green, Founding Partner and Technical Director

"It was the hardest, most rewarding thing I have ever done.
As the youngest co-founder I did a lot of failing, learning, and growing.
I am in awe of the talent we got to work with,
and I am fiercely proud of what we created."
*Teresa Howell-Southworth, Founding Partner
and Resident Stage Manager*

OVERTURE

The Last Night of the World

JULY 2006

I woke up drenched in sweat and knew something was wrong. My thermometer provided a clue: I had a fever of 102. My furniture and boxes of belongings were long gone on a Russian-owned moving-company truck and there was a good chance I'd never see any of my stuff again.

I'd sold my house to a couple from the theater and I was spending my final night on the cold, hardwood floor of the front bedroom of a house that had been both a frequent joy and a constant frustration.

I had partially fulfilled a longstanding dream of working for Disney.

Just hours before, on the night of July 6, 2006, I'd sat in the lower house, seventh row, center seat, in the empty, silent Boiler Room Theatre as I watched memories play out on a mostly bare stage, a flip-book of sorts of the dizzying previous five-plus years. I stared catatonically until my sight was blurred from tears and cigarette smoke.

I took a last climb to my meticulously organized prop shop above the backstage dressing rooms and surveyed the inventory: A vintage turquoise record player from *Grease*; a tray of well-dented metal steins from *Man of La Mancha* and *Disney's Beauty and the Beast*; a painted barber sign from

The Last Night of the World

Sweeney Todd. I ran my hands over the items tenderly, saying goodbye to just a few of my old friends.

I crawled up to my lobby display area above the guest restrooms and secured décor and wires. I'd left the theater company a non-themed display of props and set pieces, each one representing a piece of my heart and a cache of my memories. A display with bursts of light peeking through the spindles of an antique gate, shadows creeping gently around a stack of vintage suitcases, and a mini spotlight on a large backdrop from *Godspell*. It was my final inspection to ensure I was leaving the Boiler Room as poised as possible for success.

As I drove back to Inglewood in upper East Nashville, my mind flipped over the same worries. The overpowering fear that I had really screwed up. The cold realization that there was no turning back. The house was sold, my stuff bound for Moscow, and my position as Managing Director at BRT relinquished to two successors. I couldn't undo one bit of it. Jamey had made that clear. Once I closed the door behind me, there was no option to return.

I had already packed the 1997 red Ford Escort gifted to me by a theater friend with my most precious belongings: my infamous collection of Annette Funicello records; the leather jacket I'd worn in shows; the Titanic-era ankle boots that I wore for special occasions, and the tan dance shoes I wore in the finale of *A Chorus Line*; my computer and all of its peripherals; VHS tapes and DVDs and programs from the shows I'd done both before and after my country music career; my vintage Disneyland souvenir collection; and the entirety of the archives of the Boiler Room Theatre. I stuffed Buzz, my then-beloved pug, into a sliver of the passenger seat, then squeezed myself behind the wheel. Provisions were strategically placed: The Hostess chocolate-frosted *Donettes* that were my go-to food under stress, four hard packs of Marlboro Lights, and a small cooler filled with a six-pack of Diet Coke.

Only an hour west of Nashville, I was nauseated and pouring sweat. I should not have been embarking on a cross-country drive to California that day. But I felt I had to race to get to Pasadena before the movers arrived (turns out there was no worry there; it took three weeks before the "Moose and Squirrel" moving truck arrived). Plus, there was no place to which to return.

So I forged ahead...

...until I could no longer drive. My fever had hit 104, so I grabbed a room in Butthole, Oklahoma. Alright, that wasn't the town's name, but the motel room smelled like one. I stayed there for 24 hours. At some point, I called Jamey and told him, "Tell the avenging angels to back off." He still doesn't know what I meant. I don't know what I meant. I hadn't even read the Book of Revelation from the Bible yet (that would come, but not for several years). He concluded I was hallucinating. I concluded I was dying.

I blamed my illness on the incredible stress and lack of sleep in the weeks leading up to the trip. I would later learn something far more sinister was devouring my body, but that was covered in my first book.

With some foresight and a highly creative self-promotion campaign, I'd garnered enough interviews to warrant a trip to California in June 2006. Although I didn't leave with a job offer, I left with enough confidence that I would find work, or it would find me, if I were to relocate. It was an enormous risk selling a house and heading back west. If only I'd had the courage to move to NYC in 1986 or 1997, I'd have different stories to tell.

CHAPTER 1

The Euphoric Catalyst

1999-2000

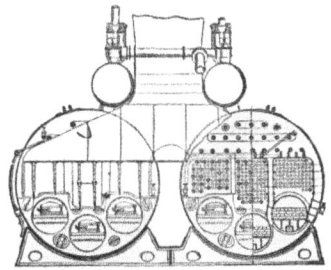

To tell the story of the Boiler Room Theatre, I must take you back to April-something 2000, the closing night of a twice-extended run of a great song-cycle musical called *Personals*. Another fledgling theater company in which I was involved had run *Personals* to sold-out performances for more than three months at a Belmont University-adjacent coffee joint, Bongo Java, in its tiny upstairs cabaret. It was the second of the only two shows the company called Euphoria! The Theatre had mounted.

In early 1999, Jamey (one of the future co-founders of the Boiler Room) hooked up with a philanthropic actor named Tobias who wanted to start a theater company. Jamey had already been at the helm of the wildly successful Avante Garage! (AG!) and was eager to start another theater and become Euphoria's artistic and musical director. I had been pulled in to handle promotions and graphic design since that was my field of expertise.

But Tobias didn't want anything steady. He had money and just wanted to give creating a theater a shot. Either Rosewater had been financially disappointing or simply not the experience he had hoped for. Jamey talked to him several times, but Tobias had moved on to different projects.

The previous year, we produced the obscure Howard Ashman-Alan Menken musical *God Bless You, Mr. Rosewater*, a show so obscure that its licensing company, Samuel French, wasn't even sure if a score existed. Finally, one was located.

During that first Euphoria! production, a core group of us formed and were eager to do another show. We thought since we had already built out the interior of a former retail storefront that had been an art gallery with seating risers, rigging for lighting, and a small stage, that all we needed to do was choose the next show. *Rosewater* was a quirky-yet-courageous choice that was well-received by critics and audiences. But Tobias couldn't make a decision, the rental term was up, and everything got squirreled away in his garage. Jamey and I talked with Toby about planning a season and finding a space of our own. I stressed repeatedly to Tobias that it would be difficult for a nomad theater company to build an audience without its own performance space and schedule of shows. But he had no intention of doing another show for a while. The "a while" turned out to be nearly a year.

So, we did the one show in May 1999 and teased a mini season in the program. Jamey, his brother Corbin Green, who is an amazing technical director, Teressa Howell-Southworth, a top-notch production stage manager, and I were gung-ho to get the next show into production. Unfortunately, Tobias snapped the purse shut and said he had no interest in doing another show anytime soon. The four of us briefly went our separate ways, although Jamey and I were constantly working together on several projects including writing and recording nine songs for a musical stage adaptation of a classic film. I sang at his wedding in October 1999, and he sang at mine in December of the same year.

It was also in late December when Toby decided he was ready to mount another show. He didn't know what show, only that it had to be small enough to fit in Bongo Java's upstairs 60-seat cabaret. I had a knack for finding shows and pitched *Personals* (written by the two show-runners for TV's *Friends*). It hit the mark and we started casting. Daniel Vincent, the late Dan McGeachy, and I were the guys. Cela Scott, Julie Durbin, and Nora Cherry were the gals. Lisa Gillespie, who I'd known since before *Rosewater,* deftly choreographed some clever bits to fit the tiny stage. It was a smart show with timely humor and songs written by a dozen or so famous composers, from Alan Menken to Stephen Schwartz. It got rave reviews.

Toby's absence from the production sat comfortably with the natural stewardship of the company that Jamey and I shared. I had such passion and protection for the little show that in an argument with the owner of Bongo Java's upstairs space about oversized prop storage, I yelled in his face, "Just whose f-cking theater is this anyway?" Well, technically it was his. At least the venue. It became of many infamous Lewis quotes.

Parallel to the success of the production was my faux-marriage, which was short-lived and nearly killed me. I spent every night for two weeks drowning my sorrow in Bud Light and bourbon on Jamey's front porch. It was there that Jamey confided in me that he really wanted to start a theater in a permanent location and offer full seasons. He wanted me to be a co-founder and do all the marketing, publicity, and graphic design, my then-career. I told Jamey I still wanted to perform.

He said, "Sure."

I said, "OK."

The Euphoric Catalyst

I really had no concept of what we were about to do. Years later, he confessed that he also pulled me in because I needed a major distraction to save me from myself, financial destruction, and the suicidal spiral in which I was spinning.

That's when the four of us broke away from Tobias. Of course, there are funny stories about both of Euphoria's two shows, but that's not relevant for this book. The main takeaway was the four folks who wanted to do more.

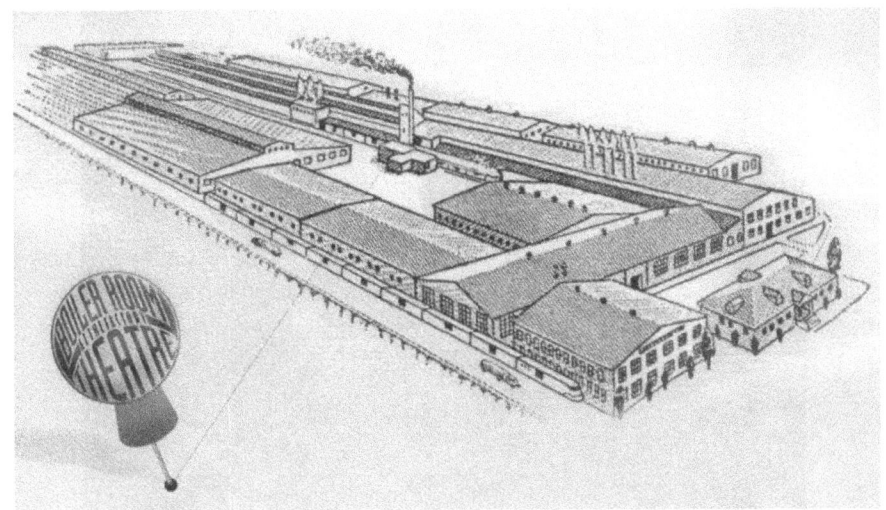

Vintage illustration of The Factory complex, circa mid-1930s. Shows location of the theater.

Co-founders (left to right) Lewis Kempfer and Jamey Green enjoy a cigarette during one of the many walk-throughs during renovations.

Our first look at the boiler room building.
Entrance to eventual lobby at center.

An original boiler door that inspired
the Boiler Room Theatre logo.

CHAPTER 2

Birds and Biohazards

JULY TO SEPTEMBER 2000

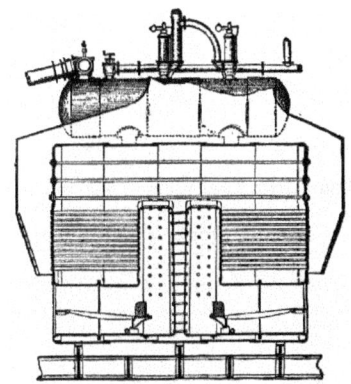

When we announced our new endeavor to our circle of friends, we were reminded constantly that 90 percent of restaurants close after their first year. I asked what the statistics were for theaters and usually received a blank look followed by, "Well, I don't know, but I'm sure it's much worse. You shouldn't try doing this."

Nevertheless, in July 2000, Jamey and I started scouting performance spaces. We didn't want another retail storefront with impossibly low ceilings and no acoustics. We didn't want a church basement, and we didn't want to share a space. This narrowed our options quite a bit. Jamey was adamant about the theater being in his hometown of Franklin, within the borders of wealthy Williamson County. I was concerned people from

Nashville proper wouldn't make the extra 20-minute drive south to see a show. I also insisted the theater had to be professional; Franklin already had in Pull-Tight Players, a well-loved community troupe.

Turns out, Williamson County was hungry for professional theater that veered away from overdone musicals like *Oklahoma!* and mindless Neil Simon comedies. Preliminary surveys and impromptu interviews revealed that people wanted to see new shows along with less-frequently produced classics. That model worked for me, but not so much for Jamey. He really only wanted to do edgy, unknown stuff. I insisted that edgy, unknown stuff wouldn't pay the bills.

But first, a space.

We looked at a few different locations including a storefront on Main Street, part of an old bank, and the second level of an antique store. The bank had promise but would have been enormously expensive to convert. We even thought about the storefront in downtown Nashville in which we had mounted *Rosewater*. And for about 30 seconds, the idea of creating a dinner theater was discussed. The startup costs would be exorbitant.

Then we found The Factory at Franklin. It was one of the first old-warehouse-turned-entertainment-and-dining destinations from when the fad was taking off across the country. The Factory had been open a year, maybe longer, and its owner wanted live entertainment to go with its eclectic shops and two restaurants. The then-owner, Calvin LeHew, had a space in mind: Building 6, a dilapidated brick building that was once the actual boiler room for the factory. Originally a bustling, sprawling industrial complex built in the 1920s, the factory had been the home of Dortch Stoveworks, Magic Chef ovens in the 1950s, and finally the Jamison Mattress company. Sometime in the 1980s, the factory complex was abandoned and fell into horrible disrepair and a homeless and a large pigeon population had both nested in the once-gleaming factory. Yet there remained in all the buildings charming remnants of industrial gear, a testament to its former life. Building 6 was no different.

Present on the first walk-through were Jamey, Calvin, and me. What we saw was jarring and overwhelming. The interior was a devastating disaster. A thick coating of pigeon poop covered the floor. An obnoxious metal support was precisely in the middle of the space—not exactly what one wants in a performance venue. A smaller boiler blocked a third of the interior. A crumbling brick half-wall held back decades-old hay and coal in a lean-to-like side room. Supposedly, the hay had something to do with the boiler functions. Someone said they burned it, while someone else said it was for emergency use to put out a fire. Hay seemed an odd choice to extinguish a blaze. In any case, the hay smelled like the 80-year-old rotting hay that it was.

The sight in the back left corner that would become upper house right (in theater-speak, left and right orientation in the seating area is always from the audience's perspective, much like stage left and right are from the actor's on-stage perspective) was vomit-worthy. A lone, exposed toilet coated with caked-on filthy nastiness sat menacingly in the corner. No doubt the homeless who had encamped in the building used it, but it had long since lost any plumbing functionality. It was thoroughly disgusting. We left knowing the monthly rent would be $3,000. That was a lot of money for a broken-down, biohazard of a building.

My first impression was that the building would not make a good theater and we needed to continue our search. That is, until I got home, and as is typical for me, creative, brainstorm-induced insomnia gripped me. I started to envision a theater inside that mess. The next morning I called Jamey and said we needed to take another look.

Lisa, the eventual grand dame of the Boiler Room, accompanied us. Her initial reaction was summed up in two words rendered with a thick Southern accent: "Oh, my." Still, she bravely picked her way around the space. I had warned her to not wear open-toed shoes. Her stomach churned from the stink of the long-since rotted hay, shards of coal, piles of pigeon poop, and disgusting clumps of homeless people's feces. Partial sunlight poured through the filthy, broken windows 20 feet above our heads illuminating the insidious yellow dust in the air. It couldn't have been safe to breathe.

Lisa shared some of her earliest memories of the Boiler Room. "The first time we walked through the space, my first thought was that Jamey, Corbin, and Lewis had lost their minds. My second thought was that we should have been wearing HAZMAT suits because we were going to catch some horrible, bird-poop Ebola virus by simply trudging through it. Then there was the ginormous boiler in the back—our namesake. Talk about taking a leap of faith and having a vision—whew. It still blows my mind that everything came together."

Corbin joined us on the second walk-through. This time we took measurements and discussed where a stage could be located. Building 6 was longer than it was wide which offered two options. Either we could orient the stage horizontally, spanning some portion of the length of the building with folding, moveable bleacher seating making it a flex space, or we could place the stage at one end of the building with a more traditional seating layout. I hadn't shared it with my soon-to-be partners, but I knew deep in my gut that *A Chorus Line* had to be in the first season. More on that soon. So I was looking at things in more than one way.

Lease negotiations were unpleasant at best.

The Factory would clean the debris out of the space, remove the small boiler and support post, and run standard electrical wiring and provide a standard breaker panel, the same as they would have done for any of its retail, storefront tenants. They would also create an opening into the hay-and-coal room that would become the lobby and do an exterior entrance treatment with brick. It sounds like a lot, but really, they were only willing to invest just above the bare minimum because the owner had never imagined it being anything more than a boutique.

We told them that theatrical lighting required much more power than a standard business. They said the additional power panel expansion would be up to us.

We said we needed restrooms in the lobby and one backstage. Again Factory management shrugged saying, "Your guests can walk next door to Building 11 to use the facilities," Calvin cooed back in his thick Tennessee drawl. He was such a Southern gentleman that you'd rarely hear him say a possibly offensive word such as "restrooms." We knew that would turn a 15-minute intermission into a 30-minute one which was not acceptable with live theater.

We weren't even going to get the attached, rear metal building that could house the dressing rooms, costume shop, set and prop storage, and cast restroom because that's where Calvin parked his tractor. The metal addition was a nightmare in and of itself. A massive, locomotive-sized boiler took up three quarters of the space. Still, the space remaining could be of vital use we explained. Calvin said he'd "throw it in" for an extra $500 per month. Such a deal.

"Is there any way the boiler can be removed?" Corbin asked.

"Not for less than half a million bucks," Calvin answered.

"Why so much?" I asked.

"Well," Calvin said in his thick Southern drawl, "It's full of asbestos." Oh, just that?

It would require a major environmental hazard cleanup project to get rid of it. But he assured us that the asbestos was sealed inside the boiler. Never mind that yellow dust falling off it.

After Calvin left us, we discussed.

"If we can't have the back building, we will be severely limited to shows like *Personals*," I said. "Without it, there's no backstage."

"Yeah, but the rent is already high as it is," Jamey said.

"We'll have to find a way to absorb the extra cost. Hell, I don't even know if we can cover the main building's rent."

"No harm in trying," Jamey responded.

It was clear that The Factory at Franklin wanted us there as the sole entertainment tenant, but the owners were not willing to invest in our success. To them, we were an unknown entity and the only modifications they would make would need to be suitable for renting the space for retail.

The project manager in me could hear the cost driving upward like the clackity-clack of the number tiles flipping over inside a 1970s gas pump.

CHAPTER 3

The Infamous LLC

OCTOBER 2000

After the fourth and final walk-through, we gathered outside to discuss our options where the Green brothers and I lit up our cigarettes and Teressa batted the smoke away from her as if she was being attacked by an angry wasp.

"So what do guys think?" I asked.

"We'll have to put in our own guest restrooms. That won't be cheap unless I can do it myself, which I probably can," Corbin said.

"I like the idea of a flex space that can be rearranged for different shows," Jamey said.

"Really? That seems so Circle Players," I said. Circle Players was a decades-old Nashville community theater that, in 2000, was producing its shows in the basement theater, the Johnson Theatre, of the Tennessee Performing Arts Center downtown. I'd done two shows there. The theater was a black box with the type of rolling, stowaway bleachers that were mentioned on one of our walk-throughs. To me, it never felt like a real theater. I felt the same way about the former art gallery with Euphoria! The Theatre.

"I know you guys will probably shoot this down, but I want to do *A Chorus Line* in the first season. It's rarely produced, so it's not like doing *Fiddler on the Roof* but it has big-time name recognition and could really drive advance season ticket sales. I think it checks most of your boxes, Jamey. I know it's not an obscure *Rosewater*-like show or an original, but…"

"No, no, it's an intriguing idea. I need to give that some thought. That would support orienting in a horizontal flex-space, though," Jamey said. "Do you think we could find the dancers?"

"Do you think it would fit in here?" Corbin asked.

"I grew up in Colorado, where Boulder's Dinner Theatre did a two-year run of the show. I saw it probably five times. Their stage isn't huge. I think they cut the line down from 18 to 16. We could do that. Plus it would save two paychecks every week," I explained. "We could fit it on a permanent stage at the end of the building and do a traditional theater setup."

"Have we decided to go professional?" Teressa asked. "Holy crap! It's cold in here," she said kicking some pigeon poop away from her.

"It would differentiate us from Pull-Tight, which would be a plus. But we can't go Equity, could never afford that," Jamey answered. Equity referred to the Equity Actors' Association, the union for professional actors from regional to Broadway.

"I think they require showers to be installed," I said like I was a union expert.

"That's BS. Tennessee is a right-to-work state. We can be professional and non-Equity," Corbin wisely explained.

"Calvin wants to see a business plan before finalizing any lease," Jamey said.

"Sounds like we need a meeting. And not in this disaster zone," I said.

Thursday evening of that week we gathered in Jamey and his then-wife Laura's duplex living room in the 100 Oaks area. It was the two of them, myself, Teressa, and Corbin's wife Letitia. I don't remember Corbin being there. I'd bought an easel with a chart pad, being the ever-mindful marketing guy.

I should mention there was a fifth, original founding partner named Samantha who had been in *Rosewater*. She supposedly had connections that could get us start-up funds and sponsors, but she ultimately didn't deliver. She bailed shortly after January 2001 anyway. The only real contribution she made was loaning us a rolling pallet of blue-plastic-and-flimsy-metal folding chairs she'd commandeered from Belmont University where she was a student and Laura was head of the theater program. The chairs were for our yet-to-be-scheduled season auditions. Samantha was unable to attend the first and most crucial meeting. The chairs were never returned. They ended up being used backstage and I spotted one in BRT's 2010 production of *Rent*. They probably ended up in renovation debris a few years later. Nevertheless, since Samantha left so hastily, we never included her when we spoke of the LLC.

Letitia led us through a ticket-pricing plan and came up with the idea of Two-for-One-Tuesdays. That idea ultimately was a winner, albeit doubled-edged. The deal attracted guests in droves, but we always lost money. Still, I viewed it as a marketing expense. We laid out a typical weekly performance schedule: Tuesday, Thursday, Friday, and Saturday nights plus a Sunday matinee. That's how we built our weekly schedule to get us started. We quickly learned that Two-for-Tuesdays hurt Thursday night attendance. We often cancelled Thursday shows or tried to sway season ticket holders to attend on that unpopular night but our efforts were rarely successful. Over the years, we tried offering slightly discounted tickets on "Thrifty Thursdays," but that rarely worked because it was too close to the weekend when people typically went out. Letitia's work gave me what I needed to create season-ticket pricing.

"Don't we need a name for the theater?" Teressa asked.

We all looked at each other, dumbfounded that we had skipped the most basic element. Names were bandied about.

"What about calling it the Green Family Theater since it's mostly us Greens," Letitia said. At that time, Letitia was married to Corbin, and with Laura married to Jamey, I was sitting in a room full of folks with the surname Green.

Teressa and I exchanged hurt looks. "Umm, it's not just Greens," she said.

"And wouldn't it make it sound like the family was green?" I added, not yielding as much as a chuckle. "Like the theater was from Mars? You know, green people? No? Never mind."

"It could be the Avante Garage Two! or something like that," Jamey said, "Although I don't know how Michael and Joe would feel." Michael Bouson, Joe Cornell, and Kathy Shepard were his AG! business partners.

"How about the Vibe Theatre?" Teressa offered.

"Sounds like vibrator, like an adult bookstore," I replied.

"The Franklin Theatre?" Laura suggested.

"That's the name of the old movie house on Main," Jamey said.

"Oh, right."

"The Williamson County Theatre or Performing Arts Center," someone offered.

"Too broad," I said. "And way too large a scope for the tiny building."

It seemed everyone had at least a few names in their back pocket, but none seemed right. Franklin Repertory Theater? It was promising, but I pointed out its acronym would be FRT which looked a lot like fart.

I had long been a student of Walt Disney and his Imagineers' stellar placemaking and theming. "It used to be the Factory's boiler room. We should embrace its heritage and history. The Boiler Room Theatre," I said.

At that moment the heavens opened and an angelic choir sang a magnificent chord.

OK, not really. But the name garnered "oohs" and "yeahs."

"The Boiler Room Theatre," Jamey said with a smile. "I like it. It works."

I had just named a theater.

We spoke about the business plan that I would write. That inevitably led to a serious discussion about liability should we not be able to fulfill the lease and leave a lot of debt on the table. We all agreed the theater needed to be a non-profit in order to apply for grants, but that process could take months to complete, and we'd lose the space if we waited. We had thrown a dart at the wall and it landed on a March opening, if all went according to an aggressive schedule with renovations and our build-out of the space. Being early October, it seemed a long way off, that is, until I built a project schedule. Then, to some of my cohorts, a May or June opening looked better. I reminded the group that we would be on the hook for rent as soon as we signed the lease, depending, of course, on how Calvin structured it. We were adamant that we should not be charged rent on an uninhabitable space. The Factory agreed with our logic.

"We can go into this as an LLC, that is, a limited liability corporation," Jamey announced. He had prior knowledge of types of business structures, probably due to his Avante Garage! days.

"What does that mean?" I asked.

"Basically it covers our collective asses should we not be successful. We wouldn't be personally liable for unpaid rent, utilities, and other debts. The company—the LLC—would be the responsible entity, and it would just go bankrupt," Jamey explained.

The Infamous LLC

It was decided that Jamey, Teressa, Corbin, Samantha, and I would be the five LLC partners. We met a week later at an accountant's office and inked the deal. I already had a good portion of the business plan drafted.

There was no turning back.

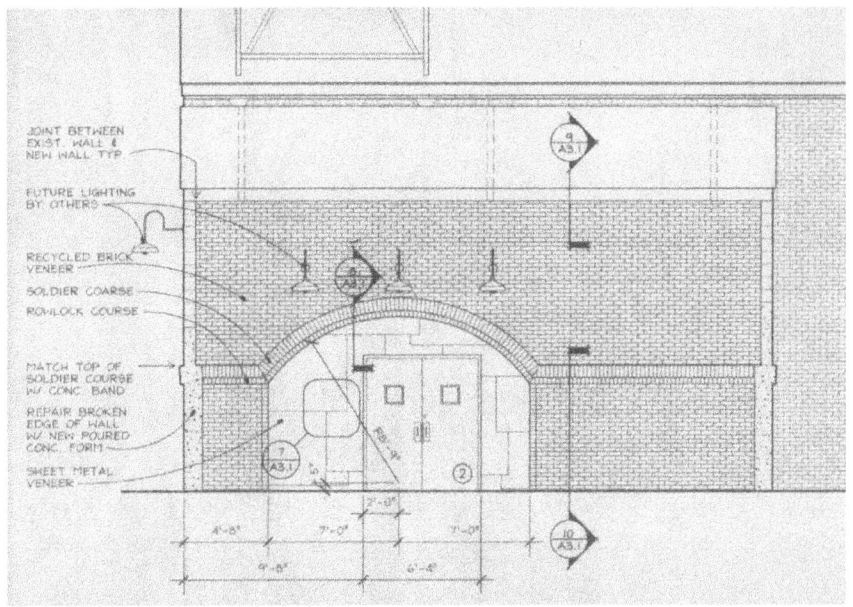

Architect plan for theater entrance.

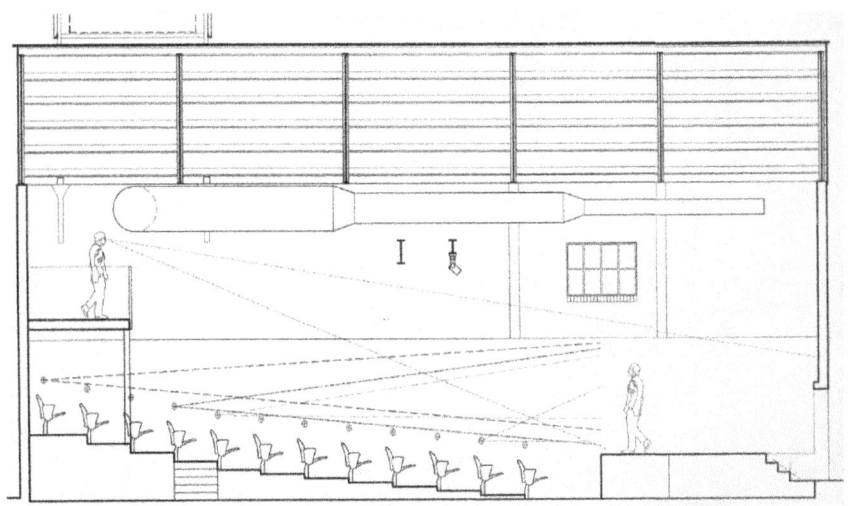

Architect plan for theater interior, side view.

CHAPTER 4

Seats and Schedules

OCTOBER 2000

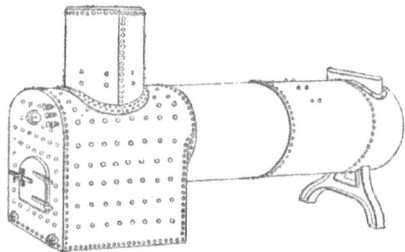

With the LLC formed and our business plan complete, Jamey, Corbin, and I met with Calvin and signed a two-year lease, the start date contingent upon the completion of basic renovations. With that behind us, we did another walk-through of the space. Two years was a scary amount of time, but we had the LLC to fall back on if we failed.

I had been inspired by Walt Disney and his brilliant theming since my first trip to Disneyland when I was 7 years old. I came home and built my own Haunted Mansion in the backyard out of two refrigerator boxes, masking tape, magic markers, and some threadbare towels as ratty drapes. It was the new attraction in my backyard theme park, Kempferland, which offered a two-hole miniature golf course, a petting zoo with my turtle, and the all-new, crawl-through Haunted Cardboard Mansion. I charged ten cents for admission and my only paying guest was my Mom.

She wouldn't crawl through the haunted boxes or touch the turtle, so I can't claim she got her money's worth.

And so with BRT, I wanted a totally themed, branded, and cohesive theater product. I wanted every possible industrial detail to be preserved, which exactly matched Calvin's vision, who had behind his desk a large framed photo of Walt Disney. I asked if the smallest boiler, the one that had to be removed from the brick building, could be moved outside and mounted on a monument slab to serve as signage. Calvin loved the idea. I asked that the sliding doors on the north side of the building remain, albeit bolted open. And I asked for the boiler door with the Springfield Boilers logo in what would become the upper house to remain as a sort of Easter egg for vigilant guests. That 80-some-year-old design served as my inspiration for the BRT logo.

"Where will people enter?" Jamey asked. There was a large parking lot immediately north of the building.

"It would make the most sense for our guests to enter from the north side," I added. "But what do we do with the hay room?"

"Your guests will need to enter through that side of the building. That little area can be your lobby," Calvin said.

"So guests will park over here," I said, indicating the north lot. "But have to walk to the other side to enter? It will be confusing." Despite my signage, it always proved confusing for guests to find the front door. It wasn't *that* hard, but people rarely read signs.

By this point, we'd decided to build a permanent stage and have a dozen or more rows of traditional theater seating. We considered a center aisle to make the length of each row shorter and easier to navigate but it didn't work for emergency egress. A center aisle also would have lowered seating capacity. The flex space idea had died with the cost of the bleachers and the overall awkwardness of it. With that being the case, the only logical placement for a lobby was the hay room. The stage size would be a little under 28 feet wide and 16 feet deep with no wing space.

"Now hang on a minute," Corbin said. "If we can rake the seating bank at a steep pitch, we could have a box office under the seating and people could come in here, closer."

"What about latecomers?" I asked. "They would flood the house with light interrupting a show. And we can't make them wait outside if it's cold."

So the hay-and-coal room, that odd little lean-to side of the building, would become the box office, lobby, guest restrooms, and eventually the concessions counter. That was a tall order for the little space, and while we made it work, it often proved less than ideal but ended up meeting our needs in a smaller way than we would have liked.

The steep grade of the seating bank would be problematic in that it would reduce seating capacity and leave no place for a tech booth. A balcony was discussed, then abandoned. So with a traditional theatrical seating plan with a gentle slope of the seats, more akin to the orchestra section of a large Broadway house, Corbin, knowing architectural standards, assessed the space could accommodate 122 seats. That is, until we realized we needed a clear spot in the front row for a guest using a wheelchair. That took us down to the magical number of 120 seats. Actually, there was nothing magical about the number; it just became so engrained in all our heads. But it also put us in a higher and more expensive tier that ultimately prevented us from becoming an Equity theater. In that case, to keep costs down, seating would have to be below 99 seats. And have showers. Still, it really wasn't a big deal as there were few Equity actors in Nashville.

Boiler Room Theatre interior on its last day in January 2014. Photo by Rick Malkin.

Just as we were wondering how we could afford real theater seats—I insisted on no folding or banquet chairs—Calvin let us know he could obtain approximately 140 seats from a local synagogue. They were vintage, which fit the look of the space perfectly. And since the upholstery was burgundy, that became our signature color, along with *A Chorus Line* champagne-gold, and black.

The most uncomfortable conversation came next: We had to plan the first season of shows. This was the fun part—to an extent. But when you get a room full of creative people together to pick shows, it can become contentious. Season planning occurred in Jamey's living room. This time it was Jamey and Laura, Corbin, and me. Teressa may have been there; Samantha was not. I knew it would be a long, difficult night.

It was October 2000, and we were stuck between a rock and a little brick building. If we waited to lease the building, we risked losing it. If we leased it too soon and opened too late, we'd be saddled with paying rent on an empty building.

We stuck with the slated March opening which put our season on a calendar-year basis rather than a typical fall-to-spring theatrical schedule. A few other theaters did the calendar-year plan too, so it was no big deal. Plus, it gave me a marketing point: That we were a year-round professional theater.

Everyone had come prepared to some degree, and I, being the most anal, had everything short of a PowerPoint presentation. I was dead-set on two shows: *I Love You, You're Perfect, Now Change* (ILY) to serve as the opener, a four-person, song-cycle show in a similar vein as *Personals*; and a summer run of *A Chorus Line* (ACL). I had both shows set in my mind before we had finalized if we would be professional or community. But I knew that Music Theatre International was only granting rights to ILY to professional companies. I'd seen the show live in Denver the previous Christmas. It was smart, hilarious, and only required a cast of

Seats and Schedules

four (who would race through some 17 characters and costume changes each in a dizzying, delightful show). I played highlights from the cast album and insisted it be our opening production. We would be the regional premiere (or at least the Tennessee premiere), it was largely unknown, recent, and best yet, the score was written only for piano and one violin. That one was the easy sell. I had laid out a draft of a production schedule for 2001 and had ILY slated for a ten-week run. It was a bold move, but I was sure it would be a hit. My partners were wary of a run of that duration, but saw the benefits of not having to build a set one month after opening. The show played to packed houses for most of the performances, except those problematic Thursdays.

Many shows were suggested for the second slot. Corbin wanted to do *Noises Off*. Over time, it became a running joke because he would suggest *Noises Off* in every year's season-planning session. It took until 2013, but Corbin finally got his show. It was shot down for the inaugural season because we weren't sure of the stage logistics in real use, and the play required the set to revolve 180 degrees for the second act. Other shows were pitched. Jamey's go-to was typically *Who's Afraid of Virginia Woolf*. Teressa, admittedly, didn't know a lot of shows and was "fine with whatever." For the second slot, I suggested a campy, Off-Broadway musical called *Ruthless!*, in which the leading role was written to be played by a man in drag. And I had my eye on the role.

But my big pitch was *A Chorus Line*. I knew with everything inside of me we absolutely had to do the show. I rehashed my story of seeing it on stage in Colorado.

"Yes, it's a big cast, but we've already determined we can fit a line of 16 dancers across the stage. I already have the two character cuts figured out." I was on fire with my pitch. "It requires virtually no set other than some mirrors and a set piece for the finale. It hasn't been done in Nashville for ten years. It's a big-name show, but it's not *Oklahoma!* or

Fiddler. You-know-who might want to choreograph, even though she hasn't seen the space yet. She's cautiously confident we can find the dancers. But she's not locked in yet. Pam Atha is a strong contender. If we pull it off—and I know we can—it will officially put us on the map. And I promise it will drive advance season-ticket sales. And I really want to direct it."

"Sounds like you have a true vision, so I'm OK with it," Jamey said, who by that point had been dubbed the Artistic Director. "But aren't the rights expensive?"

"They're not cheap, but no more expensive than most other shows," I responded.

Laura wanted one straight (nonmusical) play and pitched *A Girl's Guide to Chaos*, a sort of *Sex and the City*-type show with a small cast. We put it in the season without reading the script. You'll soon see why that was a terrible move.

Finally, everyone except me wanted *The 1940s Radio Hour* for the Christmas show. I didn't know it, wasn't impressed with the show concept, and ultimately didn't care. I thought we should have done *Meet Me in St. Louis*, but that was immediately quashed. No biggie, I thought. I knew what would put us on the map and was prepared to fall on my *A Chorus Line* sword as many times as necessary.

Immediately after designing the logo and getting my founding partners' approval, I designed the first season brochure. It was truly amazing how the pieces fit together. I was still working as a graphic designer and copywriter for a direct-mail company, and although I'd only been there a year, I had learned a lot about successful direct-mail sales campaigns. With my boss Holly Hines giving valuable feedback, the season-ticket brochure with its ACL cover art and tag line "One Sensational Season" was mailed to a list of 1,000 Williamson County residents in the main 37064 ZIP code and stuffed into 2,500 copies of a

Sunday edition of *The Tennessean*, Nashville's one daily paper. It wasn't a lot of exposure, but it was what we could afford.

That first brochure introduced local residents to "Williamson County's First Professional Theatre" and featured a stylized photo of *A Chorus Line* dancers in the gold finale costumes. I was truly blown away by the response. Every time I went to our post-office box, it was stuffed with orders for season tickets. It was thrilling, flattering, and humbling that I had created a brochure that ultimately yielded $80,000—an 800-percent return on investment (ROI). That represented a whole bunch of folks who had put their faith in an unknown entity. Between the season-ticket money and the sponsorship contributions, we just barely had enough to build out the theater's interior, finishing the transformation from a trash-and pigeon-poop-filled building into a 120-seat venue that was oozing character and rustic charm. The building was not only part of our brand—it was our namesake.

I firmly believe that the inclusion of *A Chorus Line* as our major, big-name anchor was the reason we were able to open. It had been a decade since anyone had produced the show and learning we were doing it got people excited, particularly when they visited The Factory and peeked into the space. "They're going to do *A Chorus Line* in there? This I've got to see," or a version of that statement, was something I overheard numerous times.

CHAPTER 5

Five, Six, Seven, Eight

NOVEMBER 2000

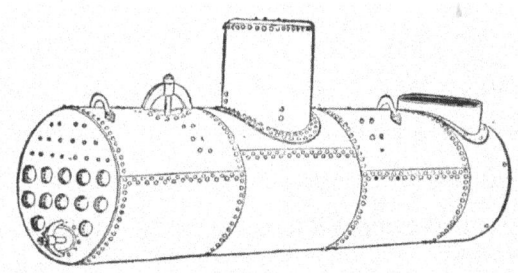

With the inaugural season set, we needed to not only generate interest and buzz within the theater community, but we also needed to make sure we could get the dancers for ACL. The latter was the main reason we held the general season auditions in November 2000. Interest was overwhelmingly positive, and we saw approximately 200 people over two days.

At this point, the fledgling theater company had no income and no funds; we all pitched in what we could. I suppose we could have held auditions somewhere in Nashville such as at Hume-Fogg High School where we would eventually hold offsite rehearsals. But it felt right to do them at The Factory, if for no other reason than to give the actors a sense of the distance to Franklin from downtown Nashville. We asked Calvin if there was a space within the complex where we could hold auditions. He was happy to help and offered a large, unfinished space at the far back end of Building 12 which was attached to the fully operational Building 11 that housed shops and eateries.

It was a mind-numbingly cold November day when we hauled in 12 sheets of luan wood to make a dance floor on top of the decades-old concrete. Corbin had the wood and a pair of industrial floor lights. Jamey set up a keyboard. We borrowed some folding tables from The Factory to pair with the blue Belmont chairs.

The far back corner of The Factory smelled like decomposing wood and dead rats. The floor was filthy and the concrete uneven. Teressa and I swept it twice and used a shop vac, but fine particles of dirt still hung in the air and stuck inside my nostrils where they mingled with half-frozen snot and burned the back of my throat. I wondered just what was in that dirt, especially after Teressa and I had climbed a ladder to the partial second floor to explore like a couple of kid sleuths, and afterward both of us blew nasty brownish-red snot from our noses. Although the four of us—technically five—had signed our names to a two-year lease, it still felt silly and fun and adventurous as well as unreal and surreal at the same time.

Scheduled audition times fell behind quickly as actors tried to find our space, our 30-degree corner of biohazard nastiness. We'd asked actors to prepare the requisite 32 bars of both an uptempo song and a ballad as well as two contrasting two-minute monologues. I was never a fan of the audition monologue. I hated doing them, and even more so, I really hated listening to them. And frequently, actors just pulled random monologues from audition books. The monologue showed me nothing helpful whatsoever. The only exception was Paul's monologue from ACL, but that was only required during callbacks a few months later, although a couple of guys attempted its climax at the preliminary auditions. An actor had to nail that approximately eight-minute-long and ultimately emotionally wrenching piece for a real shot at the role.

Teressa was trying to churn out enough coffee and hot tea to keep us warm, which we gladly shared with the auditionees.

"This is an impossible space," the choreographer complained. "It's too f-cking cold for dancers."

"Correction," I said. "It's too f-cking cold for anyone."

One of us called Calvin and pleaded our case: We needed a warm space ASAP. We had too many actors and dancers coming to make them suffer the dirty, frozen tundra of the back of Building 12. Calvin sent his general manager, Rod Pewitt, to help. His team helped move our ramshackle operation to an empty storefront inside the finished portion of the main building, Building 11. It, too, was far from ideal. It was a cramped space and barely large enough to accommodate our folding tables and allow space for dancing. But it was toasty warm. Too warm. Those waiting to audition had to wait outside in the commons area. With its all-glass storefront, our little event was starting to draw a lot of onlookers. It felt wrong for potential audience members to see the auditions. I know it made many of the actors nervous. While there was nothing to cover the windows with, the marketing part of my thawed brain figured it would boost awareness of BRT.

"Jesus," the choreographer said. "This is just as bad. Oh, sure it's warm, but there's absolutely no room to dance. But I suppose, having seen the tiny stage you're forcing me to put this on, I guess it's appropriate. This is the best you could do? This whole day is a major embarrassment. So unprofessional."

"Then leave," I said. "No one's forcing you to do anything. Pam Atha was our first choice anyway."

"No, I'm sorry. I want to do this. It's just going to be harder than I thought."

"Well turning an ancient boiler-room building into a theater isn't exactly a cakewalk," I said.

Five, Six, Seven, Eight

It was only the beginning of the choreographer's running rant about putting *A Chorus Line* on a stage "the size of a postage stamp," and how stupid I was to do that. I bluffed, hoping the choreographer would stay long enough to at least run the dance auditions. If she had walked out, I'm not sure what we would have done. She wanted to play the starring role of Cassie, but we were hesitant about production-team members taking starring roles. As the years progressed, we mostly adhered to that rule.

The back of the retail space had a premium view of the renovation of the boiler room building. Corbin, his dad (the late Jim Green), and David Suggs were using a backhoe to excavate down through eight feet of concrete and frozen mud to tie into the main sewer line so our lobby restrooms could be built. At one point, Corbin stopped by, he was covered in mud and frozen muck. I felt awful that he was doing that disgusting work in the cold as we watched groups of dancers perform the "One" choreography.

The auditions drew many familiar faces and a lot of new ones. As we expected, male dancers were hard to find, but we had nearly all the guys I needed for ACL.

At the end of the first day of auditions, I called a fantastic dancer named Lauri Dismuke née Bright.

"Hi Lauri. This is Lewis from the Boiler Room. I'm calling to offer you a part in *A Chorus Line*. I'm not sure which role yet, possibly Kristine. But block out next summer because you're in the show," I said.

Lauri was ecstatic and surprised, and in tears. "Of course, I accept. I'm so honored to get to do the show I've always dreamed of doing."

She was the first person ever cast at the Boiler Room Theatre.

CHAPTER 6

Flip This Mess

JANUARY TO FEBRUARY 2001

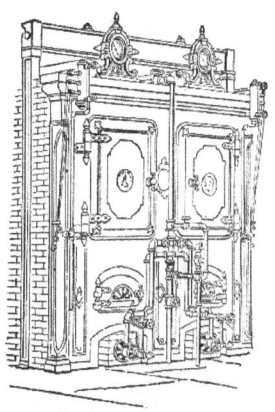

Launching a theater company is rarely an easy feat. Often, however, the fledgling theater might be taking over a space already outfitted for the purpose of live entertainment, and frequently, there is either a rich benefactor or grant money with which to work. Rarely is the task as Herculean as raising the money while building out a venue from scratch, all within a four-month period.

Renovations were underway in January 2001, but The Factory was slow doing their part, which delayed our progress. We had committed to a March 16, 2001 opening and wouldn't let anything change that. But we had so much to do: building a stage and the seating banks, installing aircraft cable for rigging lighting and audio components, painting literally everything black, and figuring out how to make the backstage building somewhat livable. Our seats from the synagogue had arrived and were in that filthy part of Building 12 where we attempted auditions. We covered them with tarps to avoid cleaning the upholstery.

Meantime, rehearsals were beginning for *I Love You, You're Perfect, Now Change* a few blocks away at Historic Franklin Presbyterian Church. The cast included me, Lisa, Paul Cox, and Cathy Motley-Fitch. Paul and Cathy came to the season auditions. Although I'd played some good roles around town, I couldn't get cast with Tennessee Repertory Theatre or Chaffin's Barn Dinner Theatre. I've always sucked at auditions. Always. I almost felt guilty, like I was creating a theater just so I could play roles I wanted.

For the opening production, Jamey was at the helm as director and musical director, Teressa was the production stage manager, and Lisa and I did props and costumes. We had a ten-week run scheduled, and for that many shows, we all agreed we needed swings (understudies), one male and one female to cover the four roles. I recommended Lisa Marie Smith, with whom I'd done *Little Shop of Horrors* in Woodbury, an ungodly long drive from Nashville out to the sticks.

"You're probably not going to want to hear this, but the guy who makes sense and has the range to cover both you and Paul is Daniel. Plus he can be the assistant stage manager (ASM)," Jamey said.

"I know you're right. It's just that the hurt is still fresh from him breaking his commitment," I said. Daniel was the guy I "married" in 2000.

"He's really the only guy who makes sense. Can you work with him and not let emotions get in the way?"

"I think so. Yeah, I mean, yes, I can. It makes the most sense. Who's going to call him?"

"You can or I can. It depends on how comfortable you are making that call."

"Well, I already called him after the general auditions telling him I wanted him for *A Chorus Line,* so what's one more call? I'll do it."

Fortunately for BRT, Daniel was available. I always felt he needed to be a part of the Boiler Room and he became another pillar, working many seasons for us. Teressa decided she needed to be in the booth to call the show. That meant an ASM was required backstage, in addition to a running crew and dressers to assist with some 68 costume changes among the four actors. Thankfully, we had Daniel, who could multitask as well as I could.

The Factory finally cleared the heavy equipment out of the main building allowing Corbin to get in and start installing the lighting rails. And the Martins—the lights from hell. Someone or some theater company unloaded those behemoth lighting instruments on us for the "bargain" price of $2,000. Their function was intended as programmable, moving lighting instruments. But they were just big, heavy, and completely useless. Sure, they looked impressive, but for whatever reason—possibly the heat 30 feet above the seating—they refused to work. They looked like heavy military artillery, as if they would launch bombs at the stage at any given moment. They were bombs alright. They ultimately cost us a much-needed chunk of our scarce startup money. In future seasons, we tried to unload them on a couple of theater companies, and finally in 2005, Corbin sold them to one of the local university theater programs for half of what we paid for them.

"Lee Co. employees work on the heating and cooling system for the Boiler Room Theatre." *The Tennessean Williamson A.M.* March 11, 2001.

Jamey and Corbin's mother Barbara and brother David worked tirelessly trying to enlist corporate sponsors. By this point Samantha was gone. She didn't bring any funding to BRT, and after I'd unofficially selected a different actress to play Val in *A Chorus Line*, she bailed.

We ended up with a mixed bag of season and show sponsors. The Franklin Marriott was solid name clout, but all they did was commit to buying a block of discounted tickets per season for around $2,500. Two sponsors who were with us from Day One until the truly bitter end—Mallory Station Storage and Discount Plumbing & Electric—were in-kind sponsors, meaning they gave us free storage space, and free plumbing and electrical parts respectively in exchange for advertising. Moody's Tire & Auto Service gave us a few bucks and got advertising on all our promotional materials and playbills. Crystal Springs (water) provided a cooler and free jugs of filtered water. We also had a restaurant and a pest-control company donate some cash. One of the most useful sponsorships was from Harpeth True Value Hardware, which had a lumberyard in addition to the materials Corbin needed for rigging. The Lee Company, The Factory's HVAC vendor, installed the heating and cooling system in the boiler building and signed on as a show sponsor for ACL. By no one's fault, sponsorships weren't as lucrative as we needed them to be. The real boon was the money generated via the season ticket campaign. I've always said it, and will continue to say it: *A Chorus Line* saved our butts and enabled us to open the doors.

And those of us who could—namely me—chipped in. By the beginning of ACL, I had emptied a large chunk of my $15,000 life savings into the brick building.

The days were ticking away as we waited impatiently for the Lee Company to finish their installation. The *Franklin Review Appeal* newspaper ran a full-page feature on our progress (or lack thereof) one week prior to opening day, including a photo of the HVAC techs and giant ductwork. Until they finished, we couldn't build the seating. It was a dizzying race against the clock and many nails were chewed to the quick.

We did all we could. We worked alongside the contractors building the stage, painting all the 20-feet-high windows black, painting the lobby and restrooms, and loading in the audio mixing board and an already outdated IBM 286 PC Corbin got for free to run lighting software. To my knowledge, that same PC programmed and ran the lighting for the entire life of the theater. As soon as we had clearance, one of the battalions from the larger brigade of volunteers came in and built the seating banks and installed the seats in a little more than a day. We had to cut corners with the railings in the house (I wanted elegant brass pipe but got two-by-fours), and the front of the tech booth (I wanted at least a luan wood covering but got black fabric). The $3,000 worth of black stage drapes that flanked three sides of the stage for "black box" shows went in the day before we opened.

And Letitia taught me about a fabulous, brand-new floor care product called Swiffer.

But chaos had yet to erupt.

THE INAUGURAL 2001 SEASON

One Sensational Season

I Love You, You're Perfect, Now Change
Ruthless! The Musical
A Chorus Line
A Girl's Guide to Chaos
The 1940s Radio Hour

CHAPTER 7

Opening Day

MARCH 16, 2001

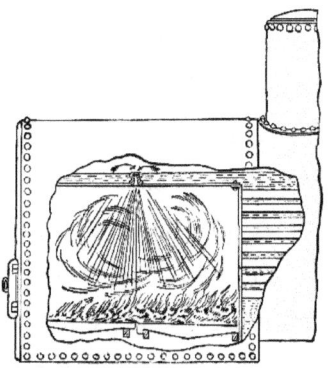

We left the theater around two a.m. on Thursday morning, March 15, 2001. Teressa had painted the stage with three coats of black paint while I was frantically vacuuming the upholstery of 120 seats. And for the last week prior to opening, Corbin had worked around the clock rigging and programming lighting while juggling a dozen other tasks. He slept for 30 minutes each day in his truck parked behind BRT. I was concerned with his being on ladders with virtually no sleep.

Jamey, Teressa, and I trickled in at various times on opening day. My Mom had flown to Nashville, her first time ever on an airplane. She's always said it took me opening a theater for her to get on a plane. And she came out solo. I was so proud of her for doing something that had always scared her. I warned my Mom it would be an exhausting day and once we were at the theater, probably around ten in the morning, I told her there was no going back home. She was a trooper and helped with cleaning and decorating the guest restrooms.

Then things started falling apart, as things inevitably will on the opening day of a new business.

BellSouth accidentally cut off our phone lines. I had ads running in every newspaper and one of the few radio commercials we ever produced playing hourly on a popular station that hit our demographics. But when potential ticket buyers called, they got the dreaded "the number you have reached has been disconnected or is no longer in service" message. We lost three hours of operational phone lines. (Fun fact: our main phone number was once country legend Naomi Judd's private line and for at least the first two years we received calls for her.)

Once the phone service was restored, and as Letitia was finishing painting the lobby, Mom, who had been an executive secretary, volunteered to answer phones. As soon as orders came in, Letitia ran the credit cards using the second line. And then for some unknown reason, Letitia yelled at Mom, which left her in frustrated tears. Each one of us broke down and cried that day.

Not long after the phones were restored, the website crashed, cutting off guests who were trying to order tickets online.

The Lee Company had to come in to fix some issue with the HVAC.

Corbin was troubleshooting the lighting system while Jamey was tweaking the audio setup. The body mics weren't "talking" to the sound board.

Around 4:30 in the afternoon, our cast of four began to attempt its only rehearsal in the venue.

The only rehearsal in the venue.

Around Corbin, center stage on a 14-foot ladder.

It hadn't occurred to any of us just how we were going to wear the body mics. Fortunately, Cathy's boyfriend, who had Broadway experience, came to the rescue. He rushed out to get surgical tape to attach the mics to our faces. The first night we had to shove the mic packs in the backs of our underwear. By the next day, a local costumer named Billy Ditty, who would eventually become quite involved with BRT, had sewn four mic belts—elastic waistbands with tan pouches for the packs. We ran the mic cords under our costumes up our backs, around one side of our necks, over one of our ears, then taped to our faces.

We managed to run the show almost twice, a show with all those 68 or so quick costume changes and shuttling a sofa and a rollaway twin bed on and offstage for several scenes. The backstage building was bare, dirty, and cold. Lisa and I had set up four small folding tables and four garment racks, one set per actor. We devised a method to stage our costumes on our individual racks in show order with a large laundry basket under each. As soon as one costume was done, it was dropped in the basket. We had two girls working as dressers, but by and large, each actor had to do the majority of his or her changes unassisted.

Meantime, a different drama was playing out in the house. Corbin was on the phone with the City of Franklin. We could not legally open the building to guests without a final inspection and sign-off. It was supposed to happen in the morning. Then they said "around two p.m." It wasn't until six p.m. when the inspector arrived and flagged a few items that he felt needed to be adjusted or fixed. It was dicey, but Corbin talked the guy into a sign-off. It wasn't like we were a retail store, where opening a day late would have been unfortunate, but not tragic. The opening night of a brand-new theater company's venue with a sold-out house was entirely different. It would have ruined us.

Opening Day

Opening week ad in the *Nashville Scene*, March 14, 2001.

We stopped rehearsal around seven p.m., just 30 minutes before the house opened to guests. No one had eaten that day and the neighboring restaurant, Bluewind Art Bar, brought over large banquet trays of finger foods. Like a pack of ravenous dogs, we dove into the food. There were some yummy, bite-sized *hors d'oeuvres* that looked like they were stuffed with cream cheese and I crammed two in my mouth. Daniel was next to me and realized what they were: Some type of crab cakes or puffs. Knowing I have a shellfish allergy, he shoved his hand in my mouth scooping out the crab. Had he not, I would have been in the emergency room and he would have had to step into my role and still be assistant stage manager.

"You are not going to miss opening night," he scolded me. "Spit the rest out now and rinse your mouth."

"Why? What?" I asked.

"Because you had a mouthful of shellfish, idiot. You're not swelling up, so I caught it in time. You owe me a drink. No, make that several drinks."

By some miracle, at just a few minutes past eight p.m., the house lights faded to black, the opening announcements rolled, and four dimly lit, cloaked-and-hooded figures took the stage singing a Gregorian-chant-style chorus of "oohs."

"And the Lord God said, let there be light," said Cathy Motley. A warm glow softly bathed the mostly dark stage. "And there was light."

"And the Lord God said, let there be man and woman," I said.

"And there was man and woman," spoke Lisa Gillespie.

"And that night, man asked woman if she was busy," said Paul Cox. The audience howled.

The sequence continued with more biblical-sounding, chanted lines setting up the evening's theme of man and woman crashing into each other in attempts to mate.

Opening Day

After this sequence, each of us ripped off our monk hoods and dropped our cloaks. The stage lights snapped to full revealing us in underwear and lingerie as the two-piece combo of piano and violin played a snappy, upbeat opening refrain.

I got to sing the first solo line ever sung on the new stage.

Throughout the opening number, we all dressed for a first date, which in retrospect, was highly appropriate. And as with all first dates, the evening had many awkward moments. Moments when lighting cues didn't work or body mics cut out. Still, the audience roared with laughter and applauded thunderously.

There were two questionable moments in the show that we figured walked the line of being acceptable to conservative Williamson County audiences. The first occurred during one of the early numbers, "Single Man Drought," during which the audience hears the internal thoughts of two women on first dates. Lisa sang full voice lamenting that perhaps being a lesbian would be preferable to the torment she was enduring looking for a man. Lesbian is inherently a funny-sounding word, and it always got big laughs.

The second instance was downright offensive for sensitive, Christian ears. In a short "commercial" for a law firm that helps dating singles achieve more satisfying sexual experiences, the firm's attorneys, played by Lisa and Paul, presented oversized checks to Cathy and I who were in the rollaway bed. Cathy's character received $5,000 because her partner was unable to locate her "g-spot." My character received a larger, $10,000 settlement because my female counterpart had refused to "go down on me." From the audience, it was a mix of uproarious laughter mixed with uncomfortable groans. The box office received a few complaints, but per the agreement a theater company enters with the show's licensing house, no lines nor lyrics may be changed or cut.

Everything else in the show hit the audience's collective comedic g-spot due to the crisp, expert writing, and timely topics.

The show received a standing ovation, and we took three curtain calls.

The Boiler Room Theatre had just concluded its first date and the reaction indicated a second date was definitely in order.

Bluewind hosted the opening night gala for us, which I barely remember other than having several glasses of champagne before talking and singing on a mic with Jamey. Then the small cast, Cathy's boyfriend, and my Mom went to some open-all-night breakfast joint in a bad part of Nashville and devoured pancakes. Apparently, the diner was a well-kept secret that only the boyfriend knew. It was only after I had some food subsistence in my burgeoning belly that I took in the details of the place. It was dirtier than a Waffle House with caked-on food and grease on the chair rails and around the perimeter edge of the wobbly table, which someone had unsuccessfully attempted to level with a matchbook. But, damn, they were some awesome pancakes.

We all discussed the first performance of the show. There is a line in ILY about someone fondling something that brought a random memory back to Mom, perhaps something her mother had once said. My Mom—God love her—practically shouted the word "fondle" because she thought it was funny. The greasy-spoon full of patrons all looked at Mom. I think she would have liked to crawl under the dirty, feebly leveled table.

For the first month or so, the Boiler Room Theatre was the talk of the Nashville theater community. We got a glowing review out of the gate from Martin Brady in the *Nashville Scene*. Brady began his review with a cursory overview of the company's origins (Euphoria! The Theatre) and a summary of the work we did to the old boiler building.

Opening Day

...

"Boiler Room has successfully inaugurated its modest but impressive new surroundings with a polished and highly professional production of Joe DiPietro and Jimmy Roberts' *I Love You, You're Perfect, Now Change*, a hit musical that has been playing Off-Broadway for about five years now...

"...Without question... the production—a Nashville-area premiere—is spirited, well-paced, cleanly directed, and features four undeniably talented performers who act, sing, and dance... with commitment, purpose, and style...

"...Of course, you can't pull off stuff like this without top-flight actor-singers. *I Love You* has got 'em. Paul Cox and Lewis Kempfer are the guys. They're not great singers, but they're certainly very good, and both know how to sell a Broadway tune, which in some ways is even better than simply having raw vocal skills.

"...The ladies are perfect foils for their belching, scratching counterparts. Cathy Motley uses her opera-trained soprano beautifully in the solo "I Will Be Loved Tonight" and leads the cast in the tongue-in-cheek angst of "He Called Me." Her acting is solid too... the lady's got great gams, and she's an attractive force onstage.

"... Lisa Gillespie, in her own quiet way, trumps 'em all, though. Gillespie... has a classic musical-comedy alto, which she uses to terrific effect throughout, especially in her solo, "Always a Bridesmaid."

"…Mostly, this production epitomizes relentless energy and an obvious dedication to the fledgling parent company's mission: classy musical theater… Those theatrical rumblings you hear are coming from the south of town, where a small band of musical-comedy kids has a new playground. Good for them."

. . .

It still stings to read that he didn't consider me a great singer. I guess people had been blowing smoke up my ass for years or Brady just didn't like me. His future comments of my onstage work only went downhill from there, although once I devoted myself to set design and dressing, I got glowing reviews from him. It was Brady's reviews of my performances that ultimately drove me to behind-the-scenes work.

HOT TIPS

Be Prepared

Any new or new-to-you theater space will have its challenges, and some venues will have quite an odd assortment. Because we chose to put a professional theater into a then-80-year-old boiler room building, we had crumbling bricks, an enormous boiler backstage that seemed to toss down yellow dust on a whim, an ancient smokestack that rocked and creaked with the slightest breeze, and much more. New actors had to be indoctrinated to the space and its inherent challenges to prevent breaking character when sounds like the Titanic sinking often drowned out the audio system. Vines grew through the bricks into the building as if they were reclaiming the space. And we had our own fauna as well.

"I miss the wildlife aspect of BRT," said Lisa Gillespie. "During the second act of *I Love You, You're Perfect, Now Change*, a pair of mice would come out on stage during the same song, every time. They would sit and listen, then after the song they would meander away.

"During the second season, if a matinee ran late, the birds that still nested inside the theater would start throwing sticks and straw down on our heads to make sure we realized we needed to speed it up."

There was also my pug, Buzz, who lived backstage in a large crate when he wasn't in the box office with me. And there was the disembodied bark of a ghost dog that only Buzz and I seemed to hear.

The lesson? Be ready for anything. Absolutely anything.

CHAPTER 8
Ruthlessly Challenging

EARLY SUMMER 2001

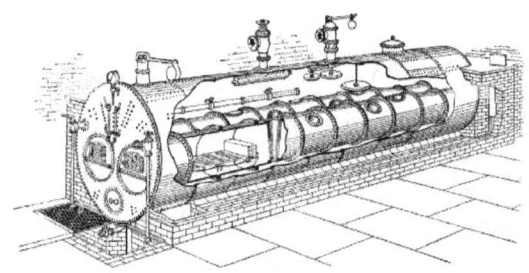

After the dynamic and celebrated opening of the Boiler Room Theatre, we plowed ahead with what we were sure was a can't-miss follow-up, a campy Off-Broadway musical called *Ruthless!* that was a send-up of *The Bad Seed, All About Eve, Gypsy,* and several other film and theater sources. We thought it was hilarious. Our audiences didn't get the jokes.

The show was written for a child actress to play the lead, Tina Denmark. And the role of the central character, the talent agent Sylvia St. Croix, was originally written for Bea Arthur, but she was unavailable and couldn't be in the show. The songs were written for Bea's contralto voice, which was so low that a man had to play the role in drag. Which then became the traditional casting. I was no stranger to drag, although it was limited to Halloween. I was already cast in the role before we announced the season. At the general auditions—which for some stupid reason weren't open to children—we found an exceptionally talented and diminutive actress named Melody Dawn Kennedy. I wanted her as my Diana Morales in *A Chorus Line*, but she insisted on no less than a two-production contract. We had her sing some stuff from *Ruthless!* and made a group decision to give her the child lead. Now, Melody Dawn brought great vocals and acting chops to the role, but ultimately, we should have cast a kid. But we weren't ready to deal with children yet. A successful children's theater and summer camp program was still a few years away.

The cast also included Lisa Gillespie as Judy Denmark (Tina's mother), Adele Akin, Cathie Correia Stamps, and Cela Scott, who had been with us in *Personals*. Dan McGeachy was at the helm as director.

The show was played on our first unit set which was basically a boring, three-sided box with a three-step staircase. It had to function as the suburban, mid-century home of Judy Denmark in the first act, then in the second, it had to transform to Judy's alter-ego character's penthouse apartment. I practically emptied my house of my mid-century furniture and created most of the set dressing. It was far from my best work, but it planted a seed, and not a bad one.

One of the features of the set per the script was a large, up-center-stage portrait of "sweet little Tina." Whoever painted it—perhaps Letitia—unwittingly made the girl's face look nearly identical to the show's costumer from hell, someone named Yoshie who, after weeks of sewing, brought in the most hideous, ill-fitting costumes any of us had ever seen. There were no more than three usable costumes, and it was a little over a week from opening night. Mercifully, Cathie, who was the director of the drama department at St. Cecilia Academy, had an enormous costume shop and saved the day. Only those of us who were around that first season knew the Yoshie story and still shudder at the mention of her name. Contractually, we had to pay her for useless garbage, barely fit for mopping the stage.

"I was truly excited to be cast as Lita Encore in *Ruthless!*" said Cathie. "We were all having a grand time, but there were crazy moments where we dashed around to help with the production beyond our official responsibility. Then, prior to a tech-week rehearsal, Lewis yelled out, 'We still need a fake turkey.' I simply replied, 'Oh, I have one in the trunk of my car.' I went to my car and brought in the $99 hard-plastic, yellowish-brown turkey. And that was that. And it became a favorite story to tell. I mean what are the odds of someone having a random prop turkey in the trunk of her car?"

I worked hard to get publicity for the show using the guy-in-drag angle. I ended up in my full drag on the entire front page of the Nashville gay newspaper of the day, *Query*. And the *Williamson A.M.* edition of *The Tennessean* ran a feature taking up half the features' front page with me getting into makeup under a headline in 72-point type that screamed "Dude Acts Like a Lady," a play on words from Aerosmith's song "Dude" [looks like a lady].

Opening night went well enough. But we knew the jokes were falling flat because we were playing to a Middle Tennessee audience who only knew shows like *South Pacific* and *The Sound of Music*. Joel Paley's script and Marvin Laird's score were smart, sassy, and played brilliantly to more advanced New York audiences. We were reminded of the old theater adage, "But will it play in Peoria?" We got a resounding "no" that night.

No opening night is ever perfect, so we cheerfully hoped for the best with the first Saturday night show. Surely *these* people would get it. And perhaps they might have if it had not been for a banana peel.

We were located adjacent to Building 8, which was home to an obnoxious, evangelical church that was always playing music at outdoor-concert levels and frequently held weddings that jammed the parking lot.

There had been a late-afternoon wedding that day and the married couple's getaway car was decorated with shaving cream and banana peels. Condoms would have been too much for that stodgy crowd. Around our cast's 6:30 p.m. call time, the parking lot had partially emptied, but a slippery trail was left throughout the lot. Lisa, who never traveled lightly and often had two backpacks and a dance bag, slipped on a shaving-cream-coated banana peel. The weight of her bags pulled her down hard resulting in a broken foot. Another cast member found her, and Jamey and Daniel got her into the building. Lisa was positive she could not do the show and needed to get to the emergency room. But we wanted to have her checked out as quickly as possible.

The audience was packed in when Jamey grabbed a mic and took center stage. "Is there a doctor in the house?" To the audience, it sounded like an old Vaudeville gag and they laughed uproariously. Again, "No, seriously. Is there a doctor in the house? We have an injured cast member."

Turns out there was a doctor in attendance, and he recommended the emergency room. We had no budget for understudies and had no choice but to cancel the show and refund all the ticket money for both that night and the next day's matinee. We were already in the hole, and this didn't help.

So, we scrambled.

The show's choreographer, Nancy Whitehead Brown, learned Cela's roles as child-actress-nemesis Louise Lerman and Eve, while Cela learned Lisa's. We rehearsed Sunday and Monday nights, cancelled the Tuesday show (refunding even more money), and on Thursday, we performed the show with the unplanned understudies. They both did yeoman's work in just a few days. But by Saturday, Lisa was back in the lead wearing a medical boot on her broken foot. It certainly distracted from the period costumes Cathie had pulled together.

But we made lemonade.

In the second act, Eve (in a nod to *All About Eve*) wants desperately to be Ginger DelMarco, Lisa's character's alter-ego. There was a gag in which Eve comes out dressed identically as Ginger. We knew we couldn't hide the non-period walking boot from the audience, so Eve came out with one on as well. That drew a hoped-for hearty laugh from the audience.

Then another injury occurred. The show seemed cursed. I had a fight scene (in full drag, of course) with the "child" actress in which we nearly wrestled for possession of a prop pistol. Of course, the fight was meticulously choreographed as theatrical fight scenes always are. But a move was missed, and I knocked the gun against Melody Dawn's mouth and chipped one of her front teeth. I was mortified; she was in shock. Ultimately the theater paid $400 to have her tooth repaired.

At the end of the show, nearly every character is killed. My gag was dying in a position with my legs wide open to reveal my industrial-strength girdle. I would quickly realize my unladylike pose and close my legs. Medium laughs.

Then Cathie was blocked to perform an elaborate dying sequence, moving from furniture piece to furniture piece and ultimately dying, draped across the back of the sofa, legs in the air in a crooked pose that looked so impossible it was a wonder and a feat of physical strength that she could hold that pose for at least five minutes. Huge laughs. Through the rest of the five-week run, Cathie's death scene took on a life of its own, growing longer and more and more elaborate. It never failed to garner one of the show's biggest laughs.

The show concluded with the much-talked-about-but-never-seen husband, Mr. Fredrick Denmark. Daniel once again served as assistant stage manager and, to save paying an actor for a single appearance, donned a suit for the last line and entrance of the show: "Honey, I'm home!" spying the carnage across the set as the lights snapped to black.

Despite all my efforts to market the show, it just didn't draw guests and barely made payroll. The season ticket holders showed up, of course, but they walked away scratching their heads not really understanding what they'd just watched. The show was a far cry from the rock-solid *I Love You*.

Toward the end of the run, we were asked to perform songs from the show at a theater educators' conference being held at Belmont University. It happened when Mom was out for her second solo visit to Nashville. We had an 8 a.m. call time at Belmont which required me getting in drag at home—a two-hour process of a close shave, troweling on a quarter pound of pancake makeup, and gluing fake eyelashes that always refused to stay attached. We'd just left my house on Sunnymeade Drive in Inglewood and I realized I needed smokes. We stopped at the nearby Mapco Express convenience store. I was driving my stick-shift Toyota truck in full drag and heels.

"Mom, I can't go into the store at 7:30 a.m. in drag. I'll get my pantyhosed ass kicked."

"Well, can you get by with what you have?" Mom asked.

"No, I'm out. You need to go in and buy them. Marlboro Lights, hard pack."

Mom was mortified. "I can't go in and buy *cigarettes!* I've never, ever done that and wouldn't know how."

"You just tell the clerk 'Marlboro Lights in the hard pack.'"

"What if someone sees me?"

"Mother, it's not like you're buying crack. If I can drive a pickup in full drag and pumps on a Tuesday morning, you can go in and buy cigarettes. Please."

Mom worked up the courage to do the deed. She came out red-faced and looking to each side as if the police would pounce at any second.

One positive thing came out of the Belmont showcase. A rep from the show's licensing company, Samuel French, was in attendance and told me I was the best Sylvia he'd ever seen and that I was remarkably believable as a woman. That's exactly what I was going for. Not campy, over-the-top drag, but Dustin-Hoffman-in-*Tootsie* legitimate female-impersonation drag.

Martin Brady didn't fully agree, although reading the review 20 years later, I discovered I fared better than I had always thought. I was stunned to read his largely positive comments about me. But overall, the show's review was lukewarm:

...

"The cozy little Boiler Room Theatre in Franklin made a nice splash back in March with a highly entertaining production of *I Love You, You're Perfect, Now Change*. Now the company returns with the second offering of its inaugural season… *Ruthless! The Musical*… this is a far more challenging piece, and on opening night, the results indicated as much.

"… The Boiler Room folks bring their zeal and dedication to the task, and there are moments when you think this zany, campy spoof of '50s movies is going to take off. Yet it never really does.

"… In a role that was supposedly written with Bea Arthur (*Maude*) in mind, Lewis Kempfer takes on the mighty task of a drag portrayal of Sylvia. Like the trooper he is, Kempfer goes for the gusto, and he certainly has taken pains to look the part. He's largely good, but it's hard to know if it's the writing or Kempfer that makes his performance seem a tad dreary at times. He's a first-rate performer, but he's better as a guy playing a guy."

. . .

Huh. Well, color me surprised. What wasn't surprising was that both Lisa and Jamey received the highest marks.

The negative *pièce de résistance* was the skewering review by Leo Sochocki, who I believe was working at the time for *The City Paper*. As complete as my six fire safes full of BRT archives are, alas, the review is missing. But he panned the show, the cast, and the set. I'll never forget one of his comments: "Would it have broken the production budget to have balusters on the staircase?"

Why, yes, Leo. Yes, it would have.

It was a missed detail between Corbin and me, and every stair unit on the BRT stage from that point forward was as complete and elaborate as necessary for the show. But it was a nasty comment, nonetheless. A ruthless comment, one might say.

HOT TIPS

Understanding Understudies

If you think you'll make it through the entire run of a show without a mishap or injury, then you haven't done much theater. Sprained ankles, torn ACLs, and laryngitis wait breathlessly in the wings for their next victim.

The point is, if you can afford understudies, or even one understudy for a leading role, or a pair of swings who can cover several roles, by all means, do it! I get it. Money is tight in most small- to medium-sized theaters and understudies/swings are often one of the first budget line items to be cut. If you simply can't afford those cast members, get creative. Maybe there's a promising young actor who would be willing (if not thrilled) to be a swing for free (if you pay your actors). Maybe there's a guy on the Board of Directors who once played Tevye and could relearn the role, just in case.

During *Ruthless!*, we got caught with our panties down. Over the course of its 14 seasons, the Boiler Room Theatre rarely had understudies or swings due to budget, but always had some talented performers who could, with cramming and intense rehearsals, step into a role. But ultimately, pre-planning is better.

And spring for balusters.

Boiler Room Voices

LAURI DISMUKE

Forever Grateful

How do I even begin to convey what my time at the Boiler Room Theatre meant to me? I'm not a writer, and 21 years have gone by since I first stepped foot into that audition—that audition that changed my life in many ways. A lot of life has been lived since then and sadly, with age, my memory isn't as good as it once was. But that was a time in my life that changed and molded the woman I am today.

In the year 2000, I decided to stop performing for a while and just teach. I was a full-time dance instructor at the Bellevue Dance Center. I had moved to Nashville in 1995, the day I graduated from college. I had received my Bachelors of Performing Arts (BPA) from Oklahoma City University (OCU) in Dance Performance. I took the role of lead dancer at Opryland USA in the hopes of performing through a contract or two and then moving to NYC. I loved being onstage and dancing was my passion, but I also had a ton of insecurities, one of the primary ones being my singing voice. You see, I was always a dancer first, but I loved to sing. Well, I loved to sing until the day one of the musical directors for my Opryland show told me that I could not sing, and he did not want me to sing in his shows. I was hired to dance, and I needed to just do my job. I was crushed. I mean, I know I didn't have the voice of some of my fellow castmates, but what he said killed something inside of me. I never sang again until the day I auditioned for the Boiler Room Theatre.

I had spotted the audition notice in the *Nashville Scene*. A brand-new theater was being built in an old boiler room building at The Factory at Franklin. For their inaugural season they were mounting *A Chorus Line*. That show meant so much to me. It was the second Broadway tour I attended in high school and was one of the reasons I wanted to major in dance and pursue the dream of being on Broadway. But to be in Broadway in musicals you needed to know how to sing, and to sing well, and I believed the lie that I was told that my voice just wasn't good enough. I wanted so badly to be in this show, but how in the world was I going to be cast when I wouldn't get past the singing part of the audition? I had been out of college for a few years, so I hadn't been to any kind of voice lessons. I wasn't even sure what song I should audition with.

Every day I would come up with 100 reasons not to audition, but one thought kept nagging me: *What if? What if I don't audition? What if I don't get it? What if they don't like me?* What if… But what if all of that was wrong and I never tried?

So, I packed my dance bag, character shoes and all, and headed to the audition. When I arrived, I handed someone my resume and headshot and I waited. I sang first. I was so nervous I think my voice shook the entire time. Then it was time to dance. The audition space was some sheets of wood on top of an uneven cement floor. I was scared I was going to twist my ankle. I learned the combination and then it was time to perform in small groups. I felt more alive than I had in a long time. I didn't want it to end. I felt like I did a great job, but then they asked several girls to stay, and I was not one of them. I was crushed. I would have loved to have been given the chance to sing and read for Cassie or Morales. I knew I could dance the roles, but once again, my voice was the problem. At least that's how I heard it in my head. I assumed that my singing cost me the job again. Oh well. At least I had tried.

I don't remember how much time had passed, but one day I got the call. The director Lewis Kempfer called me. He said that they wanted me to play Kristine (the girl who couldn't sing). I didn't even care. I was just so excited to be a part of this new project. Later I was informed that I was the very first person cast in the show and, as it turned out, the very first person ever to be cast at the Boiler Room Theatre. Little did I know how much that wonderful little theater in the red-brick building would become woven into the fabric of my life.

It was my dancing that got me cast. Once rehearsals started, I knew that I wanted to keep performing and be on stage as much as possible, but I was going to have to figure out the voice thing. I knew that "dancer musicals" would be few and far between; I was going to have to get serious about my voice. Luckily, I had become friends with Jamey, the musical director of *A Chorus Line*, and decided to ask his opinion. He said he would gladly start working with me.

A few voice lessons in and I was gaining confidence. I auditioned for the last production of the season, *The 1940s Radio Hour*. I didn't know anything about the show except the fact that it had a role for a dancer. I felt so much more prepared for this audition and knew I could do any dancing that was thrown my way. I left that night feeling confident that I would get a call. Boy, was I wrong. I did not get cast in the show. They just didn't feel that I was ready for that kind of a role yet. Once again, I was crushed. It seemed I just was not cut out for the musical-theater world.

A few months went by and one night Corbin Green called to ask if I would be interested in choreographing the second show of their second season, *Lucky Stiff*. I thought he had called the wrong person. I had no choreography experience. I had never even heard of the show. How in the world was I going to choreograph it? But that wasn't all—he also wanted me to be in the show! Lady #2 (or maybe it was Lady #1?). I don't remember all the specifics; I only remember that the role would involve me playing several characters. I told him I needed to talk to my boss at the dance studio and see if I could work it out.

The next day, I sat down with my boss, and she said that she couldn't allow me to miss classes to do the performances, but I could work the choreography part of it around my teaching schedule. I was disappointed because I really wanted to perform more than I wanted to choreograph, but I agreed to step out of my comfort zone and jump into the new challenge of choreography.

The cast was so much fun, and the show really pushed me for my first experience. There were moving and rotating doors and a "dead man" in a wheelchair. During the run of this production, I was asked to step into the role I had been originally offered for a weekend. I had exactly zero rehearsal time. I showed up, got in costume, mic-checked for my solo (yes, I was actually singing in the show) and boom—there I was onstage. I can't explain the thrill to be doing an entire acting and singing track.

It was during that exhilarating weekend that I decided to get serious about taking voice lessons and stepping into a more full-time role of performing.

During that second season, I was cast in and asked to help choreograph another show: *McBeth! The Musical Comedy!* and I collaborated with Nancy Whitehead Brown on creating the wacky dances for the delightful show. I stayed on to choreograph the small bits of dance in Lewis's *Man of La Mancha*, and it was during that time I started taking weekly voice lessons while still teaching dance six days a week at the studio, choreographing, and often performing at night. My schedule was insane, but I loved every minute of it.

Right before Christmas, the shows for the third season were announced. When I saw that *Guys and Dolls* was slotted as the season opener, I got to work. I wanted to play Adelaide so badly. I started working on "Adelaide's Lament" so I would be ready for auditions. Never in a million years did I think I had a chance to be cast. The girls I had to sing against had *insane* voices. I was still very nervous about my voice, but I walked in with the attitude that I needed to "fake it 'til I make it."

And make it I did.

When Jamey told me at a voice lesson, I nearly fell on the floor. But it was the way he told me. He said he wanted to work on "Adelaide's Lament," "A Bushel and a Peck," "Take Back Your Mink," "Sue Me," and "Marry the Man." I shot a glance toward choreographer Dietz Osborne who was working the box office phones while marking dance moves and making notes.

"Jamey, these are all songs from *Guys and Dolls*. The chorus doesn't sing all of these," I said, puzzled.

"Maybe you're not in the chorus," Jamey said. Dietz burst out laughing in the lobby. He was in on the gag.

Jamey was casting me as Adelaide. It took days for the reality to sink in: I had just been cast in my first leading role in a musical at a professional theater.

The show did great at the box office, and we played to full houses. Then Martin Brady from the *Nashville Scene* came to review us. The BRT staff always tried to keep it a secret when a reviewer would be in the audience so we wouldn't get nervous. They were successful, and I performed with no additional butterflies. I got a great review which floored me. And Lewis wanted to make sure everyone knew. He made dozens of copies of the enlarged review and plastered the backstage with them. I was embarrassed but also thrilled.

Besides being a breakthrough role for me, toward the end of 2003, the *Scene* announced its winners for the "Best of Nashville" awards. Once again, I nearly had to pick myself up off the floor. I had been awarded Best Musical Theater Performer in Nashville. That was up against performers at every theater in town: Chaffin's Barn Dinner Theatre, Circle Players, Actors Bridge, Act1, Tennessee Repertory Theatre, and others. It's an honor I've always cherished, and it boosted my confidence in countless ways.

It was also during the third season that an opportunity presented itself—to buy the Bellevue Dance Center. I had been teaching there for years, but owning my own studio never occurred to me; it was never a dream career. The outgoing owner offered me the studio at an almost unbeatable price. Even so, I'd have to go to my bank for a loan and the whole idea of being a business owner scared me and shook me to my core.

One night after a *Guys and Dolls* show, I decided to stay after and join Jamey and Lewis in their nightly "smoking in the box office" session during which business was discussed, new show concepts were born, and a lot of off-color humor was shared. I loved both guys, but I was uncomfortable with the language and dirty jokes and definitely didn't like the cigarette smoke. But in them, I had the opportunity to talk candidly to two business owners who had taken the plunge and kept the little theater alive for two full seasons. They were exactly who I needed to speak with.

I explained my dilemma and couldn't hold back the tears. I was embarrassed for crying, but Lewis put an arm around me and said, "Do you honestly think there weren't nights when I cried out of fear and frustration? Making that decision to join Jamey and take this frightening journey as a business owner that excited me while, at the same time, terrified me?"

"Yeah, I'm sure it was very hard to put it all on the line—not the *Chorus Line,* although that seems appropriate—to start this theater," I replied.

"We had a more challenging set of circumstances," Jamey added. "We had a venue, but it needed every bit of basic building infrastructure before we could even start turning this space into a theater. You already have an up-and-running facility. That doesn't lessen your fears, nor should it, but you have an infinite advantage."

"It's truly turnkey," Lewis said. "You can keep the business name, try to retain your staff and students, and honestly, no one really has to notice the change of ownership. It's really a once-in-a-lifetime opportunity and one I don't think you can pass up."

"But I don't know if I want to own a studio. I don't know if I want to teach full time. I want to perform," I said.

"Hell, I do both, Lauri," Jamey said. "It can be done, and I know you can do it."

"It's like Al said to your character Kristine in *A Chorus Line*: you just have to pull yourself together," Lewis said. "I don't say that to make light of your worries. But if you can turn off the emotion for a while and think this through as a businessperson, I think you'll feel better."

I'll never forget that night in the smoky lobby. Jamey and Lewis helped me find the courage I needed to get the loan and sign the papers. It was as terrifying as performing Adelaide, but once I got past the fear, just as I'd done with the role, I got excited. I really could do it all: teach, choreograph, perform.

A transition had already happened with BRT's choreographers. Dietz choreographed *Guys and Dolls,* and I'm very grateful as I don't think I could have handled the leading role of Adelaide, choreographing a big show on a small stage, and becoming a business owner.

Then came *Chicago*, the third show of the third season. I guess good things can happen in threes because that's when I took on the role of Resident Choreographer. *Chicago* was the biggest dance challenge, trying to make the iconic Fosse moves my own. I wanted to be considered for a lead, but was not due to being the choreographer. While it was gratifying to choreograph a show that blew the roof off the theater and blew the critics and audiences away, being in the ensemble meant that after "Cell Block Tango" (I was "Lipschitz"), the female cast members had little to do.

The situation was totally different for the second Kander-and-Ebb show that BRT mounted, *Cabaret*, in the sixth (2006) season. I choreographed the show and was in the ensemble which had a ton more female-centric numbers with a lot of stage time. I loved the show. I didn't think I would love it due to its dark and disturbing subject matter that not everyone gets, but the dancing—oh my Hell—I may have even loved it more than *Chicago*.

But back to 2003. The fourth show was *You're a Good Man, Charlie Brown*. Infusing sheer joy into the basic dance moves for the cast of six was so satisfying. I wanted to be in it but was starting to learn I had to balance being a business owner, a choreographer, and a performer. I couldn't do all of them all the time. In that way, owning the studio helped me mature, and it felt good.

Then BRT did a remount of the first season's Christmas show, *The 1940s Radio Hour*. This time Laura Skaug was the director and cast me as Connie, the dancing ingénue who also got to sing a major solo. The group vocal arrangements were difficult with tight harmonies. I had to work so hard to keep up with experienced singers who were pros at reading music.

Then, in early summer of 2004, I did my first and only nonmusical play. I played the title role in *Sylvia*—the title role being a *dog*—and I had to work my tail off. Lewis has a wonderful chapter later in this book about the show, so I'll keep this section brief.

Sylvia, meant to be played by an actress and originally played by Sarah Jessica Parker Off-Broadway, was a foul-mouthed critter. Being a devout Catholic, I didn't know if I could say the bad words written for the role. Friends said, "She'll never say those bad words. Never." Well, I did. And the show is an all-time favorite. People were shocked that I boldly used that language and were impressed with my first (and only) nonmusical role. I had no dancing or singing to lean on.

Martin, from the *Scene*, wasn't a fan of the play but gave good marks to our production. Later that year, it was staged by Tennessee Rep. It was either Martin or another reviewer who devoted his or her review to comparing my performance to that of the Rep's actress. I won "best in show" and wish I could quote the review, but sadly, it seems to have disappeared from online.

From that point forward, I was involved in nearly every BRT musical until the theater's demise. In 2004's *Nunsense*, I taught *the* Melinda Doolittle (of eventual *American Idol* fame) to tap dance.

I helped Jamey block *Sweeney Todd*.

I created the role of Candi Bradenton in Lewis and Jamey's original musical *That '60s Christmas Show* and became close friends with Megan Murphy Chambers and Melodie Madden Adams. I got to dance with Joe Truman and the whole experience was magical.

For the 2005 season opener *Grease*, I had to relinquish choreographer duties to Lori Ellis neé Eisenhauer due to studio commitments. Lewis had precast me as Patty Simcox and asked me to stage manage the show, another first for me. I worked with Billy Ditty for the first time and we soon became Nashville's version of Fred and Ginger.

120 SEATS IN A BOILER ROOM

Also, in 2005, I choreographed *Godspell* and *How to Succeed in Business Without Really Trying* as well as being in the latter.

Disney's Beauty and the Beast was the 2005 season closer, and I had been slated in advance to choreograph the enormous show on BRT's small stage. I don't know how Lewis, who directed and designed the set, made the show fit, but he did. I auditioned for the role of Belle, and along with Laura Thomas and Melodie, was kept until midnight at callbacks reading and singing over and over with Dan Whorton (who was cast as the Beast) and Erik Garcia (who was cast as Gaston). I was disappointed when I wasn't cast as Belle, nor even in the show. But when another actress who was asked to play Babette (the French maid/feather duster) turned it down, I stepped in and ending up having a blast.

We opened 2006 with *Anything Goes* with Lewis again at the helm. He told me he wanted me to play Hope Harcourt because of how I looked next to Billy Ditty, who Lewis was casting as the lead, Billy Crocker. It was the first show in which I played a leading role while handling choreography duties. Martin trashed my vocals in his review, and I learned the hard way that just because you get a leading role doesn't mean everyone is going to love you in it. Still, the show was very special to me. I got to work alongside a former student, Tosha Schmidt, in her first professional role. It was surreal to share the stage with someone I had taught to dance.

I was scarcely involved with BRT during 2007, possibly due to burn out or other people coming in with fresh ideas.

When the 2008 season opener, *Thoroughly Modern Millie*, was announced, I longed to play Millie. After all, the role required a good amount of dancing, especially tap. I was called back for Millie, which was a dream role for me, but only got featured dancer/ensemble. There was some unpleasant drama with the director pre-casting a non-dancer as Millie. I don't want to inject sour grapes so early in this book, or at all really, but the director's decision ultimately pushed away one of BRT's regular leading ladies. I had a lot of fun dancing with Billy, however, and I learned a lesson: While I had already had an incredible run at the theater, it didn't mean I got to play all the roles I wanted. People might look at my BRT career as me getting to do everything I wanted to do, but you don't get every role you want just because you're the Resident Choreographer.

In BRT's latter years, I performed in *The Rocky Horror Show* and helped stage *Parade* and *Floyd Collins*. And although none of us knew it at the time, I was in the very last Boiler Room show, *Legally Blonde*, that was mounted in 2014 at the Franklin Theatre. Like so many others, I was heartbroken to learn that BRT had lost its namesake space and the theater company was officially closed. The Boiler Room had been my second home for what felt like a lifetime. I'll never forget the many experiences and my heart overflows with gratitude for the Boiler Room Theatre.

CHAPTER 9

What We Did for Love

SUMMER 2001

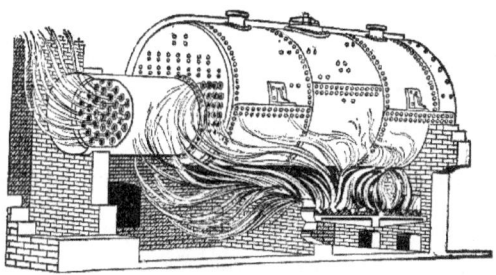

It was our big gamble, but a bet I was absolutely sure of winning. Still, it very well could have been our one big mistake. There were plenty of naysayers telling us from before Day One that we could never pull off *A Chorus Line* in the Boiler Room Theatre. Audiences were blown away and came out in droves rewarding nearly every performance with a standing ovation. It may have been one of the smallest productions ever of the show, but it had something the big productions didn't: intimacy. Guests remarked at how enjoyable it was to be so close to the actors which made for a delightful evening of theater.

As soon as we'd opened *Ruthless!* I had callbacks for the show. From the season auditions, I already had some performers in mind for certain roles, with the exceptions of Lauri, and Melody Dawn who was starring in *Ruthless!* and whom I'd already cast. Vocal callbacks were inside the theater while dance was held at the adjacent Jamison Hall. Some performers who passed the vocals didn't fly with the choreographer.

As previously mentioned, on one of the earliest walk-throughs, we'd measured a potential stage location and size and I determined that two characters could easily be cut to fit the line across the stage. The choreographer remembers the BRT management team wanting to stage the dancers in a semicircle, destroying the very basis of the show's title. Someone may have suggested that ridiculous idea, but it was most definitely not me, and if the question had actually been asked, I certainly said no.

"It's a *dance* show. There's no getting around that," she espoused.

"But they also need to be strong singers," Jamey countered.

"And some even need to act," I added.

Middle Tennessee wasn't rife with New York-level triple threats.

The typical post-callbacks scrutiny went late into the night and for days after. Strong male dancers were not a commodity in Nashville, but we'd attracted enough to cast the show.

Daniel Vincent beat out several other guys to be cast as Paul, a Puerto Rican gay dancer. Although he always admitted being a "hoofer" rather than a trained dancer, the difference wasn't noticed. And he did an amazing job with the long, emotional monologue. I thought we had him use body makeup to cover as he said, his pasty-white Irish body, but he reminded me that we paid to send him to a tanning salon. He remarked, "I don't *ever* want to be that tan again in my life."

Another guy, Jay Sullivan, was an experienced and talented actor who could move. That means someone who probably didn't study dance but could pick up steps easily. At the post-callbacks session for ACL, Jamey, the choreographer, and I did the usual ritual of laying out all the headshots of the finalists across the stage in piles that looked like a giant game of Solitaire. We were debating casting Jay. He could sing, he could act, had great comedic timing, exactly what the role of Bobby required.

"I want him for Bobby, but he admits he's never really danced," I said as we debated over casting Jay.

"Oh, I can teach that boy to dance. I'll work with him. Go ahead and cast him."

We had already pushed back hard against the choreographer taking the role of Cassie. She said it was a package deal. We said we would take it under consideration, but were strongly against it. She had been in the international tours of a couple of major Broadway dance shows for many years and had assisted renowned choreographers, so she was no slouch.

We eventually cast the choreographer as Cassie as she was a highly experienced dancer with all those impressive credentials. Even so, we all agreed we needed an understudy for her. We'd learned our lesson with *Ruthless!* The girl we were going to cast as Maggie, Emily Zeringue-Pettit, was clearly a more talented Cassie, but she looked too young to play a character who, after 17 years in the business could no longer find work and came to plead with her former lover, director Zach, for a job. When we spoke with her, she was disappointed to be cast as Maggie, but understudying Cassie sealed the deal for her as long as she could perform the role at least twice.

So now we had to find an understudy for Emily. Since I wasn't a trained dancer but was going to play Zach, I decided to mimic the film version in which Michael Douglas played a non-dancing Zach. In the show, there is a dance captain character named Larry. With male dancers at a premium, we cast choreographer Nancy Whitehead Brown in the role and called her "Laurie." She would "teach" the choreography to the dancers during the shows while I sat in the house with a microphone. And we cast Nancy as the Maggie understudy. And hence, we needed an understudy for the character Laurie, so we cast Renée Hatfull Brooks. It was Renée's first stage show ever; she had only learned to dance at the age of 28.

While the actress cast as Cassie had the stamina to never miss a show, we did promise those two shows in which Emily would play Cassie. The choreographer never agreed with having understudies and thought that it was a frivolous waste of time and money.

"Oh, great. Now I have to train another Cassie wannabe without being paid extra," the choreographer griped. "You people are nothing more than rank amateurs. I'm ready to walk out."

The choreographer's backstage behavior negatively affected cast morale. Daniel Vincent said in 2022, "I remember her holding court backstage. She was in a chair and several members of the cast were sitting around her on the floor asking her which cat they would be in *Cats*. Someone asked about me and she said, 'Oh, he wouldn't be in the show' which was a slam on my dancing. I turned around and said, 'You're right, because I hate the show and think it's garbage.'"

The choreographer never really wanted to stage the show after seeing the boiler room building and what she incessantly called a "postage-stamp stage." She was vocal about it in front of the cast, complaining the venue was too small. It caused an uncomfortable rapport between us and the cast. And every time we ran the show in rehearsal, we had to skip Cassie's big dance number, "The Music and the Mirror," because she hadn't choreographed it yet. In fact, we didn't see the number until tech week.

Even up until two weeks before opening, the choreographer was still complaining about the size of the stage and saying we were going to look like fools. The LLC had a meeting.

"Jamey, I'm at my wits' end. The choreographer seems to be miserably unhappy doing this show. She knew about the stage size going in," I said.

"What are our options?" Corbin asked.

"Well, we already have Nancy as dance captain, who honestly, could have choreographed this show. If any problems arise, Nancy can easily handle them. And the cast adores her."

"But how will this make us look? It could be negative publicity we can't afford," said Teressa.

"Yeah, I know. That's why I'm bringing it to the group. There's some pretty bad blood between the choreographer and some of the cast. I think it's impacting morale," I said.

"I hate to say it, but I don't think it's a good idea to let her go. Just can't see any good coming from this. Let's sit down and talk with her," Jamey said.

So, we had a chat with the choreographer and she acted taken aback, unaware there was any problem. Either she couldn't see it or chose not to. I could relate as I've often been in a similar position. We forged ahead. The choreographer brought her attitude down a notch, and I did my best to play peacemaker and be more respectful of her.

About halfway through the run, tragedy struck. Emily's parents-in-law were returning from seeing the show and were flying their private plane back to some other state. But the plane crashed, and the in-laws perished. Emily was out for a week. I shot the choreographer a "told you so" look regarding understudies. And our collective hearts broke for Emily and her husband. She'd been exuberant, joyful, and delightful to watch as Cassie in the two performances we gave her. Yes, she looked too young, but she had the moves and the voice.

Prior to opening, I was working with a local architect, Kenny VanHook, to figure out how we could fly scenery, that is, lowering scenic elements from above the stage. Corbin and Jamey said it wasn't possible, but when I have something in my head, I'm like a raccoon with its paw holding a wad of tin foil and stuck in a trap. To escape, the raccoon needed only to release its paw's grip. I would have made a good raccoon.

Corbin was particularly busy with his custom kitchen cabinet business that summer and had no problem letting someone else take a crack at the flown scenery. Kenny had experience flying scenery. He said all we had to do was match the peak of the roof over the stage and *voilà*, flying scenery. Essentially, making fly space out of nothing. To my knowledge, BRT never again used flown scenery and I don't know why. It could very well be because no other show really needed it.

A Chorus Line is usually played on a bare stage, at least until the iconic finale, and all the exposed brick and antique windows above (the ones we had painted black) gave us a great, vacant theater look. There are several moments in the show when mirrors typically descend (or if the theater's stage has wings, the mirrors come out from the sides). It is an important look for the opening sequence and absolutely crucial for Cassie's "The Music and the Mirror." We knew the mirror drop had to be as light as possible and using real mirrors was risky should the drop descend faster than intended. My research found that a Mylar, mirror-like material is often used instead of glass and was even used on Broadway.

The Mylar material wasn't cheap—nothing about *A Chorus Line* was cheap—and it was problematic. Prior to every show, the assistant stage managers had to use blow dryers to smooth out bubbles and ridges that had formed since the last performance. It was a pain in the ass. We ended up using the rest of the material on the shields in 2002's *Man of La Mancha*.

Then there was the finale drop. *A Chorus Line* has one of the glitziest, most dazzling finales among all Broadway shows. A big part of that is the champagne-gold costumes, but the rest is dependent upon a big, Art Deco backdrop that either travels in from either side of the stage or descends from the heavens. Kenny designed an outstanding scenic piece. Because it had to lower and be quickly hoisted back to the nether regions of the boiler building, it had to be as lightweight as possible. It was constructed of Tyvek foam insulation sheets, balsa wood, a two-by-four base, and a lot of hardware. Neither drop failed us, not once. Audiences were amazed. It wasn't a hugely impressive piece of scenery. It didn't light up or spell out "Tits and Ass" (that's a joke, by the way), but it worked. The most impressive part to audiences was that it and the mirrors were flown (theater-speak) or lowered (guest-speak) from the Boiler Room's nearly 40-foot ceiling.

I knew the weekly payroll was going to be high, which is why we charged a premium ticket price ($23 instead of $19), but it was still a struggle. The quote I received in early 2001 for performance rights was based on community theater rates, not professional rates. I tried to get the Tams-Witmark rep to play nice with me, but he'd already seen our website, the front of which splayed the tag line "Williamson County's First Professional Theater." Telling the rep we were non-Equity didn't help. Professional is professional, and as such, the rates were too. I had a contract with an $8,000 price tag staring at me and haunting my dreams. And I'd heard horror stories about other theaters' productions of ACL being shut down for a variety of reasons. It seemed to be—at least in 2001—one of the most closely monitored shows.

When I signed on to be a co-founder, I had $15,000 in savings. To get us through the opening of the theater and a week of *Ruthless!* when we couldn't make payroll, I kept tapping that account. And I'd already committed in October 2000 to paying the rental cost of $4,000 for the finale costumes. A St. Louis theater company had a nice set available for rent. I just couldn't rescue us with rights monies.

Thankfully, Cathie Correia Stamps stepped in and said she'd put the royalties on a credit card. Cathie also took on costuming the vintage audition looks as well as managing alterations on the finale costumes. It took us four years to pay her back and I've always felt horrible about it.

The famous finale "wedge." Photo by Holly Hines.

Although the cast was wall-to-wall, *A Chorus Line* never failed to wow audiences. Photo by Holly Hines.

Audiences were blown away by our production in the intimate BRT space. After all, it was a show about casting dancers for a Broadway show and was always done on a much bigger stage than ours. But guests remarked how incredible it was to be so close to the actors and that took our production to a different and exciting level. While *I Love You...* had caught Nashville's attention, *A Chorus Line* put us on the map exactly as I had planned.

The show settled in for its six-week run and other than Emily's tragedy, no one was injured. We couldn't body mic 17 people so we installed two choir mics above the stage. The flying scenery had smooth flights. And other than a couple of complaints from guests who sat beneath the tech booth where we had placed the band—they complained that all they could hear was the kick drum—as well as a few prudes having issues with the lyrics in "Dance: Ten, Looks: Three" better known as "Tits and Ass," the run was successful and largely uneventful.

Despite audiences applauding heartily and giving standing ovations, the one review we received was from Martin Brady of the *Nashville Scene*. I had hoped we would score higher marks, but alas…

. . .

> "With *esprit de corps*, director Lewis Kempfer and his mostly attractive and energetic cast manage to pull this one off. It's no easy task, though, and the results are by no means perfect… While offering no definitive production of *A Chorus Line*, Boiler Room Theatre has nonetheless delivered a mostly entertaining evening of musical theater."

. . .

HOT TIPS

Go Big or Go Home

There are instances with show selections when you have to just trust your gut and go big. If the show succeeds, it increases the theater's status. I can only speak for the shows I pitched and directed during my five and one-half years at the Boiler Room, but my big-show risks succeeded. Part of that was my perfectionist nature, a lot of luck, many prayers, elaborate sets, and casting the right people. As I've said, putting *A Chorus Line* in the first season was risky because we didn't have any experience mounting shows in our venue when the 2001 line-up was announced. Yes, there were the naysayers who thought the show was too big for the 120-seat venue. But for every naysayer there was a cheerleader singing our praises for doing the nearly impossible. It showed we weren't afraid to take risks and that we were a serious theater pushing the limits, knowing we could fail.

Sometimes you just have to go out on a limb where the good fruit is located and take a semi-calculated risk. I knew instinctively that the Boiler Room Theatre would need—no, require—a big-name anchor show which for us was *A Chorus Line*. For your theater it might be *Miss Saigon*, or *The Producers*, or *Cabaret*. ACL hadn't been done in the

Nashville area in at least ten years, and it's challenging to produce because it needs triple-threat performers. But I'm glad I pushed for it.

Is there a show that feels like a huge risk but might have equally huge rewards? Can you afford to produce it even if it requires digging coins out of every cast member's sofa and having weeks of bake sales? Sometimes you must take the plunge. You might fail spectacularly, but you will have tried.

Boiler Room Voices

RENÉE HATFULL BROOKS

Added to the Circle

Years before a successful career in theater, my number one job, like many teenaged girls in the '80s, was working as a babysitter. As I was caring for children one Friday night, I noticed that two considerate parents had rented a VHS tape for me to watch after their children were put to bed. The movie starred Michael Douglas, which sparked my interest; I recognized him from *Romancing the Stone*. Also, Janet Jones (Gretzky) had a role, who, in my young mind, was female perfection. But, even more appealing, was the picture on the cover: Dancers in flashy gold costumes with sleek, toned legs and brilliant smiles. The title, taken from the Broadway musical, was the best: *A Chorus Line*.

As I watched the movie, I was mesmerized by the story. The beginning opened with an energized dance audition that seemed to add more precision with each step. I began to care about the characters that made it to the next phase of the audition as they explained their lives with dance being at the center. They described their desperation to get the part, their complex relationships, and what they did for the love of their work. The movie finished with the emotional "cut," yet the dancers were redeemed by the famous, final number. After watching the movie and having a little bit of time before my employers came home, I rewound the tape, moved the furniture, and tried to perform parts of the dances, all the while freezing the scenes and rewinding again to learn more. I discovered that night that I loved musical theater.

After graduating from high school, I needed to move on from babysitting jobs. I was a Class I competitive gymnast and had been training since I was 9 years old. I tried for college scholarships while thinking about the possibility of majoring in dance, but I didn't know how to do that with an extremely limited understanding of ballet. I knew God had given me the ability to visualize movement when I heard music, but I didn't know how to make that *become* something. I wondered if getting into dance would perhaps lead to involvement in theater, but how could I do that with only a dream and no experience? There was also the overshadowing realization of perhaps I was too old to even begin serious dance training. Unfortunately, with injuries prevailing and a lack of direction, no college offered enough money in my chosen sport to allow me to go to school.

Years later, while trying to find my path in life, I joined the Air Force, was honorably discharged, and moved to Nashville. I had stayed in shape, and I decided to take a chance on the fantasy that still lived on in my head of becoming a dancer. I called a well-known dance school to inquire about adult ballet classes. The owner answered the phone and after politely answering my questions, asked if I had heard of their Commercial Entertainment program through a local college in Franklin which focused on dancing, singing, and acting. I asked about the acceptance of my G.I. Bill and the answer was yes—I could attend for free. I signed up right there on the phone.

College began with learning ballet, tap, and jazz, along with trying to find my singing voice, as well as involvement with acting classes. All studies led to a degree in Commercial Entertainment, which led to auditions and accepting roles in community theater productions and a few low-paying gigs. I was newly married to a man who was tremendously supportive as we both were learning what an entertainer's life would be like.

I tended to be typecast: The dingy dancer who had a few lines but never a vocal solo, unless it was supposed to imply the character could not sing, became a safe perimeter within which I could perform. After graduating, I was informed of a new, professional theater in Franklin which had the coolest name—The Boiler Room Theatre—that was auditioning triple threats for the third show in their first season, which just happened to be *A Chorus Line*. I, of course, realized that having the dream to dance in that beautiful finale with glittery gold costumes and performing the routine in my living room was quite different from doing it for real, on a real stage, in real glittery gold costumes. However, my first thought was: I can do this. I really felt that my desire could solidify a role. That initial thought, however, was followed with: *Do I have the body for it? What role could I possibly play? Could I even sing about certain subjects addressed in the show with my Christian convictions? Could I even sing at all, especially in a professional show? But wait, there was the role of Kristine! The one that had an entire song about not being able to sing!*

I chose to audition, even though I was very nervous, I tried to put forward my best effort to show them I was someone they wanted. The auditioning group was introduced to the talented director and co-founder, Lewis Kempfer, who would also play the role of the in-show director Zach. We also met another co-founder, Jamey Green, who served as the theater's Artistic and Resident Music Director. Both had hired a stunning, yet tough, choreographer, whose theater credits included [international] Broadway tours of major dance shows. I was starstruck and amazed that I had the opportunity to audition for such talented people. We were informed that all the female roles were available, except for the lead role of Cassie and, unfortunately, the role of Kristine which had already been awarded to an adorable, well-trained dancer. With that information, I stayed confident, telling myself there had to be something in that show for me. The words of the opening song, "I Hope I Get It," never felt so real.

The dance audition was first, which took place in a multipurpose hall adjacent to the theater. For some reason, possibly the way the choreographer was so thorough with her explanations or remembering that feeling I had when I first saw the movie, I nailed it. I felt secure and strong in my footing and was able to easily remember the order of steps. But oh no; the singing was next.

I saw the actual theater space for the first time during the singing audition. To me, it looked as if a small, intimate theater had delicately stepped from Broadway in New York and snuggled itself into the cozy, brick-walled space in Tennessee. There were no wings, but actors would use the building directly behind the stage for entrances and exits as well as for dressing rooms. When given a quick tour, I could tell how proud the founders were of starting this project from the ground up. However, I wasn't the only one who thought of the question: How could 18 dancers possibly fit comfortably across that narrow stage for that famous line? (It turned out that they had cut two characters because they could only fit 16 across.)

We made our way to the electric keyboard that was set up for the singing audition. I heard many fantastic singers and fought against an incredible sinking feeling. I discovered that, after about eight measures during my audition piece, the music director possessed a kind way of saying "thanks, but no thanks" that some directors have of letting you know that you would not be chosen. By the way he softly said, "OK, thank you" and handed back my music, I knew I could not be at the level they wanted. I wasn't asked to read any lines. Afterwards, as the days went by, the opening lyrics still rang true as I waited for my phone to ring.

And to my relief, it did ring. It turned out, there was something for me. Lewis asked if I was interested in being a part of the famous opening number, the one I learned when I moved the furniture all those years ago at the house where I babysat. The role was for Tricia, a dancer who was cut early, and once I exited, that would be the last of my stage time. No lines, no finale, no final bow. And no pay. Did I want that? You bet I did.

I was in! A dancer who started extremely late in life was now in the show many triple threats hoped for, even if it was for only approximately ten minutes. Expectations from the crew were high and needed to be for a show like that. Rehearsals and discussions about costumes started right away. I was to wear a leotard, tights, and character shoes, all black with cream-colored leg warmers which made me feel exactly like a dancer from the 70s. In dance rehearsals at Hume-Fogg High School, a performing-arts school in Nashville, our choreographer kept a watchful eye over our steps. At the conclusion of many physically demanding rehearsals, I would grab my bag, sweaty and happy, and leave with the other rejected characters, but longing for more, as the rest of the cast moved on with the show. I knew it was going to be great.

And it was. When we moved into the theater and all the dancers lined up, it was as if the stage was strategically built for each person to fit perfectly, like puzzle pieces. We had just enough room to execute the steps in our own space. When it was time for opening night, I had the feeling as if I could fly. My gymnast legs felt strong. As the run progressed, the joy continued, night after night, but each time my character was cut from the show, I began to linger a few seconds longer on the stage, showing my actual feelings of the sting of rejection and the desire to have a bigger role. Sadly, due to an unexpected loss in a cast member's private life, this very thing happened. The following story pains me to write.

I was in the backstage dressing room when I received the terrible news that many of the cast already knew. The actress who played Maggie and was Cassie's understudy had received the horrible news that her in-laws had tragically died in a private plane crash returning home after seeing her perform. I remember glancing at her as she sat in costume by her mirror, shaking and silently crying, and I wondered how she could possibly get through that night's show. Amazingly, she did. Because of her upcoming absence to attend the funeral, the crew made the decision to move roles by using understudies for the upcoming weekend. In the script, the in-show choreographer's role was originally written for a man, known as Larry, but our crew had easily filled this role with a woman, known in our show as Laurie. This actress was moved to Maggie's role. The next step was to fill the in-show choreographer's role with me. Since it was considered a professional role, I was expected to learn the entire show, including the finale, in three days. It was the least demanding role of all those onstage, yet I knew three days would go very quickly. With a heavy heart, I said yes. The dream was coming true, however, not in the way I wanted or expected.

I knew that I was going to do that role to the best of my ability. The crew trusted me, and I owed them and the cast my best effort, as well the audience, who would know nothing of me having to learn my part in such a short time. The crew did not coddle nor baby me, which I appreciated. The choreographer called my situation "immersion by fire" as she graciously worked with me. The dance captain, Nancy Whitehead Brown, who also played Laurie, was exceptional because she was busy with her new role as well. The cast stayed longer in rehearsal to include me. Since this was the age before YouTube, I took my notes home to work. I read the script, trying to memorize the order of the show as well as the lines that I had. Fingers as well as feet were oh-so-important to the final number, so I worked those repetitively, too, for hours. I focused on holding my hand at my hip in just the right angle and remembering to touch my hat with extended fingers as I searched my memory on how many kicks were at the end, with and without lifting the hat.

When it was time for the show, with roles swapped and shifted, it was my voice that called out the steps when the lights came up. Many dancers long for the opportunity to perform in *A Chorus Line* and, at that moment, I was living it. I made my way through, trying to soak up the experience of each moment and staying focused on what came next, all the while acting as if I was completely relaxed, although my insides were trembling. During the finale, it took all I had to get my emotions under control because I knew what had happened to put me there for that special moment. Because of the circumstances, understudies performed several shows that week.

A Chorus Line was the only show that I had the privilege of doing with the Boiler Room Theatre. I did go on to dance in other shows professionally and as of this writing, I enjoy a steady career as a choreographer. I will always remember my BRT experience and how they believed in me, how I wore the gold as I entered the stage as the first female to bow on the nights the understudies performed, and of being the leader in the famous wedge on the diagonal that I learned only after a few quick rehearsals. I'll always remember how I was added to the circle in the finale when we all removed our hats to link arms and dance as one unit. And for that, I am grateful.

CHAPTER 10

Total Chaos

FALL & CHRISTMAS 2001

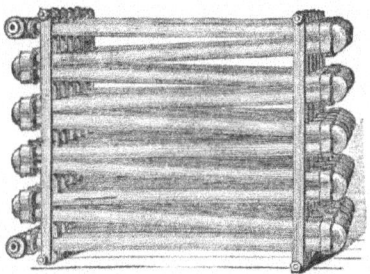

We were exhausted after a strenuous but successful summer run of *A Chorus Line*. Between the choreographer drama and Emily's tragedy, Jamey's and my attention had been completely tapped. Corbin had had a busy summer with his cabinet business. We closed the show on Saturday, September 8 with an exhausted but satisfied cast.

Two days later, the world changed.

September 11, 2001 had affected everyone in different ways, but one thing was certain: The nation was traumatized, a sense of peace and innocence was lost, and we were a little more than a week from opening the next show, *A Girl's Guide to Chaos*. The chaos part was more than we had accounted for. The LLC met to determine next steps. Would it be safe to open a show in a week? People were stunned and saddened and afraid to leave their homes. But the restaurants at The Factory weren't planning to close, so we took a cue from them.

Total Chaos

Our Resident Director and Jamey's then-wife Laura Skaug had been rehearsing the show on ACL's dark nights. It would be played on the same black-box, curtained stage that we'd opened the theater with. To be honest, I hated that black curtain because it always felt like a cop out. No time to build a set? Throw the black stage drapes up.

The first thing we had to mitigate was re-writing and re-recording the pre-show announcements. I wrote the scripts, and they had, up until that point, been full of cringe-worthy airplane jokes such as "In the case of an emergency, a mask will drop from the ceiling. Yours may be either the comedy or tragedy mask, so please play along accordingly." Yeah, those jokes were no longer funny, if ever they were.

When we rather hastily planned the first season, the theater staffer pitching a show had to have read the script and already vetted it against our expected demographic. We trusted Laura, and being so terribly busy, no one else had time to read the script. I don't blame Laura, and Jamey wanted edgy, so I have no doubt she believed it to be a good fit, but the LLC should have been more involved in the inclusion of the show. *A Girl's Guide to Chaos* was essentially four bitchy women and a bitchy waitress all bitching about life, bitching about men, and bitching about sex. We advertised it as a sort of live version of *Sex and the City*. It wasn't selling tickets, but as we would later learn, nonmusicals never drew a crowd. There *was* a crowd on opening night, the house packed with season-ticket holders, sponsors, and our new fan base.

Jamey, Corbin, and I were seated in the last row of the upper house. It would be unthinkable to not attend opening night of one of our own shows. As the bawdy, bitchy script unfolded, we each slunk a bit lower in our seats in embarrassment. Lines including blatantly vulgar words such as "c-cksucker" had us red-faced. By the time one of the characters said "sperm facial fiasco," we were totally slumped down as if we were trying to disappear into the upholstery. Some guests walked out. We got plenty of irate phone calls. We vowed to never again place a show in a season without first reading the script.

We planned the 2002 season more carefully and had a full seven-show line-up under the overarching theme of "Around the World in Seven Plays." The adventure actually began with our second go-round of season auditions, this time in our own heated space. We were still requiring an uptempo and a ballad plus a two-minute monologue. Seriously—monologues at auditions are useless. As a director, they show me nothing I need to see. But sometimes they were epic.

One young and mostly inexperienced actress choked out her two songs, then, presumably because we were doing a remount of the Avante Garage's *McBeth! The Musical Comedy!* that season, rolled out a Juliet monologue in what can only be described as a Southern valley-girl dialect. She botched the entire monologue, but the infamous line was "Romeo is *banish-shed-ed-ed* [banish'd]; and all the Disney World [world] is nothing."

Jamey and I glanced over at Corbin's clipboard. Across her audition form he'd written in huge letters, "She is banish-ed-ed-ed." I nearly bit my tongue off trying not to guffaw.

The same season also included *Little Shop of Horrors*, and because of that, we probably heard 27 renditions of Audrey's Act One-ballad, "Somewhere That's Green." One particular never-going-to-play-Audrey-in-any-universe girl was so off-key that I wrote across my audition evaluation form, "How about somewhere that's in tune?"

Our first holiday show was *The 1940s Radio Hour*, a show that I knew was special to Jamey, Laura, Corbin, and Teressa; basically to everyone but me. I didn't like the script. The first 20 or so minutes are a choreographed pantomime of the show's characters arriving and settling in for a live Christmas Eve radio show. I reluctantly played Clifton, the always-stressed general manager (which was actually appropriate) and announcer. My "office" was the lobby and as such had close-up views of confused audience members. I wanted to say, "Hey, I don't get it either, but hang in there, it gets better once the music starts."

And the show does get dramatically better when the fictional radio show goes "on the air." Jamey had assembled a kick-ass, seven-piece band with brass and woodwinds. The cast was filled with talented singers. The music was great, the comedy was snappy, and audiences left charmed and in the holiday spirit. It was a satisfying end to a roller-coaster inaugural season.

But even this show had its challenges.

The church in the next building over was always loud. Whether it was a worship service or a concert, they would easily drown out our shows, with volume levels loud enough for God in His heaven to hear. And so it was that during a Sunday matinee, a particular actor grabbed a baseball bat (I had started props for *Baby* which required five baseball bats for a production number) and marched over to the church and beat on their locked doors despite a concert in progress. He verbally threatened to break down their doors if they didn't turn the volume down. He wasn't successful. This same scene played out with the same actor during 2002's *Lucky Stiff*. It was embarrassing and inappropriate. We were all with him in spirit and probably could have staged a fight scene with actors going over carrying pitchforks and lighted torches. But that never happened.

On a lighter but smellier note, one actor had a deodorant problem. As in, he didn't wear any. His body odor was so horrendous, so noxious, it would make one's eyes water to be near him. And on stage, one can't grimace or pinch his or her nose. I suppose we could have put Vicks VapoRub under our noses as some in law enforcement do when they expect to encounter a dead body. But that rub would have glimmered in the stage lights.

That first year we did Secret Santas, the popular activity where one draws someone's name and leaves a gift for his or her person either weekly or daily. It's anyone's guess who had the guy, but I helped buy a bunch of travel-size deodorant sticks. On the final night of the show, which was the last night of Secret Santas, the actor received a gift bag with approximately 30 sticks of deodorant. It pissed him off mightily. But when he resurfaced for *Lucky Stiff*, the odor problem was gone. He must have gotten the hint. I just hope we included sticks of Secret brand deodorant to tie in with Secret Santas.

The first Christmas at the Boiler Room saw more shenanigans. One of the guys in the cast, who was partnered with a gorgeous doctor, held a cast party at their palatial homestead in midtown Nashville. There was a huge hot tub and enough liquor to fill it. A few people stripped to their undies and hurried to the oversized hot tub. I was shy and awkward as always, not wanting to show my flabby body. After the first drink, I had enough courage to strip and dip in.

Drinks continued to flow. By the fourth or fifth Tom Collins—always my go-to cocktail—I was ready for anything. So was the rest of the group that included Daniel; Allen, the guy from the show with the doctor husband; Letitia; Corbin; Jamey; two cast members from the 1999 Act1 production of *Hair* that both Daniel and I were in; the young actress who played Connie who always had rancid breath; and a couple more folks.

There was a game of Truth or Dare, then eventually a group dare to kiss the person to their right. I wanted it to be Daniel, but I was between Letitia and the gorgeous doctor. God was smiling on me that night when I realized gorgeous doctor was on my right. We went at it and it was magical under a December moon in a deliciously warm hot tub.

People started leaving and I was one of the last to exit the hot tub, quite reluctantly. At that point in my life, I'd never been a party animal, but that night I was plastered. The guy from the show and his husband wanted me to stay over and not drive. But after my buzz deteriorated by a notch, I got weepy about being single during the holidays. Then a wave of self-hatred washed over me and I announced I was driving home and "let's all pray I get in a fatal accident."

I shouldn't have been driving. I was weaving and could barely see the road. I had to navigate the challenging I-40 to I-65 lane shift, which was awful planning on someone's part. All the people heading east on I-40 had to cross over three lanes to the right to stay on I-40, while all the people heading north on I-65 had to cross over the same three lanes to the left to remain on I-65. During rush hour, it was nasty. But at four in the morning, it was no problem, other than my vision being badly blurred. I made it home to Sunnymeade without getting a DUI.

The bow on the first season's mixed package of success was that we somehow, miraculously broke even in our first business year. That's basically unheard of within the entertainment and hospitality industries. Of course, Cathie's and my infusion of cash for *A Chorus Line* helped us achieve breaking even, so the actual results were a bit skewed.

HOT TIPS

Know Thy Audience

We blew it twice in our first season, but we were learning. Trust your demographic data. We were in the wealthiest county in the Nashville area, right in the middle of the "buckle of the Bible Belt." I knew, and on some level, I think my co-founders knew that we could only go to a certain degree of edgy. *Ruthless!* wasn't at all edgy (other than a guy in drag), but it fit our business model of presenting shows that guests couldn't see anywhere in Middle Tennessee. But the show's jokes and gags were for more theatrically sophisticated audiences such as those in New York.

A Girl's Guide to Chaos was terribly shocking and crude for the far-right Christian crowd, that oddly enough, loved every second of "Tits and Ass" in *A Chorus Line*. Thus, we learned more about our guest base. Tits were OK, but sperm facials crossed the line. It echoed the punchline to the old joke about Nashville: Every intersection has a church, a Shoney's (restaurant), and a topless bar.

Although it's much more of a community-theater thing, if you have a Board of Directors or steering committee, it might not be a bad idea to have them read proposed scripts. In our case, we had an Artistic Director

(Jamey) and the rest of us were theater-savvy. They can't all be home runs, but if you're consistently not making the playoffs, something is wrong.

And mind where you store the baseball bats.

2002 SEASON

Around the World in Seven Plays

Baby, The Musical
Lucky Stiff
Little Shop of Horrors
Six Degrees of Separation
McBeth! The Musical Comedy!
Man of La Mancha
A Dickens of a Christmas Carol

CHAPTER 11

Miscarriage

SEASON OPENER 2002

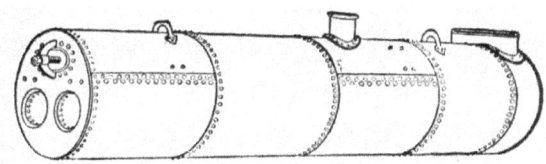

We charged boldly into 2002 and our second season in one of the most bone-chillingly cold winters Nashville had ever seen. We still had the big, empty freezer of a backstage building. I had hoped that situation could have been remedied between seasons, but we decided guest-facing changes were more important. The main thing was that we survived the first year.

The first season's lobby was embarrassingly sparse, just a folding table with a frayed black tablecloth and intermission snacks stored underneath. It was far from professional, but we had run out of time and money. I added touches such as antique "pumpkin tables" topped with faux fern arrangements and random prop pieces in the restrooms. And because The Factory started as the Dortch stove factory, I found an antique Dortch buck stove on eBay, which for a couple of years, was a charming little fixture. In late 2003, when I started creating elaborately themed lobbies, I gave the stove to The Factory to add to its exhibit collection, concluding its 70-year journey back home.

Miscarriage

The bare lobby finally took shape when, between the 2001 and 2002 seasons, Corbin built a custom L-shaped counter and desk unit. The long counter would serve as the home for the cash register, concessions, and popcorn machine. The short part of the "L" dropped down and was the box-office desk. I wished there had been a visual barrier so guests couldn't see what was usually a very messy desk when they entered the house. We never found a solution and I was always embarrassed by our clutter.

I had invested financially in the theater the first year but hadn't yet fully invested myself. I was unhappy in my current job and couldn't bear to be away from the Boiler Room. I finally realized that I wanted to be in Franklin running the place, despite there being little money to pay me. And we already had the wife of one of my partners working the box office when her schedule allowed. It wasn't a smart way to run a business, and after presenting a financial plan to Jamey, as well as practically begging, I became the full-time Managing Director and box-office dude for the measly sum of $1,000 per month. I continued to do freelance graphic design work whenever I could find it.

But to really make the full-time position work, I had to file for bankruptcy for the second time in my life. I had racked up a lot of debt from home repairs, a short-lived marriage, and the black Toyota king-cab truck I financed when I was spinning out of control after I'd been dumped. The truck was repossessed, and I bought a $1,200 beater car, a metallic blue, 1989 Chevrolet Cavalier sedan that looked exactly like Daniel's 1990 edition. We used to joke that the 1989-1990 blue Cavalier was the official car of the Boiler Room Theatre as there were frequently two of them parked behind the backstage building.

We had good publicity in the run-up to our second season as noted by Franklin's *The Review Appeal:*

...

"That the Boiler Room Theatre opened on time and that its first [show] was ready for the stage is what Jamey Green calls a miracle…

"… Tuesday, just three days before the second season begins with a production… of *Baby*, things seem to be running a lot smoother. Corbin Green adjusts lights while his brother, Jamey, plays songs on the keyboard. [Lewis] Kempfer and a group of production assistants and actors are joking around with flashlights they'll use as props… More actors come in and are greeted with smiles and hugs. There's a relaxed feeling of excitement as everyone gets ready to open the [second] season with a bang…"

...

The season did not open with a bang, rather a barely audible thud.

For the season opener, we chose the outdated *Baby, The Musical*. I pitched it, Jamey knew the great Maltby and Shire score, and it seemed like a viable second cousin to *I Love You, You're Perfect, Now Change*. We thought we'd hit the theatrical jackpot when an actress from the television series *Knight Rider* auditioned. Rebecca Holden had been a Breck shampoo girl, the second female mechanic on the car-based show, and was even immortalized in metal on the *Knight Rider* lunchbox. Jamey was the show's director and cast Rebecca as the oldest female of three couples, all being surprised by or trying hard to have a baby. I felt we couldn't miss—we had a *name* in the show.

Turns out having a *name* didn't carry much weight. All my Rebecca-Holden-centric advertising fell flat, and tickets weren't selling. The show

Miscarriage

seemed perfect for Williamson County which was chock-full of heterosexual couples having babies. Maybe it hit too close to home, akin to a busman's holiday. You know, a guy who drives a bus for a living doesn't want to take a bus trip for his vacation. It didn't occur to us that families with young children might not want to spend their valuable free time thinking about babies.

We had a stellar cast: Daniel Vincent and Erica Aubrey née Rowlett played the college-aged couple who had an "oops" pregnancy; a new actress, but soon to be a staple of BRT, Erin Parker, played my wife. We were the couple in their mid-thirties desperate for a child but unable to conceive. The silky voiced John Warren played Rebecca's husband. They were the empty nesters who also had a surprise pregnancy.

The show could have been staged on a clever set with oversized baby blocks on multiple levels, but once again, the black drapes went up. It was a drab look for an outdated show from 1983. Guests who saw the show left with "meh" expressions on their faces. (The show was updated sometime after our production and is now the only version available for licensing. Generally, theater folks prefer the original version, now unavailable, that we staged.)

Martin Brady's review in the *Scene* was dismal:

. . .

"The men all have their moments, but only Warren consistently charms. He is particularly good delivering his Act Two numbers. Vincent is generally too cornball to be believed, and Kempfer is saddled with occasionally having to interpolate a Jackie Gleason imitation into his character. (He doesn't appear to embrace this unfortunate bit of shtick, and who can blame him?)

"… As for the women, as a group they're slightly better—but not by much. Rowlett's earnest youthfulness is cute (but too much by half, probably). Holden, looking every bit the Kewpie doll, might have projected more sophistication. Parker offers the most appealing performance—she's got some personal spark, sports a twinkle in her eye and sings nicely…

"… Aside from a handful of pleasant scenes where everything good comes together, watching this *Baby* come into the world is often as difficult and as messy as, well… giving birth."

...

Ouch.

We were never sure if newspaper reviews improved or impacted our business, but reviews like the one for *Baby* certainly didn't help.

It also didn't help that the cast was a group of singing popsicles as a result of spending its offstage time in the backstage freezer. We brought in several space heaters that only managed to blow a breaker. Then one of those jet-engine-looking heat blowers was employed. Erin and I were scantily clad throughout most of the show because nearly all our scenes were in bed trying to make a baby. People thought she and I had great stage chemistry, and perhaps we did, but I think we were mostly clinging to each other to warm up.

Then there was the problem with the "star value" not delivering our hoped-for results and causing a disturbance of sorts.

One Sunday afternoon, audible to the cast on the stage, Teressa in the tech booth, and guests in their seats, there was a loud rumbling that sounded like it was right outside the side doors. At first, we thought it was another concert at the church in Building 8, but when we got to intermission, Jamey and Teressa found the culprit: A beat-up, rusted RV that looked like Cousin Eddie's in *Christmas Vacation*. Its motor belched and sputtered as if it were held together with duct tape. It was Rebecca's boyfriend's motor home that was parked on the grass next to the backstage door. She had been using it as her "star" trailer to stay warm. Teressa demanded that the motor be shut off immediately and wanted it gone after the show. It made an encore appearance at the next show, however, one of our packed Two-for-Tuesday performances, so another audience was treated to the sound of an engine on its last cylinder. Whatever transpired in the heated second-warning conversation that night had worked—the RV never again parked on the grass but was seen in the parking lot.

Baby closed with a muffled cry and became one of the shows that was only mentioned with hands shielding eyes and spoken of in hushed tones of utter embarrassment.

HOT TIPS
What's in a Name?

Just because you might attract an actor who'd been famous a couple of decades prior, having a *name* in the business doesn't necessarily mean that he or she will elevate your show to dizzying heights. Sometimes it's the person, sometimes it's the show, and sometimes it's a combination of the two.

It's also a good idea to spell out in your actor contracts—you *are* doing contracts, right?—things like designated call times and parking areas. And in regard to contracts, be sure to include a clause about participating in publicity activities which may include photo shoots, radio spots, television interviews and performances, and the like. CYA (cover your ass). You don't want your talent, particularly *name* talent, refusing to take part in publicity efforts.

CHAPTER 12

Sometimes You Get Lucky

SECOND SLOT & SPRING 2002

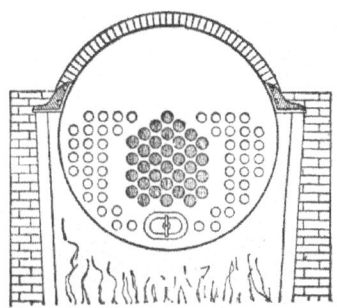

During my tenure at the Boiler Room Theatre, I maintained a massive collection of Broadway cast albums on CDs and more obscure, older stuff on vinyl. And I was always researching new shows. When we were planning 2002, I brought to the table an oddball Off-Broadway musical comedy called *Lucky Stiff*. The plot was simple. In order to receive his inheritance, a bumbling shoe salesman is required to take his dead uncle on vacation to Monte Carlo and not let anyone catch on that the uncle is deceased. Think *Weekend at Bernie's* set to a lively Lynn Ahrens and Stephen Flaherty (*Ragtime, Once on This Island*) score of infectious tunes. It landed squarely in Corbin's wheelhouse and he desperately wanted to direct it.

Lucky Stiff attracted a few new cast members who ended up becoming repertory members, that is, if we were a rep company which we were not.

But the show brought us Megan Murphy Chambers, Patrick Kramer, and Sondra Morton. Lisa Gillespie returned to the BRT stage, and Dietz Osborne also made his BRT debut. With Jamey's musical direction, Lauri's choreography, and Corbin's colorful set of doors and doorframes on wheels, it showed great promise.

It became the sleeper hit of the season. It was one of those magical moments in the theater when the right show hit the right spot with the right audience, word of mouth took off, and we were playing to packed houses. Even Martin Brady gushed over the production with his review titled "Dead On":

. . .

"A simply delightful musical comedy opened last weekend in Franklin… With its well-balanced cast and resourceful staging, this zany, highly entertaining show is the company's best overall effort since its inaugural *I Love You, You're Perfect, Now Change* nearly a year ago…

"… The players are absolutely in synch with the spirit of things. They are led by Patrick Kramer, a likable, rubber-faced comic actor who makes the most of every moment as the innocent, beleaguered Harry…

"… Everyone else is right on target too. Sondra Morton-Chaffin as the money-grubbing, venomous but ultimately harmless Rita La Porta is over-the-top funny. Lewis Kempfer as her put-upon optometrist brother gets his laughs and croons capably…

"*Lucky Stiff* is a real winner. It's worth the trip to Franklin."

. . .

120 SEATS IN A BOILER ROOM

Lucky Stiff provided a much-needed boost to the bank account after the under-performing *Baby*. The show was so popular that my successors revived it in 2007 with most of the original cast. Although the show was associated with the Boiler Room, eventually, it seemed that every other theater in town had mounted *Lucky Stiff*. But I'm proud to say that, through my research, I was the one who brought it to Nashville.

I oversaw marketing and publicity and squeezed every tuppence and half-tuppence out of the meager budget. I tried thinking outside the box, but sometimes members of our company had more daring ideas. Like the night that Sondra wrote "Buy Season Tickets" on the inside of her thighs. I call it the Spread Eagle Number One. She came out with this beauty during the song "Fancy Meeting You Here," when there was a choreographed moment Sondra did a sort of barrel roll over the twin bed on stage, spreading her legs as she performed the move. She was trying to help us grab some last-minute, remainder-of-the-season ticket sales. The night she pulled her stunt, she stopped mid-roll, keeping her bare legs wide open (she was wearing Spanx dance briefs) to display her message, all while singing. The cast was quite sure that many in the audience saw the unorthodox advertising scheme. Whether it sold any tickets, well, none of us knew for sure. But if we did, Sondra helped provide a leg up.

It was during one of the performances that Franklin was receiving a downpour with thunder and lightning. Heavy rain on the metal roof always rendered our sound system ineffective just as wind made the old smokestack sound like the Titanic splitting in two. But on that particular night, during one of Patrick Kramer's numbers, "It's Good to Be Alive," the storm was so fierce that it pushed water through the near-century-old bricks. In 2002, we kept the band in the tech booth until I "invented" the two-story set that became a mainstay and popular way to get the band on stage.

"The water was pouring on both musicians and technicians up there. So, while we were on stage oblivious to what was happening up in the booth, there was a huge crack of thunder and we lost power," said Patrick. "Well, rather than simply stopping, we all just kept performing—in the dark and *a cappella!* I could faintly hear Jamey still pounding on the soundless keyboard in the booth and after what felt like an eternity (but probably wasn't more than a second), the power kicked back on, the music came back to life, and miraculously, we were all still together!

"Those of us on stage later found out that while all that was going on, the folks in the booth were scrambling to cover equipment so nothing would be destroyed by the rain."

There was another night we caught a lucky break during yet another storm. We were in the middle of the second act's big tap number in black light when we lost power. This time it was mighty gusts of wind that made the HVAC unit on the roof and the ducts inside rattle and threaten to come apart. The old smokestack did its rock, squeak, and creak routine. We had asked The Factory to fix it, and they attempted, but eventually gave up. They offered to have it removed, but we declined because it served as a sort of "weenie." Let me explain. The smokestack was the tallest fixture amongst The Factory's sprawling campus. Disney Imagineers always placed at least one "weenie," that is, a tall feature in its parks such as the spires of Cinderella's castle in Fantasyland at Walt Disney World. Akin to one cartoon character luring another with a hot dog on a stick, a weenie's purpose is to draw guests toward an attraction. Our building was difficult to locate for our guests, so we needed all the help we could get. We needed to keep our weenie.

In the booth, Jamey pushed production stage manager Teressa into the audio mixing board to avoid a possible collapse of the ductwork. And during the several seconds we were without power, the cast just kept tapping. As before, when the power was restored, we were in perfect sync with the band. And just like in the first instance, we received thunderous applause.

The third show of 2002 was *Little Shop of Horrors,* for which I was director and set designer. The set was the first elaborate one on the BRT stage complete with a revolving center platform on which the floral shop was placed. It took some convincing to Corbin, but I got my revolve. To accommodate the third- and fourth-largest Audrey II plant puppet reveals, the floral shop unit needed to either be hidden or rotated out of view. We didn't have the stage real estate to build the set as originally produced Off-Broadway with tall, sliding scrim/screen panels. On either side of the stage, we added a portion of a rusted fire escape, a partial wall made out of corrugated metal and wooden palettes, and my favorite piece of any of my sets, a broken-down porch stoop with a dilapidated newel post and broken balusters. (See, Leo, we used balusters.) It was a great look for the conclusion of "Suddenly, Seymour."

I had played Seymour in 1997 at another theater and helped with puppet construction. But I knew we didn't have the time nor available labor to build our own set of puppets, which required a tabletop Audrey II puppet, a larger version carried by Seymour and held with a fake arm, the third incarnation that filled a third of the flower shop interior, and the final and largest version that "eats" four of the main characters. There is also a bit in the script's finale that is only sporadically done by other theaters in which the four main characters (Seymour, Audrey, Orin Scrivello, D.D.S, and Mr. Mushnick) become offshoots of the plant, each in his or her own flowerpot. In some productions, as was done Off-Broadway, vines drop from a theater's ceiling to just above the audience. I would have loved to do that, but as always, no time nor money.

I did a lot of research and finally found a high school halfway to Memphis with a nearly complete set of puppets for rent. I took Dietz (who I had cast as the sadistic dentist) and a U-Haul on a road trip hoping the puppets looked like the photos we were sent. Like a typical online blind date, they didn't look quite like their photos, but we had no other options. Today, the plant puppets can be rented directly from Music Theatre International (MTI), the show's licensing company.

We schlepped the puppets and their spare pieces and parts into the Boiler Room, laid out our haul and took inventory of what needed to be repaired or improved. The list wasn't short. Two of our regular stagehands, Beth Eakin O'Neill and Jessica Kammerud, were my rehab team.

Corbin looked at our haul. "The second-largest puppet needs some reinforcement," he said. "But the big one needs some serious rehab. We're gonna have to build a new internal structure."

"I'm going to have check with the high school we rented these from," I said.

"They should be grateful we'll be returning to them a much better puppet."

The first thing to deal with was the flimsy structure inside puppet number four, the largest. It had a PVC-pipe skeleton, but it protested and split in half during the first test. Corbin built the new structure, trying to keep it as lightweight as possible. Thank goodness we had cast an experienced puppeteer named Curtis, but even he had trouble manipulating the hunk of foam and plastic piping. He sustained a back injury during the run due to the big puppet, but like a trooper, sucked it up and carried on. I tried getting inside and couldn't even open the puppet's mouth.

We gussied up the puppets, adding new foam warts and vines and touching up paint. We built a seat for the puppeteer inside a kiddie swimming pool painted to look like a clay pot. It was a pilot's seat for a small boat with a seat belt securely anchored to the rotating platform to allow the puppeteer to move as necessary without losing his balance or sliding off the chair. For the finale, we built four pods out of backyard pond liners and fabric, and costumer Erin Parker created shimmery green capes and adorable flower headpieces for each of the four characters that are consumed by Audrey II.

The show did well enough. It wasn't the box-office blockbuster I'd hoped for, but the cast was relatively small, and payroll was manageable. The run was uneventful with no major mishaps, puppet malfunctions, or power outages. But the revolving floral shop was so heavy that it wore a deep groove into the stage floor which required us to add a new top layer.

The one review we received was by Leo Sochocki of *The City Paper*. Dietz as Orin Scrivello, D.D.S. (the dentist) received the most glowing review and Erin Parker as Audrey also got compliments on her "less vapid rendition" noting a welcome departure from the typical Ellen Greene (original cast and film Audrey). Jeremy Evans reeled from a scathing review for his portrayal of Seymour. Leo also wrote:

. . .

"The set and lighting, by Corbin Greene [SIC], are the best I've seen at [the] Boiler Room. Lewis Kempfer's staging and Jamie [SIC] Green's musical direction keep the production well-paced and interesting."

. . .

Funny he didn't mention the couple of missing balusters on the broken-down porch vignette. But it was Skid Row after all.

That summer was also the first attempt at a children's theater day camp. Janet Ivey, who had been in *Baby* and had her own PBS science show, *Janet's Planet*, led the program, but response was tepid, and we looked incapable of offering a meaningful experience. Prior to camp starting, I was going through the registration forms for accounting purposes and saw a familiar name: Country singer Billy Ray Cyrus who was a season-ticket holder. He had enrolled a female child with what seemed to be a misspelled first name that I could only assume was "Millie."

Turns out it was pronounced Miley.

HOT TIPS

Unknown vs Overdone

Sometimes, taking a chance on an unknown show can yield big rewards as what happened with *Lucky Stiff*. Not only did BRT introduce the show to Tennessee, but several other local productions were mounted based on our success. The show had a medium-size payroll which made it financially risky. But we lucked out.

When producing a well-known show such as *Little Shop of Horrors*, don't try to recreate the movie, its set, or its cast's performances. It's like the overdone riff sung by every Rizzo in every production of *Grease*: "I could stay home every night, wait around for "MIS—TER righ—ight…" With a show like *Little Shop*, make it your own whether you're the director, actor, set designer, or theater owner.

When I signed on to direct *Little Shop*, I refused to allow myself to watch the film. I did watch the original 1960s cheesy source film but got nothing out of it. I had to rely on my memories of the production in which I played Seymour—the things that worked and those that did not. The biggest challenge was imagining the show on the small BRT stage and looking for opportunities to make the space work for us, not against us. For example, the crumbling, exposed brick and rusty beams alone put us on Skid Row. We just had to add the set.

My point is that a refreshing, perhaps even innovative production will land well with theater critics and audiences. If you do *Little Shop,* save yourself a migraine and rent your puppets from either MTI or a professional theatrical rental company.

And try hard to not get behind in rent. You may have a lenient landlord, as we did in Calvin LeHew, but back-rent adds up quickly.

MORE HOT TIPS
Fun with Accounting

This was also the time period during which I led the process to take the theater from a for-profit LLC to a non-profit 501(c)(3) performing arts organization. I could go into detail, but I guarantee I'd put you to sleep. There are plenty of books and resources to instruct you through this process should that be your goal. As the theater's bookkeeper, it just meant gathering and crunching a bunch of numbers and having a few sessions with our accountant. Filing wasn't difficult, just tedious. But it did make future tax returns more challenging.

Our hope was that we could get grants. That was supposed to be Samantha's role, but of course by this point she was long gone. I probably could have learned how to write grant proposals, but I was too busy running the theater. Barbara Green got us a couple of small ones. The biggest challenge was that arts grants came through Davidson County (Greater Nashville), not Williamson County (where we were located), and that severely limited us. We were able to get minuscule discounts on fabric at Jo-Ann and on items from thrift stores, but that was about it. At least during my tenure, it didn't really make much difference nor impact on our snowballing debt, particularly in rent owed to The Factory.

Fun with Accounting

If you have the luxury of time before opening a theater company, go non-profit immediately. It will eventually pay off, especially if you're in a major city with multiple grant options.

Boiler Room Voices

PATRICK KRAMER

Worth Fighting For

In the year 2000, I heard about a new professional theater, just a bit south of Nashville. I auditioned at their first general auditions for the 2001 season and saw many friends as I looked around the room. They said they were turning an old boiler room into a theater venue. It was a mental picture my head couldn't quite unscramble. A boiler room? I'd heard of and performed at theaters in basements, cafeterias, warehouses, and old churches. But a boiler room?

Turns out, the four co-founders did something nearly impossible, but they truly took an boiler room building at a once run-down factory, cleared decades of debris, built a stage, and installed 120 actual theater seats. Never mind the enormous original boiler in the backstage building that was filled with asbestos.

From 2001 until near the bitter end, I played dozens of roles, checking many off my bucket list. I got to be in unknown shows, some of which became sleeper hits, original shows such as Jamey Green's *McBeth! The Musical Comedy!* and Lewis Kempfer's *That '60s Christmas*

Show. I played both minor and major roles in large productions. And I loved every minute of it.

Then came 2011 and *The Rocky Horror Show*. It wasn't staged frequently in Nashville due to the content, but the Boiler Room, as it had with many large productions unthinkable for the small stage, courageously grabbed the bull by its fishnet stockings and placed it in a prime spot in the 2011 season. Riff Raff was one of roles at the very top of my bucket list, and I knew I just had to get cast in the role. Competition was strong, as it had always been at BRT, and after a long, grueling callback, director Megan Murphy Chambers awarded me the role. The cast, musicians, and set were all typical top-notch BRT. The show was so popular that they brought it back in 2013 and it fared equally well. The BRT founders had always considered doing a production annually, something in the Christmas slot. But I think that *Rocky Horror* in the Halloween slot could have sold out year after year.

I'd say my biggest takeaway from those first five years was that I'll always be grateful for the opportunities the Boiler Room gave me. Allowing me to grow as an actor and forge bonds and friendships that have lasted 20 years. I believed in everything BRT stood for as a theater company and coming in practically from the beginning created a sense of family that I was willing to fight for, even during the most challenging times.

Boiler Room Voices

SONDRA MORTON

Once in a Lifetime

In the spring of 2001, I walked into a quaint little space called the Boiler Room Theatre and knew that I had entered something special. We went to see the inaugural production of *I Love You, You're Perfect, Now Change*. It's hard to put into words what it was that made BRT so special at that moment, but I would soon learn.

The second year of the theater's opening I had the opportunity to join the acting group with a little show called *Lucky Stiff*. With this show I met my best friends; friends that I have to this very day. The Boiler Room was so much more than the unique building. It was the people.

At the time, there was nothing like BRT, which already made it special, but the people inside made it magical. It was a historic little nugget of a building that within its crumbling brick walls were produced shows that were bigger than life. Whatever the obstacle, we, as a group, made it work. The production team and cast worked like a family with the same goal: To produce extraordinary theater. And we did.

It was truly amazing what BRT was able to produce on such a small stage. One of the biggest and fondest memories I have is that of *Disney's*

Beauty and the Beast. The costumes and set were like a pop-up book come to life. There were some 25 performers in impossibly huge costumes. Navigating the backstage area was certainly a challenge, but once the show was up and running, it was simply intricate choreography that we executed for countless shows in a standing-room-only run in which I believe we had a Saturday in December on which we performed three shows. Talk about exhausting. And as Madame de la Grande Bouche (aka the Wardrobe), I had the largest costume and knew all there was to know about exhausting. Whenever I feel like I have agreed to a show that seems larger than life, I often say, "This can be done. After all, we did *Disney's Beauty and the Beast* on the Boiler Room stage—anything is possible!"

Several years later, I had the chance to join in as Operations Manager for the Boiler Room. This was a whole new world. It was a side of theater I had never really seen before. It went beyond "behind the scenes" and truly opened my mind to what it meant to run a theater. It wasn't easy. My heart was often torn between the bottom line and artistic success. The challenge was to make the two cohesive. It didn't always work out that way.

I distinctly remember producing 2009's *Sunday in the Park with George*. The BRT team nailed it. It was stunning, magical, and inspiring. It was also huge and just wasn't making enough money to make payroll. I will never forget the night that I had to tell the cast and team that we had to close early because of financial reasons. Everyone was in tears, me included. These were the kind of decisions that made being on the other side so heartbreaking.

However, one of the highlights of working with BRT, besides as an actress, was growing my children's theater program, Act Too Players. During spring and fall shows, as well as summer camps including a Musical Theatre Intensive in which the young participants took part in a full-sized production, these kids had the opportunity to perform on a professional stage. They knew that performing there was special. Several of the kids even had the chance to be in BRT shows such as *Gypsy, Billy Bob's Holiday Hoedown, Assassins,* and *Annie Get Your Gun* (just to name a few). As the owner of Act Too, I am clear that BRT helped pave the way to our success today.

Several amazing actors came through the doors of the Boiler Room. Some have moved on to having theaters of their own, while others have moved to NYC. And many are still thankful for the time we had in that special little brick building. It was one of a kind. It was once in a lifetime. It was something that hasn't been recreated anywhere. It was a unique, special, and magical time in all our lives. For me personally, I am forever grateful for this time and will never forget it.

CHAPTER 13

Six Degrees of WTF

EARLY SUMMER 2002

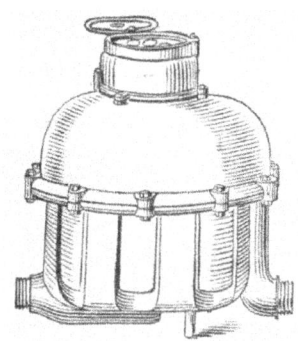

The fourth show, in what we called the first summer slot, was John Guare's award-winning play *Six Degrees of Separation*. It was BRT's second foray into a nonmusical play and became the most embarrassing production in the theater's history. A biting satire of upper-class Manhattan society members, the play's main characters are a married couple—Flan and Ouisa Kittredge—of which the husband is an art dealer. On a night the Kittredges are entertaining a millionaire investor, a young con artist drops into their lives under the guise that he has just been mugged.

The couple takes him in only to find the next morning to their horror and disgust that Paul, the con artist, is in bed with a gay lover. That storyline is barely scandalous now and wasn't much more so when we mounted the show in 2002, aside from the fact that we were in the middle of ultra-conservative Tennessee, the buckle of the Bible Belt. Audiences probably could have overlooked the gay character to an extent had it not been for in-your-face dialogue such as the line spoken by actor Dietz Osborne as Rick: "… he asked if he could f-ck me and I had never done anything like that and he did it and it was fantastic." Now, the f-bomb was only slightly less offensive than any line taking the Lord's name in vain which is why, at least while I was with BRT, we always cut any blasphemous "G.D.s," but sometimes we let an f-word fly and usually got complaints. I think the complaints for this particular line were more severe because a gay character said he *enjoyed* the bedroom activity.

Turning once again to a *Nashville Scene* review, Martin rated our production as "mixed":

. . .

"Boiler Room Theatre is currently presenting the first professional production of this script in the Nashville area… Results are mixed, to be sure… and the production is operating a little too obviously on a budget. The scenery is absolutely bare-bones, so that there is hardly even a hint of the upscale Manhattan apartment setting in which the drama ought to unfold. On a more positive note, Corbin Green, who 'designed' the non-set, also directed the action, and in this he at least displays the perspicacity to keep the dialogue and action moving apace…

"… Alas, getting there would have been more fun if Kazu Hishida, a rank amateur, were more up to the task in the pivotal role of Paul. He looks the part well enough, and

120 SEATS IN A BOILER ROOM

even seems to have some raw communication skills, yet he too often stands and declaims his words, if not with outright monotony then with barely perceptible intelligibility."

...

It was an accurate and blistering attack on Kaz's performance. The rest of the cast received ratings from decent to outstanding. Yeah, so the set was sparse, but the cast was strong—except the pivotal role of Paul played by Kaz. It wasn't our first show that received a mixed review nor would it be our last.

What made the entire Boiler Room Theatre team red-faced and want to crawl under that last row of seats again is what happened next.

Kaz took it upon himself to write a shameless letter to the Letters to the Editor ("Love/Hate Mail") section of the *Nashville Scene* directed to Martin Brady—doing the unthinkable: Asking a theater critic to come back to give him another chance at doing better. I'm hard-pressed to think of a situation in entertainment, hospitality, or any business when such a request would be acceptable.

"I'm sorry your hotel room was infested with mice and bed bugs. Please come back tomorrow night and we'll try to do better."

Or, "I'm very sorry you got food poisoning at my restaurant and ended up in the ER. When you get out, please come back and we won't serve the old fish."

Or even, "I'm sorry, Charlene, that I totally blew that major presentation for the board of directors. Can we get them to come back and I'll give it another go?"

It seems ridiculous in any of these situations.

Here's the letter:

. . .

"One more chance, please?

"This is an official invitation for Mr. Martin Brady. I would like another opportunity to 'act' for a critic who's keen to 'critique' ('A Question of Degree,' June 27). All the initial nervousness aside, more focus is now on the character instead of the many monologues. I would like to have you (a person who's cast an opinion on me) come out and reevaluate my 'acting.' Perhaps the performance you attended was a bit like a dress rehearsal, but with that behind us, I would like the chance to have my 'raw communication skills' rehashed, refried and reprocessed. Some things are better the second time around. — Kazu Hishida"

. . .

It was telling when he referred to his own acting surrounded by quotation marks, suggesting it really wasn't acting at all. It was highly unprofessional on his part and made the entire theater company look like a bunch of boobs.

HOT TIPS
Mind Your Media Manners

You might have the best publicity program and solid media relations, but it only takes one screw-up for that to come crashing down. You can't monitor the things that cast members and staff might say to others, but often that's just hearsay and easily dismissed.

But when an actor writes a letter to a newspaper editor challenging a poor review and asking for another chance, you've got a problem. The theater critic may change his or her view of the theater's professionalism and that can damage the relationship. It's hard enough to get good reviews that might bring in extra business. And with an act such as the aforementioned, the critic doesn't know if the theater company has given its blessing to the communication. If he or she assumes that actor was speaking on behalf of the theater, therein lies the problem. Although we reached out to the reviewer stating that the letter to the editor was done by the actor without our knowledge, it still put a chink in our reputation with him.

Preventing such embarrassing mishaps can be addressed in a non-Equity contract that states the actor shall not speak on behalf of the theater nor speak to the media without the theater company's approval.

But that's hard to enforce. An infraction can cause the actor to be denied future work, but in our case, the actor was terrible, and even if the media incident hadn't happened, he would not have been cast again.

Preventing incidents such as these is not an exact science. Strong media relations might help. For example, asking a reviewer that if he or she ever receives correspondence based on a review to reach out to the theater before publishing anything. That may or may not work. But it's an argument for developing and maintaining exemplary media relations.

Boiler Room Voices

BRANDY AUSTIN

Bitten

What can I say about the Boiler Room Theatre? *It is where the madness began!*

By madness, I mean the joyous, exhausting, fulfilling, delicious, depleting, and wondrous chaos of having a life in the theater. Ask any stage veteran or middle-school-drama geek and they will all tell you the same: The theater is a bug. Once it bites you, you are infected for life.

Though I may have been bitten in high school and further infected in college, my professional career started at age 19, by painting the walls and installing the seats at the Boiler Room Theatre. I do not know whether to thank or admonish them, but Jamey Green, Laura Skaug, Lewis Kempfer, and Corbin Green invited me in and gave me so many "first" opportunities. Looking back, I really had nothing to bring to the party—except cheap labor and a hunger to learn—but they made room at the table for a green youngster anyway.

At first, after the theater was painted and the doors were opened, I ran the sound board (I knew a little about sound) for *A Chorus Line* and then the light board (about which I knew nothing) on a few other shows when help was needed. I learned to run the box office on weekends, and before long I was in the booth running sound and lights for *The 1940s Radio Hour; Little Shop of Horrors; Guys and Dolls*; and many others. I ran props for *Man of La Mancha*, stage-managed and understudied *Six Degrees of Separation*, and directed for the short-lived late-night series, a show called *Nice People Dancing to Good Country Music*. I could go on and on naming shows that I helped with (or cleaned up popcorn after), but the shows were not as important as the people. The artists at BRT became Nashville theater royalty and I am so lucky to call so many of them my friends. I cannot name them all, but I would be remiss if I did not mention Steve Boysen, Pat Street, Kara Zappacosta née McNealy, Phil Perry, Lane Wright, Brad Oxnam, Pam Atha, Darci Wantiez, and our beloved Dan McGeachy—all of whom changed me as an artist or as a person at one point or another.

Years later, after grad school, I came back to BRT to direct two shows on the Mainstage: *Thoroughly Modern Millie* and *The 25th Annual Putnam County Spelling Bee*. It was incredibly fulfilling to come back as a professional director and to be welcomed with open arms in the place where I started. Since then, from tiny storefront theaters to 9,000-seat arenas, my career as a director and producer has taken me across the country and around the world. I have worked for almost every major television network, on Broadway, for feature films, in theme parks, on many national tours, and I am one of the few civilians who can say they have traveled to Guantánamo Bay, Cuba to entertain the troops. Honestly, I am not sure I would have done any of it without BRT. With so many chances to try new things and learn on the job, it started me on a trajectory that I think would have been very different had I not been welcomed into the fold.

I have as many wacky memories as wonderful ones from BRT, but my favorite experience was the first time I was cast to be *on* stage—in an ensemble role in *McBeth! The Musical Comedy!* The name of the show pretty much says it all, but the experience of working on an original musical with so many talented and hilarious people was, well, it was a blast. It also taught me valuable lessons about the type of art I wanted to make, and the kind of laughs I wanted to have. The show itself was an enormous success, and the nightly standing ovations proved what it feels like to really "bring the house down." If I wasn't fully bitten by the theater bug before, my malady was complete after *McBeth!* And it was not just me. The entire company was immensely proud of the hard work we had put in and we knew we had something special. So much so, that when two of the co-creators, Joe Correll and Michael Bouson, wrote each cast member an opening night card that read "You're the best one in the show!"—we all believed it to be true.

CHAPTER 14

Where the Wind Comes Blowing Up Your Kilt

LATE SUMMER 2002

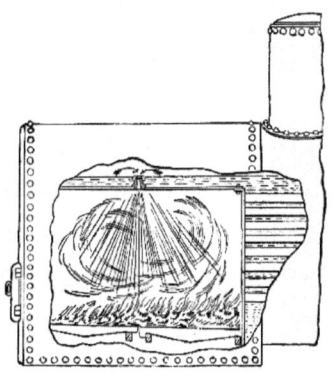

There's an ancient superstition that the title of one of Shakespeare's best-known plays, *Macbeth*, must never ever be uttered anywhere inside a theater lest unbelievably bad luck befall the company. The story goes that a coven of witches in 1606 were disgruntled that the Bard used actual incantations in his script, that has three characters who are witches, and placed a curse on the play. Ever since, in-the-know stage folk only refer to *Macbeth* as "the Scottish play." There are many notable, actual theatrical disasters surrounding the curse that gives it credence. It's said that to break the curse on one's theater, the fool who spoke the play's title must exit the theater, run around it three times, spit, curse, and then knock on the theater door to be allowed back in. (I don't think that works, but it could be a fun gag to play on a newbie actor.)

Or you can mount an insanely hilarious musical-comedy version titled *McBeth! The Musical Comedy!* and if you're as lucky as we were, this *McBeth!* (note the spelling) will cast a charm on your box office.

The show was first produced under the name *McBeth! The Murder Mystery Musical* in 1991 by Jamey's former theater company, the Avante Garage!, which was founded in the 1980s and located in downtown Nashville. Jamey Green was the musical muscle behind the theater. He and his business partners, Joe Correll, Michael Bouson, and Kathy Shepard wrote original musicals every six weeks. They would announce a season, then scramble to write the shows. *McBeth!* was one of their best. For marketing purposes, I added "*The Musical Comedy!*" to help our guests understand what we were presenting.

"The original show was very popular, but very different," Jamey said. "The musical was originally produced as a show-within-a-show murder mystery along the lines of *The Mystery of Edwin Drood.*" *McBeth!* was one of several "Rosencrantz" shows that were all shows-within-shows. The setup was that Myron Guildenstern (Jamey) and Blanche Rosencrantz (Joe) ran a theater that Blanche had inherited. Blanche had zero talent, but felt because it was her theater, she could play any part she desired. (That sounds embarrassingly familiar.) Joe created the Blanche character, a saggy, lumpy woman based on an aunt. Her performance was always purposefully lackluster and just downright bad. She had no energy, frequently looked out into the audience to see if she knew anyone, and spoke and sang in a gravelly, Elaine-Stritch voice. She was a delight.

"A lot of new material was added for the BRT production," Jamey continued. "Joe, Michael, and I did the rewrites and wrote the additional songs, mostly via conference calls and emails. Joe came out maybe ten days from opening and Michael joined us on tech week." Michael and

Joe were based in Los Angeles at that time, where Joe was a television producer.

My personal recollection was that Michael didn't care for the characterization that our actor in the titular role Michael originated, and worked with him extensively during tech week, which had to be nerve-rattling.

Jamey further explained that the AG! had a wide variety of competence in the cast from the good (Michael, Joe, Corbin, and others) to the horrendous, who shall remain nameless. "Much of the show was written and directed at the Avante Garage! to make use of what we had. The biggest challenge with the BRT production was to take really good, talented performers and replicate that without seeming to be too strained in the attempt." One of the original production's cast members was livid that he or she was not included in the BRT remount.

I'm not sure how I ended up being pre-cast as Blanche—perhaps because of playing Sylvia in *Ruthless!*—but it was back into heels again. But this time it was bad drag. My portrayal of Blanche was bawdy, gaudy, and brash, a tough broad who wore pink, cat-eye glasses, way too much makeup, and four-inch stilettos. I did some of Joe's schtick, but I largely made the part my own. I watched him on video and just couldn't duplicate his performance. I was referred to as either Blanche the Second or Blanche Jr.

Audiences absolutely adored the show and we did gangbuster business. The show had a couple of gags such as a swing that lowered from above the stage for Lady McBeth, played by Lisa Gillespie, upon which she would swing during one duet with husband McBeth. But the swing would eventually drop to the stage floor, on purpose, leaving Lisa trying to get up in a big Renaissance-style dress. Then during McBeth's solo, "Is This A Dagger," a dagger was flown to him via a fishing rod rigged above the set that would raise and lower so much that McBeth, played by Scott Rice, would have to keep up with the dagger's position, sometimes with his face against the stage floor, and at other times, on tiptoes trying to reach the weapon to keep it "before him."

A new production number, "A Royal Guest," that was a parody of Disney's "Be Our Guest," was the vehicle to get King Duncan to spend the night so Lady McBeth could kill him. It was immediately recognizable and always garnered hearty applause. Then in the Act One closer, "The Banquet," Nancy Whitehead Brown choreographed the most hilarious dance sequence ever performed on the BRT stage. It included music and moves from *West Side Story, A Chorus Line, Chicago, Riverdance,* and others, including Michael Jackson's "Thriller." It received thunderous applause before intermission where I, still dressed as Blanche, served beer and popcorn at the concessions counter. I remained in character trying to sell Mary Kay makeup and Tupperware. The tip jar was always full, providing me with much-needed cash.

The finale was a parody of the title song from *Oklahoma!* and was called *Scotland!* In between sing-spelling Scotland—"SC-OT-LAND"— we sang the title of this chapter, "Where the Wind Comes Blowing Up Your Kilt." The show sold out nearly every performance and got a glowing review from Martin:

. . .

"There are few things more difficult in the theater than successfully staging and performing an original musical comedy. It takes brains, vision, sense of craft, a little inspiration, a lot of imagination and even more hard work and dedication. All are present and accounted for at the Boiler Room Theatre, which is currently presenting a decidedly dotty and very entertaining adaptation of Shakespeare's *Macbeth*...

"… But as good as the principals are, it's the supporting cast—one of the finest that might be assembled locally for a musical—that makes this farce a real frolic… For its pure moxie and its unerring sense of joy, this might be the best show the folks in Franklin have done yet."

. . .

We could usually eke out a good-to-great review from Martin Brady once a season, but rarely, if ever, more frequently. We enlarged this one, framed it, and hung it in the lobby.

That fall marked the first non-summer, children's theater program, something that was called the BRT Harlequins. That name only lasted a year before the Act Too Players became the go-to for children's theater in the entire Nashville area. There was definitely a niche to be filled for children's theater programs, and Sondra Morton's program did just that.

HOT TIPS
Try Something New

Producing obscure or original material in a sports-oriented market such as the Greater Nashville area was always a gamble. Although the theater scene and theatergoers likely evolved after I left the Boiler Room in 2006, but in 2002, the market was pretty much "do *Oklahoma!* or *Annie*" or play to sparsely populated houses. I know that's an over-generalized statement because we introduced Nashville to at least two shows most people had never seen (*I Love You, You're Perfect, Now Change* and *Lucky Stiff*) that did exceedingly well, and other theater companies had success with offbeat titles.

We had a bit of an advantage with *McBeth!* because the Avante Garage! had a huge following, and the show, albeit in an earlier format, was already known by Nashville audiences. Still, a show that parodies Shakespeare requires some modicum of knowledge of the source material. I'm embarrassed to say as a former theater professional that I didn't know any Shakespeare other than a grueling high-school semester covering his sonnets.

I thought it was risky, but Jamey was adamant we would have a hit show. *McBeth!* proved to be another show in which the right cast melded with the right script at the right time and knocked it out of the park. But as you'll read a little later, it doesn't always work. Just know your audience as well as possible when planning seasons. And don't be afraid to survey your patrons.

CHAPTER 15

Winches and Wenches

FALL 2002

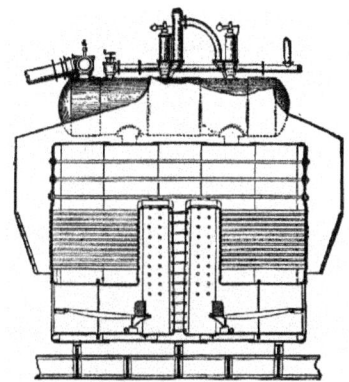

The first live musical I ever saw was in seventh grade when my music class took a field trip to Skyline High School in Longmont, Colorado. The show was *Man of La Mancha* and I was enthralled. Seeing it completely changed my odd vocational dream of becoming a taxidermist, which I had decided upon after a previous school field trip. Other than seeing the film version of *Grease* some 14 times the previous year, I knew little about musicals. Except that I desperately wanted to be in one. I was mesmerized with every aspect of the show, from the singers to the set with a giant staircase that lowered bringing prisoners into the Inquisition's prison. I bought my first cast album and sang with it. My Mom was troubled as I would belt out along with Joan Diener (the original Aldonza), "Look at the kitchen slut reeking of sweat."

The show stayed with me as I grew, but there were no opportunities to be in a production of *La Mancha*. The show is a classic, but not an overdone one. Which is why I petitioned for it to be in the 2002 season and why I insisted on directing it.

"This show perfectly fits the part of our mission statement of producing lesser-known works. It's a classic, but it's not *South Pacific*," I said. "I think enough people are at least aware of the monster-hit song 'The Impossible Dream.' There's a poetic irony there as opening this theater was once an impossible dream."

"I have no problem with including the show," Jamey said. "Hell, I might even want to be in it."

"And I really want to direct it," I pleaded like a child wanting to play outside for just five more minutes.

"Like I always say, if you have a vision for it, then do it."

Casting the leading role of Cervantes/Don Quixote was easy. The fantastically talented Dan McGeachy had played the part before, but even if he hadn't, he had the acting and vocal range the role demands. Casting the female lead of Aldonza was a bit challenging because we had a lot of talent from which to choose. Ultimately, the role went to BRT newcomer Megan Murphy Chambers. At one point in the show, Cervantes takes out a makeup kit and costume from his trunk that the Inquisition has allowed him to keep, and transforms himself into Alonso Quijano, an old gentleman who has read so many books of chivalry and thought so much about injustice that he has lost his mind and set out as a knight-errant. Quijano renames himself Don Quixote de La Mancha, and goes off to find adventures with his "squire," Sancho Panza. In a surprise turn, I cast Jamey as Sancho. He and Dan were brilliant together.

Megan quickly became the younger grand dame of the Boiler Room Theatre, her slightly older counterpart being Lisa Gillespie. Megan blossomed into an amazing actress and singer and appeared in more than

60 BRT productions. As of this writing, my research suggests she's the best and most sought-after female musical-theater performer in Nashville.

We had trouble attracting guys for the show, so Daniel and Corbin stepped forward. Allen Cox, who had been my Gregory Gardner in *A Chorus Line,* played the important role of the Duke/Dr. Sanson Carrasco. Newcomer Christopher Hamblin played the traveling barber and turned in a delightfully funny characterization. He shared a duet with Dan, "Golden Helmet of Mambrino," in which Quixote confuses the barber's shaving basin that he happens to be wearing on his head as sun protection for the prized helmet. Chris ad-libbed a take to the audience that I allowed when he proudly said at the end of the song, "That's my hat" in a strong Tennessee twang.

The other two female roles in the show were played by Pat Street and Kara McNealy Zappacosta who had been in *McBeth!* Halfway through the run, Pat was struck with the rare and incurable Guillain-Barre Syndrome and was partially paralyzed and in the hospital getting IV infusions for ten days to save her life. I'll leave her to tell that story in the following chapter.

When Pat went out sick, we pulled in Erin Parker who stepped into the role with no rehearsal. You read correctly: No rehearsal. She learned the number sung by the trio, which was made up of her character, Quixote's niece, and the Padre, in a couple of runs around the piano. On her first performance, the cast basically pushed her to where she needed to be with her lines stapled to the upstage sides of the set. It worked.

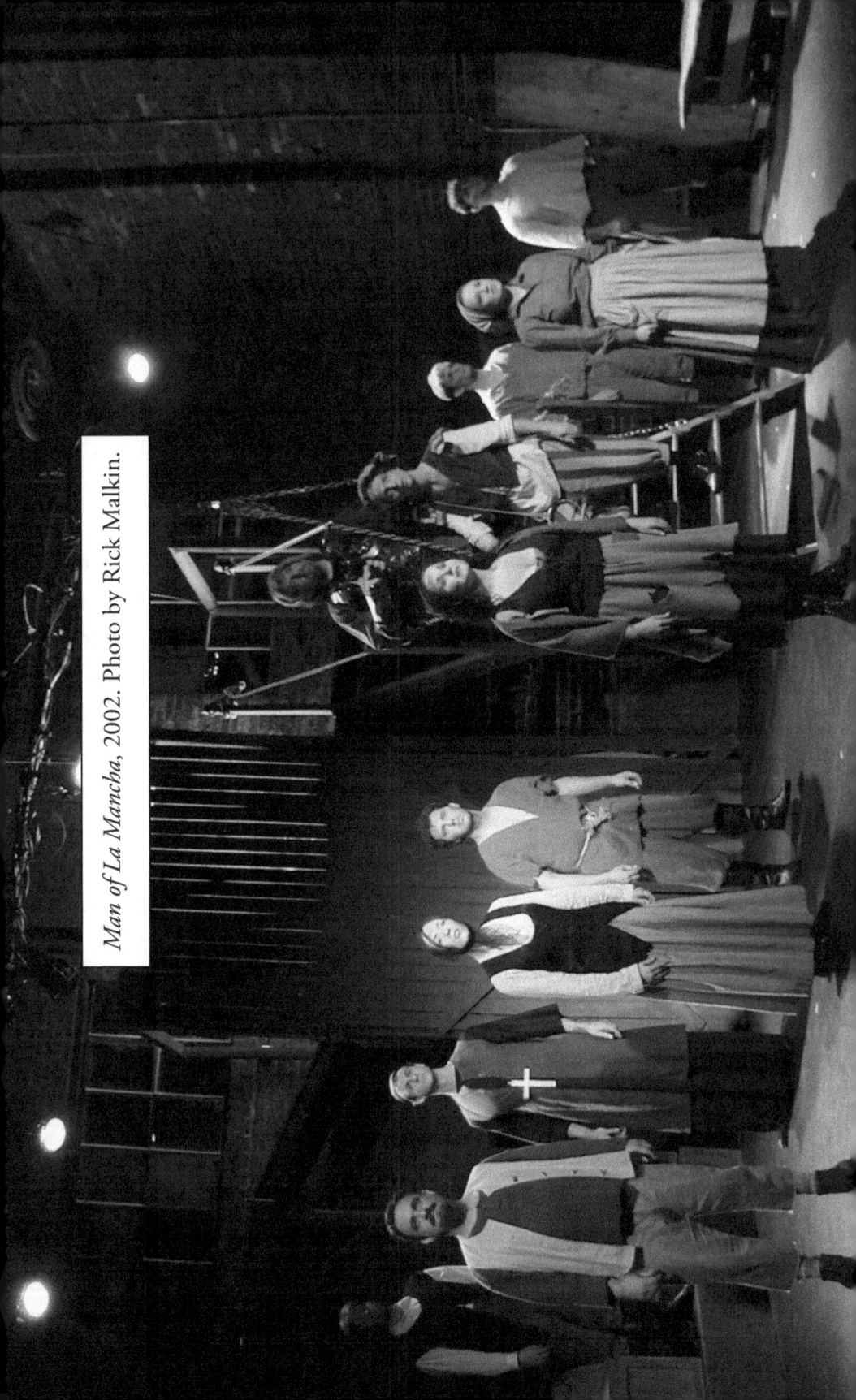

Man of La Mancha, 2002. Photo by Rick Malkin.

But then Erin went out. It may have been illness or pre-scheduled conflicts, but we had to find another actress on little notice. Thankfully, Kim Thornton Nygren had just played Aldonza at Chaffin's Barn Dinner Theatre which had already graciously loaned us the majority of its *La Mancha* props and set pieces. She slipped effortlessly into the role and finished the run. She later told me she could have played any role in the show she knew it so well. It was yet another case of our getting caught with our proverbial pants down because we couldn't afford understudies.

Alas, that wasn't the end of illness or physical issues. The role of Aldonza is a tough one that requires the actress to go from lilting ballads to high belting numbers with a large dose of gruffness. It is also a physically demanding role because the actress has to be at the center of at least three choreographed fights, one of which is the difficult rape scene. Although Megan would eventually develop rock-solid stamina with vocal cords of steel, she suffered extreme vocal fatigue during the run. There was even one performance in which we cut one of her songs and reduced another to essentially a spoken monologue with musical underscoring. We must have discussed having Kim take over the role temporarily since she'd just done it, but it didn't happen. Perhaps it was due to the intricately staged fight choreography that there wouldn't have been time to learn. Fight choreography is tricky and every actor must execute his or her moves perfectly lest anyone actually get hurt.

It's a shame that no newspaper or online media (though still new at the time) reviewed the show because some truly exquisite work was done by the actors. It was the third show I directed at BRT and many people have said it was among my finest work. I don't know if that is true, but I was proud of my cast. The set was utilitarian. Not what I would have designed three years down the road, but it worked. Again, the exposed brick worked in our favor as the setting was the below-ground, common area of a Spanish prison.

Winches and Wenches

There is one set piece in *La Mancha* that's a must: A practical staircase that lowers from above the stage. It's how the actors playing the prisoners, at least the newbies (or in modern terms, fish) are incarcerated. Some productions have used trap doors in the stage and brought actors in that way. But we had no room under our stage for a trap door or elevator setup. Under the stage was a mishmash of two-by-fours, four-by-fours, and probably a dead rat or three.

So I had to plead with Corbin to build the staircase unit. Because it had to be raised and lowered numerous times per show, and because of the winch controlling the movement, the stairs had to be as lightweight as possible. The steps were constructed of the thinnest possible plywood with a single rebar support underneath. As a result, the stairs bent with every step upon them. That stair unit eventually made its way backstage and was repurposed when we built out the backstage building's interior including the second-story costume and prop shops.

The real problem was finding a motorized winch that could handle the stair unit as quietly as possible. Corbin did an exhaustive search, but our options were limited by availability and cost. The show ended up with an extremely loud boat winch. It was deafening, really. Jamey and musical director Mark Beall tried countless sound effects to cover the noisy winch, but to do so required eardrum-breaking volume. It certainly made the stair moves dramatic. I was embarrassed we couldn't do better, but as was the case so often, money or the lack thereof was always the culprit.

We made it through the run with rotating wenches and one extremely loud winch, playing to half- or three-quarters-full houses. Ultimately, *Man of La Mancha*, although a revered classic, just didn't play in Poughkeepsie, or rather, Franklin.

HOT TIPS
No Unauthorized Gender-Bending

I've already preached about understudies: If you can possibly afford it, always have at least one—preferably a swing—at the ready to step into a variety of roles. Really, you need one male and one female swing per production unless the show is all one gender as is the case with shows such as *Nunsense*. What we could have done with *La Mancha* was to have a male swing covering all the ensemble roles and train one of the men in the cast to swing in for Quixote and Sancho. Then, we could have trained one of the two females not playing Aldonza to cover Aldonza. The right male swing *could* have stepped in to cover a female role. In a show like *Man of La Mancha,* in which every actor wears makeup to appear dirty and bruised, a male swing with a tenor voice could have covered the housekeeper or the niece in "I'm Only Thinking of Him." Daniel Vincent, had he not been in the main cast, could have easily pulled it off and with great gravitas. Of course, it wouldn't have been ideal, but it would have prevented unnecessary stress.

But beware of gender-bending clauses in show licenses. With the growing popularity of *Broadway Backwards* and *MisCast* in which gender roles are reversed for AIDS and Broadway fundraisers in concert settings,

No Unauthorized Gender-Bending

changing character genders in full, scripted shows requires permission—which is rarely granted.

Boiler Room Voices

PAT STREET

Bravo, My Friends

In Nashville in the year 2000, I had the great honor of stepping in to take over a role in *Personals*, a wildly successful musical produced by a new theater group, Euphoria! The Theatre, in a tiny space upstairs at the Bongo Java coffee shop. My daughter Cela Scott was in the show, and when it had sold out its entire run, audiences were begging for more, but extending the run meant that two actors had to drop out because of other commitments. Thus began my true association with Jamey Green and Lewis Kempfer, who would go on to start the Boiler Room Theatre, as well as Anthony Popolo, who was essential to the specialty technical aspects of *Personals* and went on to do the same for years for BRT shows.

I knew Jamey and had worked with Lewis, as well as Daniel Vincent, Dan McGeachy, Julie Durbin, and Lisa Gillespie, all involved in *Personals* from the beginning, as well as Stephen Henry, who joined the cast when I did. Dan McGeachy and I had become especially close working on *Fiddler on the Roof* at Pull-Tight Theatre in Franklin.

Many of the seeds for BRT were sown at after-parties on Anthony's back patio near the Belmont University campus. These parties would go late into the night, and while there was alcohol involved, what kept everyone there was the incredibly stimulating conversation. Between them, Jamey and Anthony had an encyclopedic knowledge of theater and cinema, while Lewis, Anthony, and Corbin Green shared a love and genius for design and invention. Since every person there had an extremely bright, creative, and energetic mind, there were animated discussions, arguments, and informal trivia contests, and suddenly you would look up and it was four in the morning.

I remember the evening on the patio when Jamey told Dan and me *sotto voce* about plans for a new theater in Franklin. The concept was to present fairly edgy, avant-garde professional theater in a town that had a long-standing community theater but had never had a professional group. Jamey had been one of the founding partners of Nashville's Avante Garage! Theatre which was known for its wacky original productions.

Although Dan and I immediately offered our enthusiastic support, there was a bit of a conflict for me because I was deeply involved at the existing community theater. In fact, as BRT was about to open, I was president of the board at Pull-Tight. There is an October 26, 2000 *Williamson A.M.* newspaper article in which I was interviewed as president and quoted as cheerily saying something along the lines of, "We welcome BRT to Franklin and don't see them as competition because their mission of producing edgy, obscure theater is very different from our family-friendly mission, and there is room for everyone!"

I spent several months of that year busily working to support both theaters. While deeply involved at Pull-Tight, I was also recruiting volunteers to help build out the physical space at The Factory at Franklin to house the new theater and spent many hours there learning from Corbin how to sand drywall (alas, never quite to his satisfaction) and lining up and securing the new seating.

As it turned out, BRT's edgy aspect was extremely short-lived. Though Williamson County and Franklin were growing, along with their citizens' level of sophistication, those things were not growing fast enough, and BRT's first and most definitely risqué show (sprinkled with blue language and references to oral sex) met with immediate blowback (no pun intended) despite being a box-office smash running ten weeks. As they began to vet shows for their second season, Jamey and Lewis regrouped because what there *was* a demand for in Franklin was this new, sophisticated space with professional standards and quality theater. And although BRT's future seasons were packed with shows that competed with Pull-Tight's lineup, the two theaters peacefully coexisted within their own niches. BRT provided professional theater and Pull-Tight continued its tradition of community theater, offering development of amateur actors and tech crews and a price of admission allowing folks to bring the entire family.

I was able to perform onstage in several BRT shows including *Nice People Dancing to Good Country Music*; *Les Miz!*/*A Tale of Two Cities*; and *Man of La Mancha*; I stage-managed some, produced one, and directed one (*Crimes of the Heart*), but mostly I was very present for many years working in the lobby, helping paint sets, or gathering props. My daughter Cela was in two shows before she left for college in Los Angeles, *Ruthless!*, and part of the run of *A Chorus Line,* and my sons Connor and Aaron Scott both spent a lot of time at BRT running lights and sound.

Some of my most dramatic memories come from *Man of La Mancha*, directed by Lewis in 2002. Dan McGeachy was playing Don Quixote and I was in the ensemble of prisoners, as well as playing Housekeeper/Maria. A story I love and have told often happened during rehearsal, when we prisoners were sitting on the stage surrounding Dan for the first time he made the transformation from Cervantes to Don Quixote. He had a small mirror mounted inside a crude makeup box and some primitive greasepaint, and we watched as with a few strokes to his face, Dan completely made the character transformation with body and facial expressions alone, all while singing with his glorious voice. It was truly a magical moment and one we were all moved by every night.

A young Megan Murphy Chambers, who was playing Aldonza, breathed out, "I want to have that. I want to be that good."

I give myself credit for saying, "Megan, you *do* have that. All you need now is experience." I'm happy to say she went on to prove me more than correct.

The second significant event of *Man of La Mancha* was that I got deathly ill and had to drop out of the show, so it was my turn to have someone take over my part. I developed Guillain-Barré syndrome, a disease in the ALS/Lou Gehrig's family that can be fatal if not stopped in time. During the show, I began to develop tingling and burning in my palms and soles of my feet, which progressed to increasing weakness and then paralysis of my legs. There was a scene during the song "I'm Only Thinking of Him" where we had to kneel, and as the nights went on, I became more and more fearful that I was not going to be able to rise from kneeling at the end of the song. I was having increasing trouble even climbing the two steps from backstage to onstage. I had been seeing doctor after doctor who could not tell me what was wrong. I was so consumed with worry about it that one night I missed my cue as the Innkeeper's Wife, and Marc Mazzone, who played my husband, had to spend about 20 painfully long seconds sweeping the stage and ad-libbing about where his spouse could possibly be. The next morning, I got out of bed and fell on the floor because my legs would not support me. I ended up being hospitalized for ten days, although my son Aaron carried on with running lights for the duration of the show.

The following year, Lewis began developing symptoms akin to Multiple Sclerosis that his doctors had a very hard time pinning down. I developed a suspicion that Lewis and I had both fallen victim to some substance or chemical in the old boiler room walls or equipment. During *La Mancha*, I was also serving as stage manager for the show, and every night I would arrive and sweep the stage, stirring up and breathing its dust. Lewis was always intimately involved with the physical space, either building and decorating sets or displays in the loft of the lobby, and I think our immune systems could not handle whatever was in there. I will never know for sure, but I was less involved at BRT following that.

BRT struggled with many challenges over the years, but it stands as a glorious achievement. The intimate and classy space. The unique energy of the team that built the theater and kept it going. The level of professionalism of the performances, direction, music, choreography, and costumes. The many ingenious sets and lighting designs by Corbin and Anthony and Lewis. The slick programs and promotional materials designed by Lewis. The great photography by Rick Malkin. The Disney-level lobby displays Lewis would do for each production were worth the price of admission themselves. Popcorn, beer, and wine coolers that could be enjoyed during the show were a new thing for Franklin theater and made for a fun and comfortable evening. The Engineer's Club and other levels of patronage made people feel special and a real part of something. Many of Greater Nashville theater's best actors, singers, and dancers graced the stage, both those who had already made a name for themselves and those who were on their way to doing so. Many of them would go on to entertain us at Studio Tenn, Nashville Rep, Nashville Opera, Broadway, and even *American Idol*, but all of them miss the Boiler Room.

Those of us who have worked behind the scenes keeping a theater running know it is a herculean and sometimes thankless task under the best of circumstances. Lewis and Jamey and many others created something beautiful and shining and made it last for 14 years, and everyone who looks back on it now sees it clearly as a Golden Age. An incredible accomplishment. Bravo, my friends.

CHAPTER 16

Length Matters

CHRISTMAS 2002

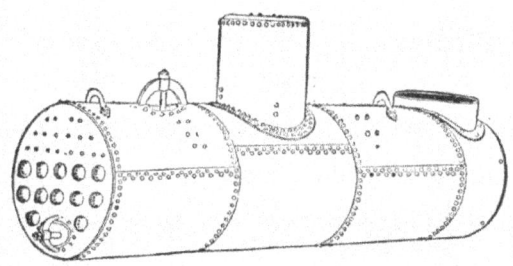

We closed the 2002 season with a hilarious 43 minutes of Christmas comedy. *A Dickens of a Christmas Carol* offered about 25-percent bang for the 100-percent buck. And actually, we had sold season tickets based on the holiday show being the musical *She Loves Me*, but due to a decision by Jamey, we swapped it for *Dickens*. It was kind of a "dick" move on our part.

The play was truly funny and Laura Skaug's direction was, as usual, first-rate. The show's premise is that a traveling, British theatrical troupe is performing *A Christmas Carol* and has a leading lady in the play-within-a-play who is not feeling well and an unprepared understudy fills in with script in hand. Add to that the purposely hammy acting, costume malfunctions, blown cues, and wrong entrances coupled with a rickety set, and it was a typical, proven Boiler Room production. The grand finale is the entire set collapsing. Corbin designed a wonderfully cheesy

Length Matters

set that comprised studio flats all connected with an assortment of latches and metal pins. In the final scene, the flats fall one by one on top of each other revealing a mess of a backstage. It all worked beautifully.

The cast was stellar, led by Lane Wright, along with Marc Mazzone, Douglas Goodman, Sondra Morton, Beth Eakin O'Neill, and others.

But it was way too short. (That's what she said.)

It wasn't until the final dress rehearsal that we realized just how brief this gem of a play was. So, as house manager, I had the unpleasant duty of delaying curtain (start of the show) by ten minutes. Then intermission came within 20 minutes. So once again, I'd stall, stretching the break from 15 minutes to as many as 25. Even so, the audience was out the door in less than 90 minutes. I was embarrassed because I knew they didn't get their money's worth. We should have timed the table read and added a one-act play, 30 minutes of Christmas music, or even a band of dancing pandas.

There were complaints. Audiences loved the play but were left wanting more and wondering what to do with the rest of date night. I may have refunded some ticket purchases. We were continuing to learn as we went along, and this was another tough lesson.

Martin Brady's review was glowing and didn't mention length. Thank goodness. He wrote:

. . .

"Mark Landon Smith's fractured script... leaves the actors plenty of room to make merry under Laura Skaug's swift, competent direction.

"... Lane Wright is the egotistical actor [play within a play actor] playing Scrooge. He's bigger than life and perhaps is all the more humorous because he successfully plays things so straight.

120 SEATS IN A BOILER ROOM

"… Avid theatergoers are alerted to Boiler Room Theatre's seasonal offering, a spoofy romp based on—but a far cry from—the Charles Dickens classic.… In its lovably daffy way, this lighthearted take on Dickens makes for solidly alternative family holiday fare."

. . .

It was a nice review to cap off an uneven season.

HOT TIPS

Don't Alienate Subscribers

Measure twice, cut once.

We really ticked off some guests who had bought season tickets based on getting to see the rarely produced and grandiose *She Loves Me*. A swap for another musical might have been more palatable, but the switcheroo to a play that was less than an hour long was a bad decision. It's a tough enough job to attract guests; don't do what we did and scare some of them off.

2003 SEASON

Sentimental Journey

Guys and Dolls
The Musical Comedy Murders of 1940
Chicago
You're a Good Man, Charlie Brown
Cat on a Hot Tin Roof
Smoky Mountain Mist
The 1940s Radio Hour

CHAPTER 17

Gamblers and Drunks

SEASON OPENER & SECOND SLOT 2003

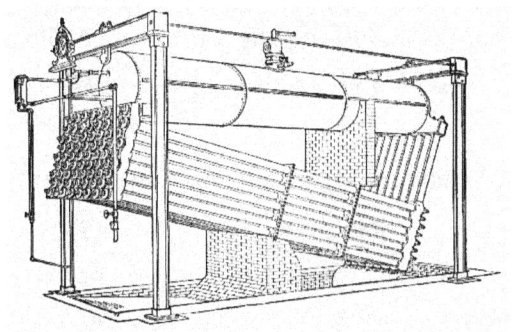

The winter hiatus between late December 2002 and January 2003 was an exciting time as the theater was finally getting a proper backstage. Once again, Corbin and his dad, Jim Green, were hard at work, this time lining the inside walls of the metal back building with studs, insulation, and sheet rock creating a cozy dressing room with one side for the guys and one side for the "dolls." Actual costume racks, makeup-station counters, and exposed light bulbs surrounded the perimeter of the mirrors. A wall and door were added to seal off the last third of the building, which we used for scenery, paint, and concession inventory storage. With the existing roll-up door, we had a functional set storage area, albeit not large enough to serve as a set shop.

An in-kind show sponsor provided carpet, and an assortment of chairs, including those blue ones from Belmont, were placed throughout the dressing rooms. We still only had one backstage bathroom and rigged a curtain to provide privacy for whatever gender was assigned to the smaller of the two sides. Sometimes it was guys, sometimes dolls.

Additionally, a second story was added for costumes and props storage. The lightweight, creaky, and pliable staircase from *Man of La Mancha* was installed to reach the second floor. It always felt like a gamble whether one would make it safely up and back down. Especially with an armload of costumes or box of props.

The floor was built flush to the behemoth boiler filled with asbestos. In particular, my prop shop (I was the resident prop and set dressing guy) was closest to the boiler and a film of that noxious yellow dust always coated my bins and shelves.

If I haven't already dropped sufficient hints, the 2003 season opener was *Guys and Dolls*. It was perfectly placed so that we could offer a Valentine's Day couples' package with *prix fixe* dinner next door at the reimagined Saffire restaurant. Lucky patrons would receive goody bags with candy, a commemorative mug, a rose for the lady (or one of the two guys in some cases), and a post-show champagne reception. We were able to charge a hefty price and sold every seat.

Jamey pulled double duty on the show, as he frequently did, as director and musical director. I'd told him I wanted to play the male lead, Sky Masterson, mostly because he had the great songs. But I never felt fully in character and Martin Brady noticed. In his review he wrote, "[Daron] Bruce and Kempfer, while competent in their roles, lack charisma. This is particularly true of Kempfer, who sings well enough but simply doesn't possess the edgy masculinity one expects in his role." That zinger began my slow move away from being on stage to designing the stage.

The women, of course, fared extremely well:

. . .

"The lead females, Megan Murphy [Chambers] and Lauri Bright, are talented and appealing, especially Bright, who was apparently born to play Miss Adelaide, the long-suffering cabaret dancer who's been waiting 14 years for gambler boyfriend Nathan Detroit (Daron Bruce) to marry her. The poised and professional Bright delivers her material with sexy charm and wit—and she's got great gams to boot."

. . .

But again, the breakout star was Megan. Evans Donnell, in a 2019 stagecritic.com review of Nashville Children's Theatre's *Auntie Claus,* states that:

. . .

"… good fortune has long smiled on any production with Megan Murphy Chambers in it, and the tremendous triple-threat performer is perfectly cast as the flamboyant doyenne of NYC's Bing Cherry Hotel…. Since I first saw her in Boiler Room Theatre's 2003 production of *Guys and Dolls*, I've known I'd never see anyone, anywhere, whose timing, singing, movement and acting choices is any better than hers. No matter how many times one's seen her, every appearance she makes onstage is a great gift."

. . .

Gamblers and Drunks

It was a good attempt at a set. It wasn't my design, and I would have done things differently, but it wasn't my place to do so. It was mostly composed of tall flats in various heights and colors to suggest the skyscrapers of 1950s New York City. The windows were abstract, skewed shapes. It was an interesting look. But after the first night, one of the windows appeared odd. It was missing its top line. Upon inspection, I discovered the windows had been created with electrical tape and the heat was making the tape fail. They should have been painted on, but time was always in short supply. So before every show, two of the techs stapled the tape back in place. We were still learning.

The run was mostly unremarkable. Again, we had no understudies or swings and there was, yet again, another emergency that was forcing us to pull in anyone we could get. In this case, it was Jeremy Evans who played Seymour in 2002's *Little Shop* who did the show with no rehearsal.

Then there was the Tuesday morning around 3 a.m. when I received a call on my landline from the Davidson County Jail. Daniel Vincent, one of our chorus men and lead dancers, had an unpaid speeding ticket in Indiana and a suspended license. A burned-out headlight got him hauled into the clink and mine was the only landline phone number he could remember. I rushed downtown to find out how to get him released. Bail was set at $1,000. I called Jamey, explained the situation, and asked permission to pull $500 from the BRT account. I had already pulled $500 from my own, but daily ATM withdrawal limits left me needing to find the balance. Because we had a show coming up that night, it was deemed essential to spend the money.

I found a bondsman and the financial arrangements were settled. I figured I could still get home by 5 a.m. and resume sleeping. No dice. It seemed Williamson County also had a warrant and around 9 a.m., when I had hoped to pick up Daniel, I learned he had been transferred to the Williamson County Jail. He was stuck there until around 3:30 p.m. I paid more bail and raced Daniel to my house to shower and shave, then it was back on the road to just barely make call time. Daniel was a featured dancer, and had I been unsuccessful in springing him from the slammer, the show would have suffered from his absence on that sold-out Tuesday night.

Then we experienced our own Janet Jacksonesque costume malfunctions one night when, during the Act Two Hotbox Girls' number "Take Back Your Mink," in which the girls stripped down to bustiers, one of Erin Parker's nipples popped out for a cameo appearance. Pasties were issued the next night.

I was also "lucky" enough to contract pleurisy, an inflammation of the membranes surrounding the lungs. It made sustaining notes difficult and also robbed me of 50 percent of my vocal ability. Maybe that's when we were reviewed.

I also discovered that I look *really* bad in any kind of hat, particularly an ill-fitting fedora. I looked like a toad in a hat.

But the real joy came in the form of an annual honor bestowed upon one actor or actress per year by the *Nashville Scene's* Martin Brady. (The honors were announced in October 2003, hence the early reference to *Chicago*.)

. . .

"Best Performance in a Musical: Lauri Bright

"The moment she stepped onto the Boiler Room Theatre stage as Miss Adelaide in *Guys and Dolls*, Lauri Bright captured her audience and recaptured the essence of classic-era Broadway musical performance. As gangster Nathan Detroit's put-upon, long-pining, 'Noo Yawk' nightclub-singer girlfriend, Bright nailed the great Frank Loesser songs—'Adelaide's Lament,' 'Sue Me' and

'A Bushel and a Peck'—and offered a touching and hilarious portrait of the marriage-minded female in extremis. Bright also often works as a choreographer for BRT—case in point, the recent production of *Chicago*—but here she proved she was a star."

...

As the person who chose Lauri as the first person to be cast in a BRT show, I couldn't have been more proud.

The Musical Comedy Murders of 1940 was the ho-hum show that filled the second slot of our third season. The plot begins with the creative team for a recent Broadway flop in which three chorus girls were murdered by the "Stage Door Slasher" assembling for a backers' audition of their new show at the secluded estate of a wealthy benefactress.

Not much to tell, but it had a stellar cast including Sondra, Megan, Daniel, Dan, Patrick, Douglas Goodman, Beth Eakin O'Neill, Neely O'Brien Green, Sloan Yarborough, and Jennie Lee Frank-Gambill.

The set was fun to create and was one of my first detailed interior unit sets, built in conjunction with Corbin. He and I became a great team, building (Corbin) and dressing (me) some increasingly amazing sets. This one featured sliding panels, revolving bookcases, and secret passageways. I needed to fill four bookcases with books and hated the way painted books look. So I scoured every thrift store in Nashville and a Nashville library sale purchasing at least 1,000 volumes. That gave the set a great realistic look paired with the deep burgundy wall color I had chosen.

We did receive complaints about a bit of staging that I will call the Spread Eagle Number Two (remember, Spread Eagle Number One happened in 2002's *Lucky Stiff*) that came directly from the script. Beth, as the German maid, gets in a choreographed struggle with a male character, and in a series of moves ends up on top of a desk, legs wide open with the guy facing upstage (away from the audience). It was a funny visual bit, but one that offended some of our devout guests.

CHAPTER 18

And All That Spray Paint

SPRING 2003

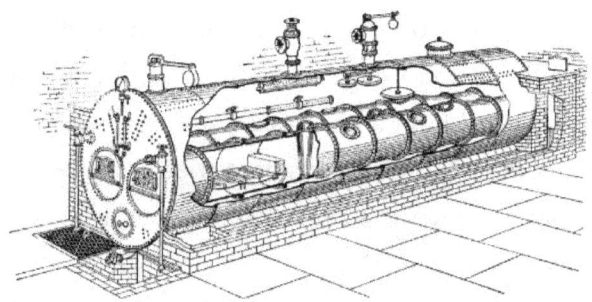

We arrived in New York City around six in the evening on my birthday and got to the hotel by seven. We being me and some guy I was briefly dating who bought me a trip to NYC for my birthday. What was his name? Brent? Trent? Brett? Doesn't matter. We were staying in Times Square and his idea of dinner was a choice of either Applebee's or Olive Garden. Um, no. I sure as hell wasn't going to eat at some chain restaurant we could go to in suburbia. The rest of the trip continued to disappoint in this way, but the reason for going was for me to see *Chicago* on Broadway before I directed it. The movie had just come out and was wildly popular. The stage show in New York had been running for some time. I left wanting my production to be a blend of both, but probably leaning a bit more toward the film.

And All That Spray Paint

Boiler Room Theatre seasons were planned months in advance of the late January opening of the first show of a calendar-year season. Because we first opened so early in the year, we didn't follow the usual fall-to-spring season schedule. So when we put *Chicago* in the 2003 season, we were only vaguely aware of a film version of the show possibly being released at some time in 2003. We must have gotten in under the wire to obtain rights to produce the show. Once the film hit, rights for all productions were cut off (except Broadway). We placed the show in the hit-or-miss third slot. I had pushed for the show and to direct it, insisting that it was the right show at the right time.

Which brings us up to mounting the show, post-NYC. Based on a combination of the *Chicago* stage set and that of the original Broadway production of *Grease*, I built a non-scale, cardboard version of my show concept: A two-story set. It hadn't yet been tried at the Boiler Room, but would eventually become the standard configuration for most, but not all, big musicals.

My concept was simple, really. A second-level platform for the band with two large sets of stairs at stage right and stage left, and a main playing area on the stage level. But part of my concept was an elevator that would execute the iconic rise of Velma into position for the opening number, "All That Jazz." Both Broadway and the film had the elevator and by God, I wanted one. Because we didn't have any depth under the stage, the elevator would be on the stage level and lift to the second tier.

Based on *Man of La Mancha*, we didn't have great experience with mechanical set pieces. But there was a construction elevator that had been stored in the corner of the backstage building that Corbin thought we might use one day. But of course, it needed a motor. Any motor Corbin could find was still either cost-prohibitive or would be too damn loud. We landed on a hand-cranked rig that required two of the male actors to operate. It supposedly had a safety catch so the actress wouldn't come crashing down if a hand or gear slipped. I'm not sure if that was actually true. And there may have been a scary moment in a tech rehearsal.

With my set concept approved, I was excited to present the model to the cast at the read-through, and it was received with a chorus of oohs and ahhs. It was the same realization I'd had with *A Chorus Line* and *La Mancha*. We didn't have width or under-stage depth, but we had height. And just as that height paid dividends in *A Chorus Line*, it paid off in spades for *Chicago*. The BRT double-decker set was born.

There had been a bit of a stink among three of the co-founders about the casting of Velma and Roxie, with my choice for Roxie being a non-dancer for a dancing role, but we finally resolved it when I played the director card.

By our third year, we had a better go at finding triple-threat dancers and Lauri was now at the helm as our Resident Choreographer. That once-timid dancer from *A Chorus Line* had already become a capable singer and actress.

Many, but not all, BRT shows suffered a cast-member injury. We were rehearsing offsite in the dance studio of Hume-Fogg High School (for the performing arts) since we couldn't be in our space on show nights and really needed mirrors. I'd cast Dan McGeachy as reporter Mary Sunshine because the man had an insane, four-octave range. On one of the offsite rehearsal nights, Dan dressed in full drag to adopt and embody his female role. I should know from my turns in heels and hose. Dan was picking his way up the sloped faculty lot where we parked, lost his footing, and either sprained an ankle or broke a foot. There was poor cell-phone reception in the school, but we managed to get a feeble "help me" call from Dan. He had to go to the emergency room in full drag. Oh, to have had a camera. Being a trooper, he did the run, albeit in a gray wig and using a walker. He was delightful. But there would be an eventual kerfuffle in Martin Brady's review.

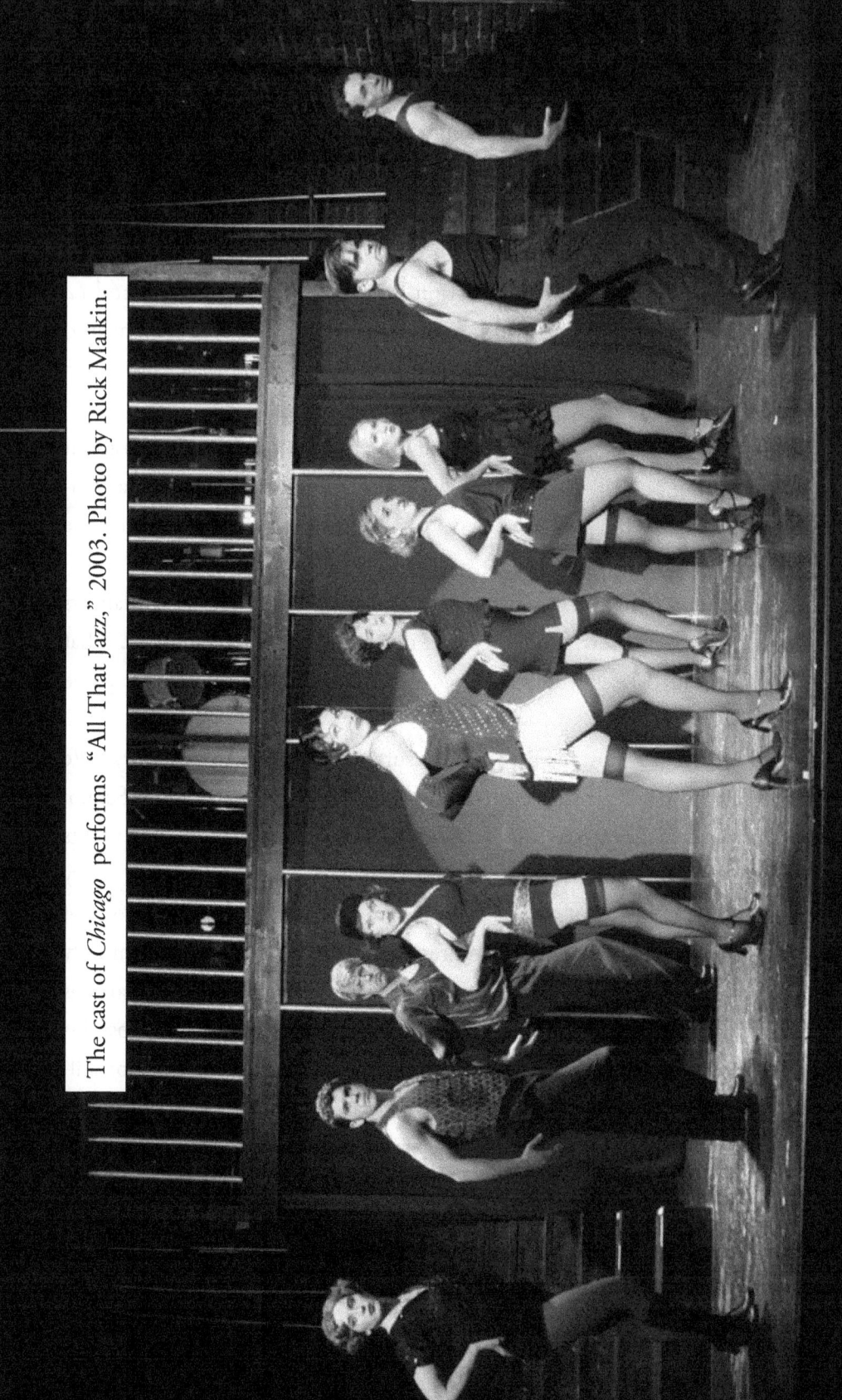

The cast of *Chicago* performs "All That Jazz," 2003. Photo by Rick Malkin.

Building the set, I had a small crew to help me paint dozens of lengths of PVC pipe that would serve as non-practical jail bars across the top level as a railing and elsewhere on the set. We always made a mess painting on the stage because tradition was that we'd put a thick, fresh black coat of paint on the stage after the final Thursday night dress. So we didn't give it much thought using metallic silver spray paint on the stage. Spray paint is usually latex-based and we always painted the stage with black latex.

Daniel was running box office on opening day and was the first to notice.

"Lewis, you've got to get down here immediately. There's a problem with the stage," he said.

"What kind of problem?"

"The black floor paint has bubbled up and is peeling. I don't know why. But there's no way anyone can dance on it."

"Well, crap."

Upon closer inspection with Corbin, all the places we'd spray-painted the PVC pipes silver were the areas where the black paint wasn't adhering. At first, I thought it was no big deal. Most of the show took place inside a prison, so a rough stage floor would work. That was until Daniel put on his dance shoes (he was in the cast) and tried some steps. He both slid and got stuck during a double pirouette. Pat Street was part of my paint crew and I called her to come help. My theory was if we ran a couple of belt sanders over the stage to rough up and remove the silver paint below the black, we could make do for opening night, then paint afterwards. Except the sanders weren't providing any improvement, mostly because metallic spray paint isn't like regular spray paint.

We had twice rented the theater to a local ballet group. I called them in a panic to see if they had a Marley, a broad term for a variety of PVC and vinyl materials that in varied thicknesses provide a smooth dance surface. They had one but didn't know its size. Daniel and I took my

Cavalier and raced to Brentwood to pick it up. Thick as a wrestling mat, the Marley was insanely heavy. We hoisted it into my trunk only to later find it had badly dented my back end and the trunk lid no longer closed. We tried to lay it out on stage, but it was too big for the main playing area and cutting it was out of the question.

We were running out of time and options.

The sanding had merely removed the black paint leaving us with a slippery semi-silver floor. As cast members started to trickle in and tested it, the results weren't good. Teressa, who was stage managing, recommended we "Coke" the stage. It was a decades-old theatrical trick. You'd make a lightly diluted mixture of Coca-Cola and mop the stage with it. It gave the dancers some grip but made pirouettes nearly impossible. Fortunately, *Chicago* was a Fosse show and didn't have many, if any, pirouettes. With the cast in agreement, we used the best available option.

To truly fix the paint mess would require one or two coats of oil-based paint. Because of drying time, we had to get through the first three shows, then on Sunday night, lay the oil paint allowing it two days to dry before the next show. It worked, but had created a bigger problem: Unless we wanted to always use oil-based paint, which we did not, the stage floor would have to be totally sanded down. But Corbin had been wanting to add another layer of Masonite on top of the existing stage to deaden sound for some time, so now he had the perfect opportunity when *Chicago* closed.

With regard to closing, we could have run the show for a year with sold-out houses. The demand was so great that we couldn't add enough shows. But we couldn't extend—the cast had other commitments and we'd sold a seven-show season that we had to fulfill. So the show closed as scheduled. But guests clamored and called the box office asking in their endearing yet annoying way, "Do y'all still have the *Chicago* playing?"

Our guests always added a "the" in front of all show names. It seemed to be an aspect of Southern dialect.

"Do you have the *Gypsy?*"

"Yes, but she's practicing her strip tease."

"Do you have the *Grease?*"

"Yes, but it's being used to lube an '89 Cavalier."

And so forth.

I was thrilled to get at least one great review as a director. F. Daniel Kent in *Out & About Nashville* said:

. . .

> "Although many are impressed by the film version, the full impact of *Chicago* as it was meant to be seen cannot be experienced in its entirety until one sees it on the stage, and the Lewis Kempfer directed show delivers that impact in spades…
>
> "… the performance of the evening is without a doubt Lori Ellis's portrayal of Velma Kelly who belts out her tunes in a powerhouse performance that rivals such classic performances as Bebe Newarth's [SIC] portrayal of Kelly [SIC]."

. . .

He was spot-on about Lori. She was a gorgeous Sheila in *A Chorus Line* and would go on to be (at least in my eyes) a great Mama Rose, and a perfect Rizzo. But she really did shine in *Chicago*. I always told Lori that she was the only woman who could turn me straight.

With the floor tragedy and Dan's injury behind us, the run of the show was fantastic, playing to sold-out houses every performance. And

And All That Spray Paint

trust me, that's a thrilling, exhilarating feeling. *Chicago* is a bawdy show and based on the movie that had just been released, guests should have seen it coming. During "Cell Block Tango," five female characters got in position on the black "cabaret" chairs, and upon Velma's spoken cue, they all performed the Spread Eagle. Number Three if you're counting.

We got a good review from Martin at the *Scene*, although he literally spent one half of it writing about the film. Under the headline "Stage Trumps Screen," here's what he had to say:

. . .

> "Boiler Room producer Lewis Kempfer directs the production and generally speaking, does it nicely... There is one artistic misstep in this show. The part of tabloid reporter Mary Sunshine is attributed to an aging thespian named Patina O'Swett, who arrives onstage using a walker... far more problematic, the "actress" is the subject of a hammy gag toward show's end—one so irrelevant to the source material that it comes off tasteless and self-indulgent, not to mention unprofessional. If director Kempfer is willing to dispense with such in-joke amateurism, he and his company have a pretty nice show."

. . .

I was in shock that Martin had said such things about my direction and had accused me of shoving a drag joke into the show. At the risk of "pulling a Kaz," I scanned script pages and emailed them to him explaining that the "in-joke amateurism" is written into the script and at BRT we stayed true to the writers' original intent. That intent, by the way, is lawyer Billy Flynn explaining to the jury and the audience that things aren't always what they appear to be. At which point Mary Sunshine rips off his wig and dress. I asked him to print a retraction. It must have killed him to print his *mea culpa*. Perhaps if he'd spent less time trying to be a film critic, he might have researched that the supposedly amateurish bit was legit. The week following his barbed review, he wrote:

. . .

"In last week's review of *Chicago*, I took the Boiler Room Theatre to task for a piece of stage business deemed to be 'amateurish' and not a part of the Bob Fosse-Fred Ebb script. In fact, the scene in question, involving a male actor playing a female character, is spelled out just so in the original version, as first performed on Broadway. The recent Academy Award-winning film of *Chicago* eschews this comic bit, and some other stage productions have done likewise. BRT stayed true to the source material. I apologize for the false assumption."

. . .

That made up for every lukewarm to scathing review he gave me, both up to that point and thereafter.

HOT TIPS

Stick to the Script, Not the Floor

Don't be afraid of taking creative chances when staging shows. Now, you can't add or delete dialogue or add songs that weren't in the stage version to which you have a license. You do have a license, right? Don't try to mount a production without one: You *will* get caught and could get sued. If the rights are too much for your theater to bear, consider finding a large performance space and packing in guests for three nights of shows rather than over the course of two, three, or four weeks. BRT eventually did occasional productions in this manner, although it had more to do with venue renovation challenges.

My production of *Chicago* stayed true to the original script, as you've read. I didn't try to recreate the film nor could I duplicate the Broadway staging, which I really don't care for. The huge innovation was the introduction of the double-decker set that opened up a world of new possibilities, all variations on a set-design theme.

And if a theater critic is flat-out wrong with something in his review, don't be afraid to call it out to him—just do so professionally. Theater and critic relationships are tenuous and fragile things that are easily quashed. As the iconic BRT saying went, "Don't Kaz It Up."

And latex paint and oil-based spray paint do not pair well.

CHAPTER 19

Dogs and Cats

SUMMER 2003

I grew up with few opportunities to perform. My biological father dumped my Mom when I was 6, and her second husband abused us both psychologically and physically. That encompassed my first 14 years and self-esteem and anxiety issues were well engrained. Despite the father, my family had no money. Without a father who was a film or Broadway producer, I had to find or make my own opportunities. Like creating a self-promotion kit to get into the select choir in tenth grade at my new high school. Or taking any crappy theater role in Denver for the experience on my resume that would allow me to launch myself into the smallest dinner theater that perhaps ever existed. All this while an acquaintance from Denver was *en route* back to NYC to star on Broadway. I say all of this because I made some bad decisions when better opportunities came my way, particularly the *Rent* tour in 1997 and the season of leading roles at a professional repertory theater in Florida in 1998. In both cases, my anxiety took hold of me and the voice in my head told me I would fail anyway. My original decision to help co-found BRT was an easy one. If I co-owned a theater, I could get any role I wanted, right?

Not so fast.

The mostly friendly disagreement about my not casting his choice for the role of Roxie in *Chicago* came back to bite me in the butt when Corbin held auditions for the revival version of *You're a Good Man, Charlie Brown*. To me, I thought I was perfect for the titular role. After all, I was the real-life counterpart of ole Chuck and I could sing all of his songs well. Although the cartoon character is mostly bald, in the revival, Charlie was played by Anthony Rapp (the original Mark in Broadway's *Rent*) who had plenty of hair. So I figured I was a shoo-in to play Charlie Brown.

When the guy I'd cast as my sad sack Amos in *Chicago* was at callbacks, I had a sick feeling in my stomach. Mark was stocky, shorter, and had a bald head. Another opportunity gone. I got cast as Schroeder and found the role disappointing, but suitable. Mark's wife Kelly was cast as Sally, Charlie's sister. Nope, nothing weird to see here, folks. It was, after all, Tennessee.

But as Schroeder I got to wail, showing off my highest range in the song "Beethoven Day." Still, I resented Mark and the director all during rehearsals. But the opening night audience reaction to my big Beethoven number told me I was in the correct role. Dang it. I wasn't always right.

Charlie Brown is a pretty simple show, but has some deceptively tricky music, especially "Book Report" (aka "A Book Report on Peter Rabbit"), and my role had a full-on patter song within the contrapuntal music. It was just a memory exercise for me and I got it quickly. We licensed the revised show that included additional Andrew Lippa songs such as Sally's "My New Philosophy," a duet with my character.

The set was simple because it was a rehash of the *Lucky Stiff* set: All blue flats topped with the same white cloud cutouts. Again, I thought we could have done better. What wasn't simple was the choreography, well, at least not to ole double-threat me. Actually it was simple. It's just that I barely qualified as a "singer who could move." I struggled through each dance section and in Charlie Brown fashion, may have knocked my head against a wall. I had a way with developing my own version of workaround moves that would blend with the others. It was a trick that rarely failed me, the equivalent of a novice singer going for the lower note instead of the written high one.

Mark was truly the onstage embodiment of the titular role. He was a pro and rarely made a blunder, but one evening when he was supposed to be listing the things he wasn't good at as the lead-in to a number, he said "I'm no good at stickers" rather than "I'm no good at stick ball." It was one of those brilliantly flubbed lines that had the other five Peanuts biting their cartoon lips. We all laughed when we got offstage—how could anyone be bad at "stickers"? Missing the page altogether?

Another night there was a malfunction backstage with Lucy's costume or mic-pack. Sally and I were onstage calling out, per the script, a handful of character names. But no one came out. The band vamped and Kelly and I started naming every Peanut imaginable.

"Peppermint Patty!" she said.

"Marcie!" I added.

"Violet!"

"Little Redheaded Girl!"

"Pigpen!"

"Shermie!"

"Danny! Sandy!" Kelly said.

"Now you're just doing *Grease*."

"Oh. Are we even supposed to know about that in our world?" she asked.

"I don't think so."

Communication amongst management was rarely our strong suit. While I often complained I was the only one who cleaned the theater or took out the trash, Jamey and Corbin *did* help. At the end of each performance week, after the Sunday matinee, I would collect all washable costume pieces in a black trash bag to take home to wash. I set the bag by the backstage door as I finished my routine tasks. When I was ready to leave, the bag was gone. I looked frantically around the backstage area and throughout the theater. It wasn't there. I caught Jamey just as he was leaving.

"I had a trash bag full of the costume laundry sitting by the back door. Now it's nowhere to be found," I said.

"Oh, crap," Jamey said. "I thought it was trash and took it to the dumpster."

By that time, the restaurant next door had dumped several bags of their greasy trash in the common-use dumpster. Jamey ran to the bin and literally jumped in, digging through the mess.

"Found it!" he said.

Upon inspection, thankfully none of our costumes had been stained with grease. Disaster averted.

I publicized the hell out of the show and some newspapers gave it a good review (neither locatable online nor in the BRT archives). One reviewer made a special note about Kelly's "extensive dance background" which became a running backstage joke because, while Kelly had studied theater in college, her dancing was only a step above mine.

It was a standard five-week run but seemed interminable through a sweltering summer with a failing AC system. Mostly, it was a summer of calls at the box office from guests wanting to see "the *Chicago*." Ticket sales made me say "good grief!" every time I looked at the financials—the show didn't sell nearly as well as it should have.

The summer of 2003 was the first with which we partnered with the Jan Williams School of Music and Theatre under the expert direction of Sondra Morton. It was a little clunky, like a jet experiencing a bumpy climb to cruising altitude. But Sondra put together a comprehensive theater day camp program that concluded with showcase performances. Sondra would continue to grow and expand the program using BRT as its home base for year-round offerings. We were mightily blessed to have the influx of camp funds (we took 50 percent of tuition) and it became our primary source of income for half of each year, the other half coming from season-ticket sales. Without these two crucial sources of income, we would never have survived.

To keep single show ticket prices competitive, we usually just barely made payroll each week. Children's theater and season tickets covered most production costs and whatever we could throw at rent. Although I didn't care for—OK, let's be honest: I despised—children—I grew to accept their snotty-nosed presence in the flourishing children's program. They were messy and played with the Mainstage show's props backstage, but over the course of the next two years, I realized just how vital the program was.

It took longer than it should have to realize that children's shows—that is, shows performed by kids—were a real moneymaker. Every kid in each show likely had at least 12 adoring family members and family friends who wanted to see little Charlie or Charlotte perform. There was a reason every performance of every "Sondra" show sold out. She was a sharp, smart businesswoman who knew that large casts brought in large crowds. I just disliked kids so strongly I refused to see it.

Immediately after *Charlie Brown*, Sondra's recently minted Act Too Players—they had been part of the Jan Williams School of Music and

Dogs and Cats

Theatre before a big falling out—were loading in the set for their summer show. At that point, the first two weeks of the three-week summer camp were held offsite. But then the kids came in for their final week and production on the Sunday night after we'd closed the Mainstage show. There was a steep learning curve to sharing the venue with our own children's program. We'd eventually learn to co-exist better, but not in 2003.

Show strikes were always on Sundays because our productions' closing nights were on Saturdays. Strikes often started much later than they should have. Jamey had church responsibilities which meant we never saw him until almost 2 p.m. Corbin had family commitments and usually couldn't arrive until late afternoon.

Although the set for *Charlie Brown* was simple, it still required clearing the stage of large set pieces such as benches, the huge doghouse, and the mini baby grand I'd played as Schroeder. I'd arrived around 11 a.m. to clear props and start getting them upstairs or ready to be taken to offsite storage. Around noon, Sondra's crew arrived to load in the summer show. Her people just started pushing their way onto a stage with a set that hadn't yet been struck. I was in one of my trademark acrimonious moods and was ticked off that I didn't have any help, and that Act Too was aggressively taking over.

I get it now. Sondra had one day to load in the set and program lights in preparation for the final week of her program's "hell week." So, to make my displeasure known and to send a clear message to Sondra that the Mainstage show always took precedent, I quickly grabbed the smaller pieces and threw them out the stage door onto the grassy area out back. I was offered help, but in my funk, I ignored the offers and continued to drag things offstage, pushing, pulling, and kicking as necessary, especially the huge dog house. I threw out my lower back simply because I wanted to make a point. My reputation at BRT was starting its descent. I remain embarrassed to this day and apologize once again to Sondra for simply doing her job. Financially, the Act Too program is what usually saved our collective butts.

Cat on a Hot Tin Roof occupied the second summer slot and was a surprise critical success, selling even better than *Charlie Brown*. Go figure. But it had a stellar cast led by Kelly, Dietz, Dan, and Mary Bea Johnson, and was under Laura's expert direction.

Laura had the concept for a set comprised of scrim walls to reveal secondary action on the Southern home's gallery (exterior second floor wrap-around porch). As I was getting more vested in set design of most of BRT's shows, I didn't like the idea of white scrim. Instead, I found several bolts of a sheer green fabric with vertical lines in Nashville's "garment district" which was really just a couple of fabric stores. I had the shop put the fabric on hold and took a two-yard sample to Laura. I explained it would accomplish her vision while adding color and texture to the set somewhat suggestive of the green iron lace of plantation homes in the Delta. She liked it, I bought it, and it worked beautifully.

Two of Nashville's theater critics gave us high marks. Evans Donnell of *The Tennessean* had the following to say:

...

> "Boiler Room Theatre's *Cat on a Hot Tin Roof* is ready to howl… The play's leads are particularly adept at revealing the raw anger and pervasive pain beneath the poetry of [Tennessee] Williams's dialogue… J. Dietz Osborne gives us an enviably cool Brick… His interplay with [Kelly] Allen's character has the appropriate mixture of indifference and tension. And his moments with Dan McGeachy's magnificently ruined aging lion of a Big

Daddy are charged with the anger and frustration that have been building between father and son for years…"

. . .

And Martin Brady was seemingly shell-shocked:

. . .

"When I first got wind that Boiler Room Theatre, typically known for its devotion to musical theater, was taking on Tennessee Williams, I was skeptical. The Franklin company has mounted a couple of straight plays in its two-and-a-half-year history, with mixed results. The prospect of a Williams work, with all its steamy emotionalism and bigger-than-life characters, crowded into BRT's intimate, music-hall-like venue seemed a potentially dim one. The question had to be asked: Are these musical-comedy actors versatile enough to shed their hats and canes and get into Southern Gothic? The surprise answer is yes."

. . .

Thanks for the lack of confidence, Martin.

Chicago had brought in massive ticket sales, but it was a hefty payroll to meet each week. We figured we'd make up for it with the small summer shows, but they barely brought in enough. We had already been getting behind on utilities and credit-card payments as well as the steep $3,500 per month rent. At one point we owed as much as $40,000 in back rent. Our descent into financial quicksand was well underway.

HOT TIPS

Right Show, Wrong Time

Planning a theater's season is a lot like a crap shoot. We tried to adhere, as best we could, to our mission statement of producing new works, edgy shows, and reimagined classic shows in an intimate space. But we also had to scrutinize every production choice. Would it sell? Is it appropriate for our guests? Thankfully, we got better at the selection task with every new season. But even when you think you've got a sure thing, like *You're a Good Man, Charlie Brown,* the show fails to do as well as expected. We always had trouble selling tickets in the late spring to early summer due to proms, graduations, and vacations. If you've got a slow period at your theater, mount the least expensive show with the smallest cast possible, then just white-knuckle it and ride it out. It might even be an ideal time to try out an original show with no rights to pay, or even a series of new original works.

CHAPTER 20

Something Witchy This Way Comes

FALL & CHRISTMAS 2003

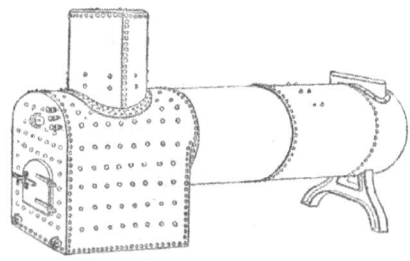

The last part of 2003 is somewhat of a blur to my partners and me. As the theater's bookkeeper, I was keenly aware of our finances. By the end of the summer, things weren't looking good. We'd blown through the summer camp money that sustained us one half of every year and had yet to launch the 2004 season campaign. We were still hopelessly behind on rent and the "we need to sit down and discuss this" meetings with The Factory had begun.

One of our first-season benefactors recommended we do a benefit concert, and make it catchy and clever and an annual thing. I was usually the king of catchy and clever, but came up as dry as the dry ice I'd soon be schlepping.

We gathered a cast of many of our stalwart performers including, not in any order, Lisa, Erin, Dietz, Dan, Megan, Lauri, Lori, Mary Bea, Corbin, Scott, Sloan Yarborough, Neely O'Brien Green, John Warren, and me. I wrote the script for John who was the emcee, Jamey and I came up with the set list, and the cast had one rehearsal. Some folks reprised numbers they'd done in our previous shows, and others had to learn new material to step in for former cast members.

The Factory begrudgingly allowed us use of the lawn between the Boiler Room and Jamison Hall where we erected an ugly, standard-issue event tent to hold the silent auction and serve *hors d'oeuvres*. Megan and I pulled the event together working around the clock the week of the benefit. There was no budget for décor. Hell, there was no budget at all, hence the need to do the benefit. We found $500 for the tent rental, and the neighboring restaurant, Saffire, donated the food. Megan and I dragged nearly every prop and small set piece out of the upstairs prop shop and created little show vignettes in the corners of the tent.

For the stage set, we pulled out three of the 24-foot-long vinyl banners which had advertised shows on the side of the building and hung them from the stage-curtain rigging interspersed with long swags of cheap white fabric. Corbin rehung over the stage the huge chandelier from *The Musical Comedy Murders of 1940*, and we had an instant, but effective set.

A lot of season-ticket holders and our sponsors stepped up with donations for the silent auction. We did the concert in two acts to allow for last-call bids. Our dedicated team of Laura Skaug and Pat Street managed the auction and tallied the amounts due from the patrons for when they left the show.

The cast was in black-tie attire. A local tux shop donated rentals of tuxes for the guys and the women were encouraged to wear their favorite little black dress. We began the show just as we did on our very first opening night: Four hooded figures (Erin and Corbin took over Cathy and Paul's roles) appeared on stage as we recreated the opening to *I Love You, You're Perfect, Now Change*. Throughout the evening, costume pieces were added as necessary such as bowler hats for the *Chicago* portion of the show. It was a who's who of Nashville musical theater and was warmly received.

We netted a not-so-grand total of $7,000 which barely made the effort worthwhile. But we had to try to stop the bleeding that had just begun.

The next show, *Smoky Mountain Mist*, was another Avante Garage! reboot, but unlike *McBeth!*, it was a serious musical that did not reside inside the Rosencrantz Theater universe. The show is a love story set in the Smoky Mountains of East Tennessee and involves a mortal man (Corbin) falling for a beautiful mountain witch (Neely). It was a perfect pairing and it was during this show that the two were engaged. But the show was a hard sell because it was unknown and challenging to describe by phone to guests.

One of the show's co-writers, Kathy Shepard, spoke fondly of the show. "Wow. So many memories. That was my favorite of all the shows that I wrote with Jamey, Michael, and Joe. During the run at the Avante Garage!, I played bass. At BRT, I was on the steps [built into the mountain set] playing banjo. I always dreamed that the show would live on and maybe be performed somewhere in Gatlinburg on a long run. We put a lot of heart into the creation."

We—that is, the LLC—must have been out-of-our-minds exhausted because the only thing anyone remembers is the dry ice. Corbin built two dry-ice foggers out of 55-gallon drums fitted with fans and dryer hosing. It created a wonderful effect—if the house manager was vigilant enough to kill the air conditioning at key moments throughout the show.

Otherwise, the low-lying fog was sucked up through the still-squeaky HVAC unit on the roof. The only place in Nashville to buy dry ice was downtown near the football stadium. And since I lived closest to the shop, I became the dry-ice wrangler—that is, procurer—for the show.

Although I wasn't involved with set design or dressing, I did create the first of many "totally themed lobbies." Sometime before the benefit, I'd taken a solo trip to Disneyland. It was the first trip during which the idea of somehow becoming an Imagineer became front of mind. I'd bought my first digital camera and took photos of the incredible detail inside the parks. I came back inspired.

To tie in with the show, I created a quaint boutique environment called "Witch-Mart," a place where a witch or wizard could "buy" eyes of newt, poisoned dragon liver, brooms, hats, cauldrons, wands, dog napping baskets, and the like. I utilized the large open area above the restrooms which would become a key area for my displays. While Pat Street and her crew were building a paper-mache mountain on stage, I was dragging and/or tying to the roof of my Cavalier dozens of limbs from a downed tree behind a defunct restaurant across from the Mapco Express convenience store at the rear entrance to "our" parking lot.

Back in the lobby, I attached these dried-out tree limbs to the electrical conduit in the corners behind the concession counter, bowing over the area to close it in, to make it feel like one was in a shop that was in a semi-outdoor space—a place that could have been right out of a Harry Potter novel. I installed more branches in the space over the restrooms, with tree limbs jutting out to continue the tree-branch ceiling. I used the two rounded window frames we'd borrowed for *Man of La Mancha* the previous year because I had yet to return them. I hoped Chaffin's Barn would never miss them because they were such cool set pieces. Up above, I added the suggestion of a witch flying away from the shop on her broom with a shopping-trip's worth of supplies. Down below, I covered the entire handicap ramp railing with willow twigs.

Between the tangle of extension cords and half of a downed tree to create witchy ambience, I could have gotten the theater shut down by the fire marshal. It was only after going to work for the Mouse that I realized just how many violations I'd broken. But that first themed lobby awakened something in me—the desire to create truly magical sets and props.

We closed the 2003 season with a remount of *The 1940s Radio Hour*. Without hurting feelings, I believe this was a far better production. Laura Skaug directed, we had a much-improved set, and I got to play the crooner, Johnny Cantone, the role Corbin played in 2001. The show brought at least one new and important talent to BRT with the casting of Corrie Maxwell (formerly Miller) née Westerman. In the Boiler Room's latter years, Corrie became another grand dame of BRT, playing roles including Muzzy in *Thoroughly Modern Millie*, the Baker's Wife in *Into The Woods*, the titular role in *Annie Get Your Gun,* and a slew of others. During my tenure, Corrie played mostly small, character roles, with the exception of Sister Robert Anne in *Nunsense*.

I was thrilled to play Cantone as opposed to the angry, flustered floor manager, Clifton. As Cantone, I got to show off some baritone croons and had a nice, drunk scene. While I still leaned on the Meisner Technique I'd learned at Actors' Bridge, my preparation for the drunk scene was definitely Method. I would slip into the back section of the metal building, past the dressing rooms, smoke a Marlboro Light, and guzzle a beer from the stock rack I diligently kept organized and inventoried. The beer gave me a bit of a buzz which helped me get into the character's head for his monologue. If we were even reviewed by Martin, I'm sure I got a lukewarm mention. Which was unfortunate, because in the Cantone role I found the Sky Masterson characterization I needed months before.

The show did well enough at the box office but should have played to packed houses. I heard comments from some guests such as, "You're doing that show again already?" Jamey knew of a theater that rolled out the show every Christmas and I think that was his original intention. But just as in 2001, audiences were confused by the 20-minute pantomime. I was thankful we'd plopped a new (and yet unwritten) original musical in the upcoming 2004 season's Christmas slot.

The lackluster sales didn't propel us into 2004 as they should have. Plus, season ticket sales were down, mostly due to a line-up of lesser-known shows. As I helped strike the set, carefully preserving the Masonite floor painted to look like aged hardwood, I had a foreboding feeling about the season ahead.

Boiler Room Voices

STEVE BOYSEN

The End of Innocence

It was a sunny and hot May day in 2001. I remember it well because I was working backstage at the CMT Awards in Nashville. In between escorting country-music stars like Keith Urban and Faith Hill from their dressing rooms to the stage, during rehearsal, I had been somewhat distracted by the thought of the phone call I was potentially missing. Since it would be a few more months until I owned a cell phone, I knew if I was to get a call, it would be at home.

After rehearsal, I rushed home to grab a few things and check messages before heading back to the arena downtown for the evening's awards. Unfortunately, the only message on the machine was one from my mother reminding me to "wave to the camera" as she would be watching from home back in Texas. But as I shrugged and turned for the door, the phone rang.

"We want you to play Mark," the voice said. "That's awesome!" I shouted, momentarily showing my young age as a 20-year-old college student who was hungry for a part in a musical.

The End of Innocence

On the other end of the line was Lewis Kempfer, director of the upcoming Boiler Room Theatre production of *A Chorus Line*. It was the call I had been hoping for. We spoke for a bit and agreed to the terms before Lewis ended the call by saying, "See you at rehearsal."

At this point in my life, rehearsal and performing were all I knew. Born in Texas to hard-working parents, although both my mother and father were good with their hands, neither was exactly considered to be artistic. That said, my parents recognized my dramatic flair and knack for entertaining people, and enrolled me in a local children's theater program in the Houston area. I also fell in love with country music during this time and started singing regularly with local bands. By the time I was in high school, I'd already had major roles in more than 30 productions.

If I wasn't in the classroom, I was at rehearsal or on stage, a trend that only continued during my college years. Having escaped the eyes of Texas, I moved to Nashville in 1999 to attend Belmont University, where I quickly discovered the school's music and theater programs. As a freshman, I was virtually stunned when I was given the part of the Scarecrow in the university's musical-theater adaption of *The Wizard of Oz*, my childhood, all-time favorite film. While juggling classes, I continued to audition for and appear in various plays and musicals at Belmont. I stayed so busy, I didn't have time to think about anything else—or anyone else. Dating was not for me at the time. Then by the spring of 2001, I also started auditioning for other theater companies in the Nashville area, working with a few. This round of auditions was what led to my eventual casting with the Boiler Room Theatre.

Although *A Chorus Line* would be my first on-stage experience with BRT, my relationship with the new theater didn't start with the call from Lewis in May 2001. It actually began the year before, when one of my best friends (who was also a Belmont student), shared the news about our theater director's spouse co-founding his own theater company at The Factory in Franklin.

Wow! I thought at the time. What an exciting and unique opportunity!

As it turned out, my friend Brandy and I became rather close to our director, Laura, and her then-husband, Jamey Green. In fact, Laura and Jamey invited us to check out the new space while it was still under construction. I even recall spending a Saturday cleaning and painting the interior—and feeling a sense I was helping to bring to life something so very special.

By the time *A Chorus Line* opened in summer 2001, I felt I had come a long way, both professionally and personally. It was only the previous year when I first began experimenting with my sexuality and began confronting the reality I was hiding my true identity as a gay man. After all, on stage, I was used to playing macho roles like Danny in *Grease* and Curly in *Oklahoma!* But by 2000, I sensed I was running away from the man my heart wanted to love. And although I ultimately played the role of wide-eyed Broadway newbie Mark, I was initially considered for the part of Paul, a gay character himself. Though I feel I could have gotten through it, I honestly don't think I had the emotional stability or dark complexion to play Paul at that time, and so it wasn't meant to be. By the summer of 2001, I was only out to my best friend Brandy. To everyone else, I was just Steve. The lanky, goofy kid everyone could rely on for a laugh and a song. But when I was around Brandy, I felt an immense weight lift. It was clear I was living a double life. But with *A Chorus Line*, I felt far enough away from the confines of conservative Belmont and, in turn, had the courage to show the cast and crew my true colors for the very first time in my life.

Rehearsals were exhausting. And the dancing. There was *so* much dancing: Ballet, jazz, tap, modern and, unfortunately, I did not consider myself a dancer. Granted, I moved well, but this was something on a whole new level for me. And for this show, you had to act, sing, and dance equally well. You know, be a triple threat. In order of "threats," I considered mine to be singing then acting and then music history. Dancing was near the bottom and certainly not amongst the top three.

Our choreographer was intense and pushed us. After all, she had performed and toured professionally for years and expected her cast to rise to the occasion. However, at the time, I felt very insecure and almost threatened by her professional credentials and brash persona. I mean, this was a woman who I considered to have done it all and seen it all. From the way she barked at us, she wasn't taking nothin' from nobody. *Yikes!* Thankfully, by the end of the run, the choreographer softened with me a bit and seemed pleased with my performance overall. *Whew.*

I fondly recall some of the other actors and actresses featured in *A Chorus Line*. Both Lori Ellis née Eisenhauer, and Keely Singer née Busteed, along with Van Dobbins III, were already friends and fellow students at Belmont. The production went a long way with helping Van and I grow a bit closer, as I always felt a bit of rivalry with him. (In my mind, he somewhat resented me ever since I, as a freshman, was cast as the Scarecrow in *Oz* while he, as a junior, was cast in the chorus.) But by our time together in ACL, we were on an equal playing field and I grew to admire Van's talent and drive. His performance as Richie, along with Keely as Val and Lori as Sheila was perfection.

Jay Sullivan, who played Bobby, was someone I initially didn't know from Adam. When we met, he introduced himself as a student of Florida State University. But all I knew was that he was a dreamboat. Though he was 100-percent straight at the time (and still is), I dreamed we'd ride off into the sunset together someday. And although we fell out of contact once he went back to school shortly after ACL ended, the crush I had on him at the time humorously resulted in my professing my sexuality to him, and eventually, others in the cast as well. In fact, there were several gay actors in ACL. But there was nothing sexual going on; we were there to do a job. But it was nice to be surrounded by so many out-and-proud gay actors living their truth.

Closing night of ACL occurred on September 8, 2001. Ending the show was an emotional experience for me. Simply driving home from the theater after the final performance, I cried like a baby. And while a part of me felt sad about the new friends I would no longer be seeing on a daily basis, another part of me felt determined to be myself at Belmont.

Then tragedy struck.

On Tuesday morning, September 11, 2001, just a mere two-and-a-half days after my wonderful experience with ACL came to an end, America's innocence also ended at the hands of terrorists when nearly 3,000 innocent people lost their lives. As I stood in a circle with other students as the horror of the day's events cast an eerie shadow, something changed in me, a change that had started with ACL and ended with 9/11. As a result, I no longer feared what other people thought as I realized how fleeting life can be. The very next day, I started opening up and coming out to friends and family, something I wouldn't have dared to do just a few months prior.

The year after *A Chorus Line*, I was offered a role in the hilariously campy BRT remount of Green's original *McBeth! The Musical Comedy!*, but unfortunately, I had a conflict with the rehearsal schedule, so it wasn't meant to be. However, since my best friend was in the show, I made it a point to be on the front row *twice*, each time laughing so hard that I slid out of my seat.

Over the next few years, I had the opportunity to attend many BRT productions and each seemed to get better than the one before it. In 2008, I was offered the leading role of Jimmy in BRT's production of *Thoroughly Modern Millie* which reunited me with Jamey, who was the musical director, and my best friend, Brandy Austin, who was the show's director and who, by that time, was also directing productions across the country. My experience with *Millie* at BRT opened up another door as well. A casting director was in the audience for one of our evening performances and, after meeting with her for coffee the next day, I was offered the opportunity to reprise the role of Jimmy at a regional theater in Houston later that year. Of course, I jumped at the chance at my family being able to see me perform regularly since they were living in Houston at the time. It was a thrilling experience I owe to BRT.

Now, 21 years after *A Chorus Line*, I think back to my coming of age and the innocent summer of 2001 and all I can do is smile. Smile a huge Texas grin of memories of the incredible talent around me, the thrill of being in the iconic show many only dream of being in, and hearing our director, Lewis, dressed all in black, barking orders at us (*ooh la la*) from the dark house as his character Zach. It was a bygone era, though I couldn't have known it at the time. And though having the opportunity to be part of BRT's inaugural season was an opportunity for me to improve my dancing, singing, and acting chops, the real lesson it taught me, both as a performer and human being, was that I could *do* something I loved while, simultaneously, *be* someone I loved. And like the hokey pokey, that's what it's all about.

2004 SEASON

Ignite Your Imagination

Gypsy
The Last Five Years
Hamlet! The Melancholy Dane! The Musical!
Sylvia
Nunsense
Sweeney Todd
That '60s Christmas Show

CHAPTER 21

Let Us Try to Entertain You

SEASON OPENER 2004

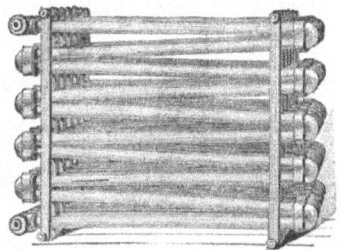

We turned the corner into 2004 with only three weeks to pull together a behemoth of a show, *Gypsy*, which was under my direction. It was our first Mainstage show that required a slew of children to play key roles. I enlisted Sondra to cast, direct, and manage three casts of five kids each. "I don't want to deal with the kids at all," I told Sondra. The show had a large cast, a full eight-piece band, and a large payroll.

Season ticket sales had fallen short of my projections and the previous show in the Christmas slot didn't do blockbuster business, so we went into the new season at a disadvantage. I'll admit it wasn't the strongest season line-up. While *Gypsy* was one of the two big-name season anchors, it didn't draw much attention. The season also had a recent Off-Broadway musical, *The Last Five Years*; another Avante Garage! "Rosencrantz" show; a small, mostly unknown play, *Sylvia*; but did pack a punch with *Nunsense* and *Sweeney Todd*. It also had the yet-to-be-written *That '60s Christmas Show*.

Gypsy had some powerhouse talents including Lori Ellis neé Eisenhauer as Mama Rose, Daron Bruce as Herbie, Melodie as Louise, plus a supporting cast that included Megan, Corrie, Dietz, Sloan, Thomas DeMarcus, and the always-fabulous Billy Ditty.

The show challenged my directing skills. I had such trouble with a crucial second-act scene between Rose and Louise that I brought in Laura, our Resident Director. I just couldn't pull the performance I wanted from the two leading ladies. The problem wasn't with Mama Rose.

Martin saw the flaws in the production, praising the ensemble characters but giving negative notes about the leads. In his review, he wrote:

...

> "With that in mind, Lewis Kempfer's direction emerges as serviceable, but it's only ordinary when the somewhat tawdry script demands more intensity. (On the plus side, Kempfer's production and set design use the small Boiler Room stage effectively, taking us through various locales on the vaudeville circuit.)"

...

It's interesting that when I started doing some serious set design work (with an eventual portfolio for Disney in the back of my mind), it was Martin who gave me compliments, a trend that continued. Overall, Martin thought the production was average at best and even called Jamey's always fantastic band "tinny."

120 SEATS IN A BOILER ROOM

I had brought back my double-decker set with the band on top. I wanted the stage to look as much like an Orpheum Circuit venue as possible and started with a pair of faux proscenium arches. The faux part is that they didn't meet in the middle and connect. But the tops were out of normal view and the audiences' minds could finish the arch mentally. The arches had elaborate molding, several layers of paint to achieve an aged look, and even ledges halfway up to hold gilded urns with fake greenery. Billy Ditty was a miracle worker and sewed the 20-some-feet-long, faux proscenium drapes as well as the heavy drape that hid a pull-out center platform, which allowed us to preset scenery and props and not lose more than a few seconds between scenes. The proscenium drapes completed a marvelous look, and although each was only 24 inches wide, there was plenty for Melodie to work with for her striptease segment. The arches remained installed for a few seasons, were taken down for a couple of shows, and even were covered for part of my scenic design elements for *Grease* in 2005. They were eventually struck permanently, although I'm not sure when, but definitely enjoyed a long lifespan for set pieces.

I also used, to questionable effect, a pair of revolving cylinders that were closed on one side and open on the other. This provided another opportunity to preset scenery and for actors to be spun out on cue. I even had faux footlights glued on top of the hardwood-floor panels left over from *1940s*.

It's hard to discern if a review positively or negatively affects a show's ticket sales without asking each guest (and even then the answers might be inaccurate). But Martin's lukewarm review didn't help the faltering sales. We couldn't even sell out the Valentine's event. What saved us financially were the three casts of child actors. That amounted to approximately 15 children who all had parents and relatives coming to see their budding thespians.

Sondra's solid work with the kids further cemented the value of our partnership with her Act Too Players. I felt embarrassed by, perhaps ashamed of, the many times we had to lean on the children's program just to make another week's payroll. Working with children was always a horror to me, but it did sometimes produce hilarious quotes and anecdotes.

A classic moment happened during one of the show's performances, and involved the nearly identical younger version of Dietz, who played the adult Tulsa. The cast had nicknamed the boy "Dainty Dietz," a play on Baby June's older incarnation, Dainty June. For the song "Mr. Goldstone, I Love You," we rotated a multitude of guys through the thankless role of Mr. Goldstone, an older man who only appeared as a prop for the song. It was my turn for the walk-on during a Sunday matinee and was backstage early. As the director, I figured it would be a good chance to see how backstage operations were progressing.

The kids were required to do a quick change during "Baby June and Her Newsboys." Toward the end of the song, the boys changed into military costumes for the finale. Dainty Dietz was near me, backstage left, when he said loudly to his dresser trying to get him into a jacket, "I can't find the hole!"

That line immediately became part of BRT's lexicon just as much as "I'm no good at stickers" or "they know we're back here," the latter spoken by Dietz during *Little Shop of Horrors* when before the show I asked the cast to be quiet while backstage. They all thought it was hilarious. I was pissed. Which they also thought was hilarious.

A couple of weeks into the run, a box-office staffer tentatively arranged to take the show "on tour" to a fledgling theater company in Donelson that used the cafeteria of a senior center. We hastily agreed on a fee to cover cast payroll and transport of the scenery and costumes. The only set pieces we could feasibly take were the two revolves. Once loaded into the senior cafeteria that always reeked of overcooked meatloaf and elderly people, we rigged a mid-center-stage drape in lieu of our clever sliding scene-setting platform.

Problems with the audio system stripped us of using our body mics. The lighting system comprised two 1970s school-theater rails, but the little lighting console the Donelson venue owned failed to operate the shoddy lighting. So we were reduced to an assistant stage manager standing at a light switch backstage operating our two lighting looks: On and off. But the shows were matinees, and the cafeteria had uncovered windows along the tops of the two long walls. Which meant that a between-scenes blackout was impossible. It was a disastrous attempt to generate a few bucks, but it cost us more than the paltry fee. It was a huge undertaking to move the show, smaller set pieces, and all the costumes and props. Never again, we said. And as far as I know, such a futile feat wasn't tried again.

The show taught the world that "you've gotta get a gimmick." Sadly, our production of *Gypsy* did not.

CHAPTER 22

A Miracle Should Have Happened

SECOND SLOT 2004

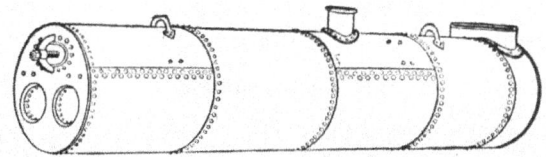

I was relieved when *Gypsy* closed and we moved on to the two-person show, *The Last Five Years*. As was the case with many of the show selections, I had suggested it. The musical had had a recent, successful Off-Broadway run. It has an almost entirely sung-through, incredibly complex score by Jason Robert Brown and a convoluted plot that Franklin audiences just couldn't grasp.

The female character, Cathy, tells the story of a five-year relationship that left her broken, starting at the end and working backwards in time. The male character, Jamie, starts his version of the story at the beginning and moves forward in time sequentially. As written, the couple are only on stage together when their stories cross paths at their wedding. More recent productions have had both characters on stage at all times. I thought the show was brilliant, but like others we'd done or would do, it didn't resonate with our I-only-know-*The-Sound-of-Music* audiences.

A Miracle Should Have Happened

I desperately wanted to play Jamie. I had the vocal and acting chops and practically begged Jamey to let me do the role. No dice. That production was the first time we'd brought in an outside director, that is, outside our small, core group of Jamey, Laura, Corbin, and me. The Boiler Room cast member who directed had, by that time, completed two solid seasons with BRT and was loved by everyone.

But he and I never got along. The rift may have begun prior to *The Last Five Years*, or the disagreement on tech week may have triggered it. The director had a minimalist vision for the set with the blasted black drapes and a garden arch as the focal point with the band behind it. I had major issues with the design. First, it wasn't much of a design. During the middle of tech week, cheap, dollar-store vines had been stapled to the arch. It looked awful. Corbin agreed and after the final dress rehearsal when it was just Corbin, Jamey, and I, we *de-vined* the arch, pulled the staples, and repainted. Then as was customary, I was left alone to clean the entire theater and paint the stage floor. When the director arrived on opening night, he was mighty pissed to find his vines missing. Jamey had to intervene.

It's not that I had anything against artificial plants, vines, or flowers. Hell, they're a set designer's best friend. Even Walt Disney Imagineering uses artificial for everything above a park guest's head (the stuff below is real and maintained by each Park's horticulture team). My problem was that the vines were flimsy and cheap and too few. Five dollars' worth of crappy vines looked exactly like five dollars' worth of crappy vines. Had the arch been covered adequately with lush greenery, it might have worked. But it still wouldn't have been the set I would have designed.

The second issue with the set design was being able to see band "gack" (e.g. cables, fans, amps, music stands, and music lights). It was one of my pet peeves that had the ferociousness of a pit bull. When I directed and had a band onstage, I always masked them from the waist down and tried in vain to get them to wear matching shirts or sport coats. The visual distractions of a sloppy onstage band were capable of pulling an audience member out of the story.

Assuming a show had audience members.

I honestly thought we would draw an audience. It was a love story. It was a musical. It had the word 'f-ck' in it. And that last thing still didn't fly in Franklin. I'm a Christian, but I'm also a theater guy and a playwright, and sometimes a cuss word is needed or it changes the cadence of a line. For example, at the top of Act Two when the now-married Jamie sings "A Miracle Would Happen," he has a line about being attracted to other women at industry parties (he's now a published author) which includes the line "since I can't f-ck her anyway." For our fragile audiences, the offensive word was changed to screw. Totally blew the humor of the line.

It had also happened during *A Chorus Line* when my business partners and the actress playing Val weren't comfortable with one of her lines that had, admittedly, the blasphemous "God d-mn." As in "… she came home one Christmas to visit, and they gave her a parade. A God d-mn parade!" That was an instance in which removing the highly offensive "G.D." robbed the line of its rhythm. Yet in the same production, I allowed Diana to say "Jesus Christ" as an exclamation of frustration during her solo "Nothing." I thought removing one offensive instance would appease audiences. It didn't, and I should have kept the script as written, as dictated by the contract.

But for *The Last Five Years,* audiences weren't buying tickets and even season ticket holders weren't making reservations. We cancelled several performances, and the ones we did, often had no more than 18 people in the audience. Yes, the story was a little confusing, but Erin Parker's majestic voice on Cathy's songs was blissful and Tim Carroll as Jamie sang capably.

But there were more problems.

Tim's mother had a dance studio in Building 8 at The Factory complex and lots of money. Tim and a Broadway friend wanted the Boiler Room venue, knew we were struggling, and made an offer. Jamey declined and we chose to forge ahead.

The Last Five Years was supposed to bring in enough at the box office to propel us into the next show, but even with its two-person cast and a seven- or eight-piece band, we came nowhere near breaking even.

HOT TIPS
Don't Change a Word

Every show contract from a licensing company I've ever seen has a clause in it that states changing the script, adding or removing dialogue and/or adding or removing songs is strictly prohibited. This is the licensing company protecting the playwright's work to ensure the original intent of the show remains intact and is presented thusly. There are several of these companies, and the big players include Music Theatre International (MTI), Tams-Witmark, Samuel French, and the Rodgers and Hammerstein (R&H) Organization, which seems to have created a separate licensing company called Concord Theatricals since the Boiler Room closed. MTI and Samuel French tended to be a bit more forgiving, while Tams and R&H had no problem shutting down productions.

Yes, we changed scripts by removing or changing profanity, although not always. We didn't seek approval to do so and probably should have. The best bet is to produce shows exactly as written. The old adage "It's easier to ask for forgiveness than permission" rarely applies when dealing with licensing companies.

Boiler Room Voices

MARK BEALL

A Very Bright Light

Before discussing my first musical at BRT, we need to go back in time, before Jamey, Corbin, and Lewis had the wacky idea to turn a decades-old building into an intimate theater venue.

For I contend, that the first BRT production took place before the theater in Franklin was rented, before the birds living in the rafters were "gently" escorted to a new abode, before the stage was built, before the lobby was constructed, even before the famous Boiler Room Theatre logo was painted onto the old boiler on the parking-lot side of the building.

Very few ticket holders, if any, ever saw the actual monster of a boiler that was left inside the theater's backstage building. It was in the way as BRT grew and needed more space for costumes, dressing rooms, and general storage, but I always assumed that the cost to have it removed would've been enormous, and as Lewis stated, The Factory said it would be a half-million-dollar environmental hazard cleanup. And no one had that kind of money.

Yes, before BRT opened their first show in Franklin, there was a show staged and produced which involved a great many people, who would one day be part of the BRT family: *God Bless You, Mr. Rosewater* as detailed at the beginning of this book. I played "Keyboard 2" in the small pit band which included future BRT drummer and photographer Rick Malkin, and of course, pianist and music director and future Boiler Room Artistic Director Jamey Green.

Actually, my association goes back to even before *Rosewater*, because my very first experience performing a musical in Tennessee, was with Jamey when he was the music director of *Nunsense* at Chaffin's Barn Dinner Theatre. I had limited theater experience in Ohio and New York, so it seems that I need to thank (or blame) Jamey for starting my musical-theater career in Tennessee. Truly so, for while I was performing at Chaffin's, Michael Edwards got a call from Jim Crabtree, Artistic Director of the Cumberland County Playhouse in Crossville, Tennessee. Jim needed a keyboard player for an upcoming production, and Michael must have liked my playing. I called Jim and got hired to play in a new production and ended up working in Crossville for two decades. So, getting to perform in my first show at the Boiler Room Theatre was simply completing a large and long circle that began with Jamey at Chaffin's in 1989.

The first show that I played at BRT was their famous production of *A Chorus Line*. "Famous" because *everyone* questioned how a show with so many dancing actors could fit on the small BRT stage. Guess what? They did it, and it was great. Audiences ate it up. This show set the high standard for future Boiler Room shows.

Let me explain something to y'all. (Those involved in theater probably already know this.) A music director (MD) is the person who is in charge of the music—easy, right?

If you ever get to look into the pit of a musical in New York City, you will likely see a person leading the orchestra with a conducting baton. Most theater companies outside of NYC have that person conducting as they play a keyboard. Anyhow, BRT was like most theater groups in the area, and the MD would play keyboard. The pit band or "orchestra" could consist of as many instruments as the budget and space would allow. At BRT, when I would play under Jamey's direction, I would normally play from music scored for "Keyboard 2." It has been common for many years, that orchestrators will use the second set of hands to cover instruments that may not be feasible to have in the production. For instance, it is unlikely in Nashville to see a 20-piece string section playing a musical. So "Keyboard 2" will usually have a different score than the full score in the book the MD uses. There might be a need for sounds emulating strings, organ, woodwinds, brass, and even percussion instruments such as bells, timpani, marimba, and vibraphone.

Every theater has a unique sound system. What was great at the Boiler Room was, that when the musicians played in the tech booth, they were very close to the sound-board operator. (This later changed with the advent of Lewis's two-story set design that was successfully employed many times.) That made communication during a pre-show sound check and the tweaks made during tech week easier than having to yell at an operator 50 feet away.

Because of the small size of the theater, certain instruments like trumpet and trombone would not be amplified. Drums in the tech booth were usually played on electronics, because having an acoustic drum kit up there would have required a drum cage (acoustic isolation) and microphones. The electronic kits sounded fine and were much easier logistically. But I was reminded that Rick played acoustic drums for *A Chorus Line,* and guests seated in the upper house heard more kick drum than anything.

I was fortunate to serve as Music Director for numerous shows at BRT. Here's a summary:

Assassins. Who knew that a show about death could be so entertaining?

Clue, The Musical. We had a wonderful cast doing their best with an inane play. I had a major goof-up one night when I missed my stage cue to start a song.

The actors waited a moment or two before realizing that I had gone "up." The great Dan McGeachy decided to prompt me by saying, "I think a song is about to start."

Godspell. The set was an abandoned theme park and the band was positioned inside a broken-down roller coaster. Whee!

Into the Woods. The rare show that Jamey Green did *not* MD because he played a leading role (The Baker).

Man of La Mancha. Here was another show with Jamey playing a lead acting role as the trusty squire Sancho Panza, trying and failing to control Dan's Don Quixote. The band was in the tech booth for this late 2002 production. Have you ever tried to climb up a ladder using just *one* leg? I had to one Tuesday night, because the day before I had outpatient knee surgery.

Sweeney Todd. What an astonishing production. I believe that Lewis outdid himself when he combined prop razors his Dad fabricated and devised a squeeze-bulb that would spurt fake blood as Sweeney knocked off his victims. The technical aspects of this show included the complex set piece that encompassed the barbershop with the slide for the dead bodies to be delivered to the meat-pie shop below. Musically complex as well, this may have been the tech week with the longest rehearsals I ever experienced at BRT.

The Last Five Years. Easily the hardest keyboard score I ever played at BRT. Thanks, Jason Robert Brown!

Among the shows for which I played second keyboard were *Annie Get Your Gun, How to Succeed in Business Without Really Trying, Little Shop* of Horrors, and probably a dozen I've forgotten. One I will never forget is *Sunday in the Park with George*. Technically, this was a show that BRT should not have been able to produce, not unlike so many others. In typical BRT fashion, they forged ahead and were able to birth a stunning production of this Sondheim masterpiece.

Two shows in particular hold special memories. A fantastic cast (and band) made *Jesus Christ Superstar* one of my favorite musical adventures at the Boiler Room. On closing night during the final bow, the actor playing Jesus, took a knee and proposed to the actress playing Mary Magdalene. She said yes and the theater almost blew apart from the applause.

For *My Fair Lady,* the band was over the stage, with a few members playing in the newly carved-out room behind the upstage wall on the second level. Before one performance, I planned a gag for Jamey. I planted a little black box in the room behind the wall that I worked via remote control that operated my trick box that emulated fart sounds placed near Jamey's feet. Of course, I was careful to choose spots in songs when the electronic expulsions would not be heard by the audience. When Jamey heard the fake farts, he swung his head to give dirty looks into the band room with that parental "don't make me stop this car" expression. I wasn't fired, so no harm, no foul. And great fun without the foul fragrance.

In total, I worked on more than 50 Boiler Room musicals and found every show to have its own challenges and rewards. Every cast, crew, and band becomes an ersatz family, but BRT transcended that, and the people with whom you worked, year after year, really became a family. And like every family, there *were* a number of crazy cousins and insane uncles that sometimes made you say, "Well, bless their heart!"

It makes no sense to me that BRT is no longer with us. I understand why, but there are days when I simply do not wish to accept the reality that there's no longer a theater space in a former boiler room at The Factory at Franklin. When the Boiler Room Theatre got screwed out of their lease, the Middle Tennessee arts community lost a small but very bright light. How many lives were touched by BRT? There is no real way to say, but if you think about all of the actors, technicians, and musicians who gave of themselves, you must ask who was the beneficiary of all that talent and energy? I believe it was the guests who faithfully squeezed into that intimate space and were treated to emotions and thrills that you just can't get from a Netflix subscription.

Did BRT give more than it received? Without question, I say yes.

CHAPTER 23

Just Too Damn Melancholy

SPRING 2004

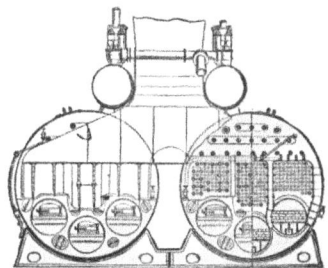

To appease my bruised ego from not getting to play the character Jamie in the previous show, Jamey said he needed me to reprise my version of Blanche in the remount of the Avante Garage!'s wildly popular *Hamlet! The Melancholy Dane! The Musical!* Blanche plays Ophelia, and as such, has a leading role. It was supposed to be a consolation prize, but when we planned the season, I imagined myself doing both roles. Perhaps it was kismet; I would have taken the low turnout of *The Last Five Years* personally.

With no royalties to pay and a small onstage band, we figured making payroll for the large cast would be a cakewalk. After all, the show had been one of the biggest hits ever written and produced by Jamey's former theater company.

We figured incorrectly.

We thought we'd get a swarm of audience members, rather we got crickets. And more than just the kind who parked themselves above stage left in a pipe that served as an echo chamber. *Those* crickets were damn annoying, especially during soft, emotional moments in shows such as during Paul's monologue in *A Chorus Line.*

I started to panic right away because I did the theater's accounting. We had a 17-member cast and a five-member band, and it took all of our available funds to make the first week's payroll which was only for three shows. The upcoming weeks were five-show weeks and I was shaking in my high heels.

We borrowed money and used cash advances from my credit cards to make the second week's payroll. There were only season-ticket holder reservations and a handful of Two-for-Tuesday prepaid tickets on the books through the remainder of the five-week run. And of course, season-ticket money came in as much as six months prior and by May, we usually had just enough to get by until the lucrative Act Too summer-theater-camp registrations and fees came in. But that year the twain did not meet. Season ticket money was gone too soon.

It was at this point we called an all-cast emergency meeting during which we laid out the options.

"Thanks, everyone for being here," said Corbin.

Jamey added, "We've never had to do this and are doing it red-faced. We're embarrassed to gather all of you. Lewis can explain the circumstances."

I took the stage. "You have no idea how difficult it was to call this meeting. It's quite humiliating. But the reality is we can't make payroll for next week and possibly the remainder of the run," I said. "We're in a very bad place being at least 12 months behind on rent to The Factory. Thankfully, they've been flexible and patient with us accepting $500 here and there. But their patience is nearly depleted. We are behind on the electric bill and have begged the utility company to not shut off our power.

"We are dead serious when we say that we're on the verge of closing the doors permanently. We know that many of you have been with us going back to the first season and have frequently heard that you consider BRT home."

"So do we," Jamey interjected. "We want this to remain everyone's theater home. But we need your help." He nodded at me as my cue to spill the beans.

"Here's the thing. We can continue the show's run with the caveat that payroll may not be met, or we can close the production and pray for the best."

Corbin was much better at delivering succinct messages. "What Lewis means is that if we keep the run going, we need a majority of you to forego getting paid."

Hearing the words cut through my heart. We never wanted to be in that position. An audible group gasp and an assortment of "Oh my Gods" and "Damn that really sucks" declarations could be heard above the din of the cast muttering to each other.

"You don't have to tell the group if you're willing to give up pay. This can all be confidential, so nobody feels ashamed," I said.

The cast wasted no time in responding. It truly felt like the run-on-the-bank scene in *It's A Wonderful Life*. Dan McGeachy was the first hand raised. "Not only will I perform without pay, but I'll also see what I can contribute financially," he said.

Four more hands were raised as I made a tally of the responses. I don't recall nor is it relevant to include who said they'd go without pay. And although I'd made it clear that individual responses could be private, there were a few people who publicly admitted their situation.

One actress, reminiscent of Miss Davis in the run-on-the-bank scene who asks for only $17.50, said if she could just get 50 bucks to pay her cell-phone bill, would do the rest of the run for free. It was more touching, in a way, than the many people who said they'd work without pay.

And then like the man in the film who asks for his full $242 and states that "$242 wasn't going to break anybody," one of the leading actresses said, "I love BRT and I'm so sorry the company is in this position, but there's no way I can give up being paid. I'm working five jobs plus this show, and I can't make rent. I want the run to continue because I love the show, but I can't go without pay."

"We totally understand and as Lewis said, no one was required to state their position, their vote, as it were," said Corbin.

A couple more cast members came forward to say they were in a similar position. We didn't fault or think less of these folks and appreciated their candor and bravery.

All in, at least 85 percent of the cast had volunteered to go without pay. Later, when I frantically punched the numbers into the box office adding machine, I delivered my verdict to Jamey and Corbin. "There are three cast members and the full band who cannot give up pay. As such, it will be damn close, but we can keep the doors open. I'll need to cancel all advertising. We need to run no HVAC unless absolutely necessary. And that running gag I do as Blanche with Jamey about no dry cleaning? No dry cleaning."

And like the run-on-the-bank scene, we just barely finished our run without having to shutter the business.

It's a shame that much of the comic brilliance in *Hamlet!* and the joy of being on stage were lost on me because I was too busy being George Bailey trying to save the Building and Loan.

But there were priceless, comic moments and gags such as the one during the finale when all the chorus girls come out with fake donuts, cinnamon buns, and sweet rolls attached to the breasts of their leotards. Myron (played by Jamey) comes center stage to scream at Blanche, "Stop! What the hell is this?"

"What the hell is your problem?" Blanche replies, stepping out of the box office in a leopard-print robe.

"Those costumes. That's not what I asked for!"

"You told me the girls should all come out wearing pastries," Blanche explains.

"Pasties! I said *pasties!*" Myron screams.

"Oh. Well, I thought it was kinda weird, but I figured it's Denmark and danishes…"

"Pasties, not pastries" had our small but appreciative audiences in proverbial stitches.

None of the BRT casts in the Avante Garage! shows were ever able to recreate the perfection that Michael and Joe brought to their roles. In *McBeth!*, Scott couldn't deliver what Michael wanted in the "Edgar" role he had created. Dan came much closer in *Hamlet!*, but I think there remained disappointment.

The converse situation happened to me in Joe's "Blanche" role. Joe was quite happy with my characterization, yet I was mad at myself for being unable to recreate his rendition of the character. Blanche was supposed to be awkward and dumpy, and in the process, hilarious. I tried, but all I could manifest was a big, bold, brassy broad with big boobs that would have fit in with the *Saturday Night Live* "Coffee Talk" skit cast. I tried hard during *Hamlet!* to bring more hints of Joe's Blanche into my performance since she plays a leading role, and perhaps I did, but I was disappointed in myself and somehow took it upon my well-padded shoulders that the abysmal turnout was somehow all my fault, that I had failed the show in its marketing, that I hadn't accurately communicated to ticket buyers the delightful comedy it was, or that my idea of Blanche doing the radio commercial was a poor decision.

Thank God we were given the gift of survival and the chance to plod ahead and to try to, as the saying goes, turn the Titanic around.

CHAPTER 24

So, A Dog and Five Nuns Walk Into a Bar...

SUMMER 2004

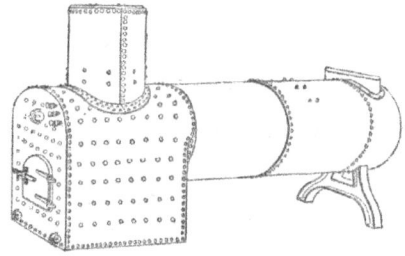

The extreme stress of the *Hamlet!* scare shook me to the core. How long could I go through these hits and misses, spurts and flops, being in the black, then in the red, then only to repeat *ad nauseum*? I had cofounded the Boiler Room partially for selfish reasons: I wanted to get the parts I wanted to play. That worked the first season but, to a great extent, hadn't since. I felt it was owed to me: After all, I'd put my life savings into the theater. What I couldn't see clearly at the time was that despite my desire to play a certain part, it didn't necessarily mean I was right for it. *The Last Five Years* was still a fresh wound.

Nearly shuttering the business hurt, but I was in good-riddance mode. I had to think about life beyond the Boiler Room. Jamey's drinking intensified as he finalized his divorce with Laura. Corbin had a new love, and his cabinet business was still booming. Teressa had moved on. Was there simply no one left who even cared if BRT survived?

If my dream of working for Disney were to ever happen, I'd have to earn my bachelor's degree. I had culled together random credits in Phoenix but without access to financial aid, finishing college was never going to happen. Then, a sign from God. Actually, it was a sign from Trevecca Nazarene University, a billboard on westbound Interstate 40 near the Charlotte Avenue treasure trove of thrift stores. The school had a 13-month degree-completion program. It was a grueling, relentless program that required one night of attendance per week in addition to around 20 hours of weekly homework. Pile that on top of my 95-hour weeks at BRT, and that's how I famously put in 120-hour weeks. My cohort's night was Thursday which meant I would have to miss every show's final dress, except for two when I could utilize my allowed absences. I allotted those to *That '60s Christmas Show* and *Grease*.

I amped up my set designs, imagining each to be a Disneyland project that required the utmost attention to every creative nuance. All the while, I was documenting every detail of every design for some sort of eventual pitch to the Mouse.

BRT's quiet salvation began with a small play, A.R. Gurney's *Sylvia*, a 1995 Off-Broadway hit that mercifully had a cast of four. It was a touching show about a childless couple whose dog makes a profound influence on their lives. Sylvia, the dog, is written to be played by a human. In director Lane Wright's production, it was played by our Resident Choreographer Lauri who had already proven her acting chops in *Guys and Dolls*. It was a challenge for Lauri only in that the role has a lot of foul language since Sylvia the dog has quite the potty mouth.

The play required little for a set: just a sofa, a chair, a coffee table, and three walls. I borrowed a Victorian settee and an Oriental rug from Chaffin's Barn and brought in an upholstered chair from home. We used spare paint from previous shows for the set which had three upstage windows overlooking a New York City backdrop that someone painted for us for free over Joe Correll's *McBeth!* drop. The prop budget was kept under $50. Costumes were from stock and the cast's own wardrobes. The final scene required a projected image of the "actual" dog. I found a Kodak Carousel at thrift and paid for it personally. The production budget, without royalties, was $130.

House capacities were not unsurprisingly small as we were best known for our musicals. But we sold enough tickets to make the minimal weekly payroll and even pay a few bills. I of course called in every possible favor to get rack cards printed and an ad placed in the *Scene* on opening week. Word spread and more butts began to warm seats. Had we, like a dog toy, squeaked by?

Irony has always been a key component of my personal life. That spilled over to the Boiler Room. Fewer than three months after nearly shuttering the theater, a miracle was delivered by five nuns. Rather, five actresses dressed as nuns. The middle of the 2004 season was perfectly tailored to our plight: A small, but popular comedy, and a rip-roaring, roof-raising, knee-slapping hell of a great show that, without the tent, delivered revival to the Boiler Room Theatre.

We knew *Nunsense* would be a hit; it usually is for probably every theater anywhere. Actually, it *had* to be a hit; it was our Hail Mary pass. For BRT, its timing was nothing short of divine. It's funny, really. One of the big duets in *Hamlet!* was "Get Thee to a Nunnery," which I performed in bad drag as Blanche/Ophelia with Dan as Edgar Douglas/Hamlet. The song is a send-up of the scene in which Hamlet is telling a crazed Ophelia to get to a convent to ostensibly be healed. I wonder if every night as Dan pointed viciously at me, he might have unknowingly been pointing a couple of months into the future. That is, perhaps, pointing BRT to get itself to a theatrical convent with wise-cracking nuns.

Because the show is written to be played on a Catholic school's cheesy stage setting for *Grease* and already knowing I would insist that *Grease* be our 2005 opener, we built two units that would be repurposed in the latter show: The slumber-party bed and the soda fountain. For *Nunsense* they were stationary. For *Grease,* they became components of one of my signature "pop-up" book sets where set pieces pulled out, spun around, or otherwise transformed into something else.

Personally, it was the show during which I grew my prop-building skills. I built the Sister Mary Annette puppet and crafted the Carmen Mirandaesque fruit hat for a Sister Robert Anne gag.

The bone that *Sylvia* threw us provided the impetus to put everything we had into *Nunsense*. Had the show flopped, we wouldn't have had a prayer of surviving.

Director Corbin Green assembled a heavenly cast that included BRT stalwarts Megan and Corrie, plus Stephanie Jones and Melinda Doolittle. The role of Mother Superior had to be recast due to illness after publicity shots were done and rehearsals had begun. Sondra Morton stepped in flawlessly and effortlessly. I had to Photoshop Sondra's head onto the body of the original actress in all the publicity photos for posters, ads, and rack cards. No one was the wiser.

The production received its sole review from Amy Stumpfl of *Nashville City Paper*:

. . .

"As Williamson County's first resident professional theater company, the Boiler Room Theatre (BRT) offers the perfect venue for *Nunsense*. The intimate, movie-style seating helps sets the stage for the nuns' benefit show and enables the sisters to interact with the audience… From the moment the sisters take the stage, the audience is treated to outstanding comic timing…

"But it is the multi-talented Megan Murphy [Chambers] who steals the show as the absent-minded Sister Mary Amnesia… Her over-the-top facial expressions alone are worth the admission price, particularly in "So You Want to Be a Nun." Her hilarious bit with Sister Mary Annette—a puppet with a rather nasty attitude built by prop designer Lewis Kempfer—keeps the audience in stitches… As usual BRT musical director Jamey Green is fantastic."

. . .

Nunsense was the blessing the Boiler Room desperately needed. While we had walked away from *Hamlet!* with collective tails between legs, from opening night, our five nuns brought the house down. Performances sold out quickly and more were added. While we had no idea how our fourth season would unfold when it was announced in the fall of 2003, *Nunsense* was perfectly slotted. Soon we were back in the habit—you knew *that* joke was coming—of producing bona fide hits.

CHAPTER 25

Saving the Boiler Room

LATE SUMMER 2004

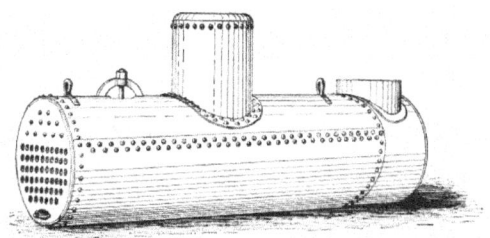

As part of my coursework at Trevecca, I was required to write a graduate-level thesis about making some improvement at my place of employment. The problems in which the theater was mired provided the perfect material. I presented my thesis topic proposal on July 15, 2004, and the timing could not have been better.

The purpose of my thesis was to determine whether a change in programming and market positioning, along with improved guest service, would increase season and individual ticket revenues at the Boiler Room Theatre by 40 percent over 2004 campaign revenues.

The problem I stated was that the theater was at risk of closing due to poor customer service and an unfortunate selection of shows. The future of the Boiler Room would be determined by the success of the 2005 season campaign as well as a dramatic improvement in guest service. If ticket revenues, specifically 2005 season ticket revenues, did not increase by the projected 40 percent, it would be difficult, if not impossible, for the company to survive. If the projected revenue increases were to be achieved, the company would have to produce in 2005 the most ambitious and aggressive schedule of productions in its history, thereby improving market share and guest loyalty.

Phew. Glad we got that stuffy, academic information out of the way.

First, guest service. It applies to every type of business. Provide great service and yield great results. Do the opposite and watch your company fail.

During the first two years after I quit my day job and made the Boiler Room Theatre my top and only priority, part of what I promised Jamey was that I would cover the box office Monday through Friday from ten in the morning until six in the evening unless it was a show day and then my shift would be much longer. Who am I kidding? Every day was long. I was either sourcing props, painting and dressing sets, creating marketing materials, buying concession items at Sam's Club, cleaning the theater—you get the idea. I usually had a part-time staffer cover Saturdays if someone was available.

And I would gladly do any task including cleaning the restrooms rather than assist guests on the phone. I admit it now; I wasn't always pleasant to deal with. And I wasn't reliable. I should have fired myself from box-office duties, which I eventually did. But until we had steady revenue again, I had to buck up and do the right thing. As good as I was at being my own boss for creating marketing campaigns or dressing sets, I was a miserable employee who could never manage to get the box office opened on time. I was usually one or two hours late.

It wasn't the first time I'd worked a box office nor was it the first time I'd delivered poor box-office service. When I was 19 and trying to eke out a meager living at Ye Olde Wayside Inn Dinner Theatre, one of my duties was running its box office. I lived in downtown Denver and made a 50-mile commute to earn, if I recall correctly, less than minimum wage to answer the dinner theater's phones and do some marketing design for the owner.

But I was 20.

Which meant I didn't know how to manage my time.

I'd go out to the underage bar and stay out too late, then be unable to get up on time for work. Every day I had to make two trips from my apartment to my car, and subsequently two trips from the car into the theater, to haul my boombox, typewriter, portable light table for manual page layout, and at least one backpack crammed with crap. Often the owner of YOWIDT would already be working the phones in my absence, and depending on her mood upon my arrival, I'd get a gentle head shake and "tsk-tsk" to the stern "this is the last time you come in late" lecture.

The problem then, as it was with BRT, was that I despised dealing with the public. I had no patience, especially for people who didn't know what they wanted or were rude. At the Boiler Room, my level of service varied from friendly car salesman if a guest was buying tickets to rude collection agent if a guest was a season-ticket holder and only needed to make a reservation.

On too many days at BRT when I was running late, I'd call Jamey, who lived near the theater, to cover phones until I could manage to get my rear end down to Franklin from East Nashville. Sometimes it worked because Jamey taught many of his voice lessons at the theater, but once he had started with a student he couldn't be expected to play box office. More often than not, especially by 2004, we missed more calls than we answered. And it negatively affected sales.

And when we did answer the phone, we rushed guests through their ticket purchases. And if one was a season ticket holder—one of the people who, year after year, gave us money in advance that kept us afloat—too often they were forced to take off-nights because we so desperately needed to sell premium-night seats.

I couldn't take all the blame, though. We had a small stable of folks who could, in a pinch, work a box-office shift. But those people, usually cast members, often had to bring babies or young children with them and as such had their own challenges getting the box office open on time.

But poor service and unfortunate show selections were the double whammy that nearly shuttered the Boiler Room.

Improving guest service was a relatively simple task: Open on time, answer the damn phone, and be friendly. It took time to retrain our guests that we *could* provide reliable service. It's not often that a business gets a second chance after blowing the basics. Thankfully, we got that chance.

Nunsense proved the point I'd made at the beginning: We needed to do shows people knew. That we couldn't just do edgy, unknown stuff and expect to survive. I had to convince my partners that for the upcoming 2005 season, we needed to hit it out of the park or close the theater. And that meant doing a full season of shows people knew while still avoiding *Oklahoma!* and *South Pacific* (although we did consider the latter).

I created each season's theme for marketing purposes, and for 2005, I went full Disney with "Classic Tales" and a season brochure that looked just like something Disney would produce. The season even concluded with a Disney blockbuster.

As we were considering the season's lineup, I made the journey to see *Disney's Beauty and the Beast* at Cumberland County Playhouse in Crossville. Their stage wasn't *that* much larger than ours, although they did have actual wing space and two side "stages" or playing areas. OK, their stage *was* a lot larger than ours. But as I watched, I imagined the behemoth show on our postage stamp, scribbling notes and diagrams, and after the show, was convinced we could pull it off. But it would be a harder sell to my partners than *A Chorus Line*.

I made my pitch.

"Guys, if we don't sell double the season tickets we have the last two years, we're never going to climb out of this hole." I explained my vision and it was met with grunts and groans.

"You know I never wanted this theater to do stuff people could see anywhere else," Jamey said.

"Lewis might have a point here," Corbin said. "If we do a year of name shows and do them better than anyone else, he's right—we will survive."

Jamey was slow to come around to Corbin's Gloria Gaynor refrain. Most of the shows up for consideration made it into the season including *Grease*, *Godspell*, and *How to Succeed in Business Without Really Trying*. After describing my take on how we could do *Grease* and make it fresh, he warmed to the idea.

Then came the hard sell for *Beast*. Neither Green brother was convinced we could do it. I'd come prepared with rough set sketches and a plan that utilized two main units that rotated and opened, along with three backdrops to provide the settings. I also asserted that I wanted to direct.

"Where the hell are we going to put the band?" Jamey asked.

"Sure as hell not on stage," I replied.

"The show's score needs more instrumentation than we can ever fit in the booth."

"I know. Remember that Colorado dinner theater that did *A Chorus Line* on a stage not much bigger than ours? Up until a few years ago, they did all their shows to tracks."

"Canned music? That's not our style," Jamey said.

"Just this once. We assemble a small orchestra. You take them into a studio and record the show's performance track. It can work and it doesn't mean changing our precedent of live bands. Just do it this one time. Trust my gut instinct, please. If we put *Beast* into a season chock-full of name shows, we'll sell more season tickets than we know what to do with."

In addition to the aforementioned shows, we added *On Golden Pond, The Secret Garden,* and one recent Off-Broadway hit, *Epic Proportions.* A huge team effort was required to make *Beast* fit and work on our stage, but it did, and guest heads nearly exploded (in a good way) when they saw how well we pulled it off.

HOT TIPS

Keep Your Customers

You've busted your butt to open a theater and attract a guest base. Don't blow it by ignoring the basics: Provide great service and a product your customers want. Do those two things well and you *should* be able to thrive.

Also, be mindful of just how many season tickets you're selling and when to say "sold out." We got a bit carried away with the sales that poured in. After barely surviving the first half of 2004, it felt so amazing to find our mailbox stuffed with orders every day. With only 120 seats (or sometimes 118 or 127), we should have left more headroom for individual show tickets. It wasn't a problem on the slightly lesser-known shows, but for *Grease* and *Beast*, we had to add shows from our cache of season-ticket money just to fit everyone in. And it dipped into money we needed elsewhere.

CHAPTER 26

The Best Audition Ever

SEPTEMBER 2004

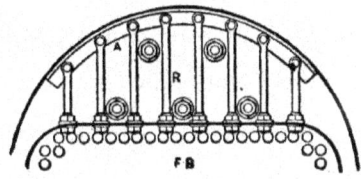

Each year we held general auditions for the upcoming season. It was a mostly useless exercise, but a tradition we'd started prior to opening the theater when we needed to make sure we could get dancers for *A Chorus Line*.

For two grueling days, Jamey, Corbin, and I, along with Lauri and whatever guest director was slated for the next season, would listen to mostly non-castable auditionees drone on through overdone songs and mindless monologues.

Early on, probably out of sheer boredom, the Green brothers and I would write humorous and often disparaging comments on auditionees' score sheets. We all have favorite audition moments such as the aforementioned "Somewhere That's in Tune" girl and Corbin's "banish-shed-ed-ed" actress, although the term "actress" is probably too generous.

By the time we held the 2005 general auditions, we had dropped the two-monologue requirement. Unless a person was a non-singer

The Best Audition Ever

auditioning for a straight play, we just didn't have the patience to hear stinky *Streetcar* or deadly *Death of a Salesman* cuttings, or even worse, those generic monologues from books of generic monologues with generic monologue titles such as "Steve," "Gordon," Ali," and "Pam."

There was the infamous girl who broke down during her song crying, "I knew it when I was in front of my bathroom mirror." That line made it into the script for our 2007 original, *Billy Bob's Holiday Hoedown*. Hey, as a song in the musical *The Life* teaches, you take what you have and run with it!

Then there was the woman who came dressed in full Velma-from-*Chicago* costume—including wig—one full season after we'd done the show. She tried to razzle-dazzle us with off-pitch singing and downright disturbing choreography during which she entangled herself in a folding chair. Think Kristen Wiig.

There were so many memorable moments, it made the annual ritual almost bearable. As had been the case for at least two years, Daron Bruce was our audition accompanist. He was a capable piano player with serviceable sight-reading skills.

But not always.

The 2005 season would include the biggest production ever staged at the Boiler Room, *Disney's Beauty and the Beast*. One actress handed her music to Daron for Belle's Act One ballad, "Home," that was added for Broadway.

Daron shot a puzzled look toward Jamey, then asked the girl, "Is this from the cartoon?"

"No, it's from the Broadway show."

Daron's classic response: "Oh. I only know the songs from the cartoon," as Jamey made his way to the keyboard.

But never in BRT's history had there been an audition as wonderfully awful as A Cappella Girl. There is no record of her name, so I've created one. Also, due to copyright rules for inclusion of lyrics in published books, I've had to adjust a bit. She sang a few correct lyrics, but mostly she screwed them up.

A mildly attractive girl in an ill-fitting sundress skipped into the house, handing copies of a hand-lettered resume to each of us.

"Hi, I'm Annie Garson. I'm 36, a soprano on good days, an alto on others," she said, laughing at her own lame joke. "I'm Annie, as in…" Then, singing:

"THE SUN'LL COME OUT, MAÑANA
"And my last name is Garson, which is:
"GARSON WITH A G
NOT LARSON WITH AN L
'CAUSE LARSON WITH AN L
GOES 'LUH' NOT 'GUH'"

Immediate, awesome freakiness.

"Hi, er, Annie. Just give your music to Daron. What will you be singing for us today?" Jamey asked.

"Um, I don't have any music. I sing this Acapulco," Annie said, again laughing at her own joke. "Your new season is so inspirational that I have a special treat for you."

"This I've got to hear," Corbin said.

"I've written a medley of songs from your upcoming season," Annie proclaimed. "OK. Oh-my-God-oh-my-God-Oh-my-God I'm-so-nervous. Deep, cleansing breath. OK."

"SUMMER LIVING
HAPPENED SO FAST
SUMMER LIVING
HAD SUCH A BLAST
SUMMER DAYS

The Best Audition Ever

>   DAYS...
>   DAYS...
>   *(key change)*
>   DAY BY DAY
>   DAY BY DAY
>   OH DEAR LORD"

"Oh dear God," Jamey muttered.

> "OH PLEASE JAMEY AND CORBIN
> CAST ME I PRAY
> TO SEE ME MORE CLEARLY
> LOVE ME SINCERELY
> CAST ME NOT QUEERLY"

"Oh. Em. Gee! I really love gay people! Never mind that last word," Annie said.

> "DAY BY DAY — AY — AY — AY"
> *(another key change)*

Daniel had been running the video camera in between checking in auditionees.

"You getting this?" I asked.

"You better believe it," he said. (Sadly, the videotape was lost at some point over the years.)

Then, to the melody of "Do, Re, Mi" from *The Sound of Music,* she sang:

> "THEY SAY THERE'S A CAT
> UP ON A ROOF
> A ROOF THAT'S TIN AND
> VERY VERY HOT!

120 SEATS IN A BOILER ROOM

AND RUSTY!
I DON'T KNOW WHAT IT'S DOING UP THERE"

Next, in a paws-up *Cats* pose:

"HI, I'M MAGGIE. I'M A CAT"

Then, a la Cassie in "The Music and the Mirror,"

"AMUSE ME, GOOD NEWS ME
MEOW MEOW MEOW"

Next, a ridiculous Southern accent appeared.

"Oh, Brick. Ah, Brick. Where's Big Daddy. Why do you have a cast on your foot? Are you gay?"

"WELL I'M ALONE
UP HERE
ON THIS HOT! TIN! ROOF!
GUESS I'M NOT THE FIRST
TO HAVE MY HEART TORN IN TWO
GUESS OTHER EYES HAVE CRIED
THE WAY I DO"

"That actually rhymed. Huh," Jamey said.

"I'M HOPEFULLY DENOTED TO YOU, JAMEY!"

Then turning upstage, Annie sang:

"TURN YOUR BACK O, MAN
FOR I SWEAR YOUR FOOLISH WAYS
(still another key change)
AYS — AYS — AYS
A WAY UP NORTH, THEY GOT A NAME
FOR EARTH AND WIND AND FIRE"

"I didn't think we were doing *Paint Your Wagon*," I said. By this time I had moved to sit between Jamey and Corbin.

"THE FIRE'S A MESS, THE RAIN IS MOE
AND THEY CALL THE WIND
MARIAH—
CAREY
(*laughing*)
I'VE JUST KISSED A GIRL NAMED MARIAH
Prithee, Hamlet, prithee.
I LOOK PRETTY
SO GOSH-DARN PRETTY
I LOOK PRETTY, VERY PRETTY AND GAY"

"Now you're talkin', girl. Go on with your bad self," said Daniel who by now had taken a seat in the house.

"AND I FEEL SAD FOR ANY GIRL
WHO ISN'T ME TO—
DAY BY DAY
Lookout!
CAMPTOWN LADIES SING THIS SONG
DOO DAH, DOO DAH
CAMPTOWN RACETRACK
FIVE HUNDRED MILES LONG
OH, THE DOO DAH DAY
G'WIN TO RUN ALL NIGHT
G'WIN TO RUN ALL DAY
BET MY MONEY ON A BOB—
TALE AS NEW AS TIME
QUEER AS IT CAN BE
BEAUTY AND THE BEAST"

Annie ended her epic audition in the dying-swan ballet position announcing, "And scene."

Lauri laughed out loud at the ballet pose while the rest of us sat stunned.

"OK, well, thanks. Next!" I said.

"Oh! I've also got 'Can't Help Lovin' Dat Man' in my car if you need something else."

Jamey put an end to the fun. "Oh, I think we've heard plenty."

Annie left the theater.

We all burst out laughing.

"Corbin, you arranged this whole thing, didn't you? Is she some friend or something?" I accused.

"That was either the most brilliant comic audition or she's straight out of the nuthouse," Jamey added.

"I wish I could take credit, but no, you can't make this stuff up." Corbin said.

Straight from the Kaz playbook, Annie called Jamey the following week.

"Oh. Em. Gosh. I think I did terribly," Annie said. "I had something from *The King and I*. Maybe that would have been better."

Jamey's response: "Yeah, it might have."

HOT TIPS

The Occasional Joys of Auditions

Monologues are a huge waste of time. Actors hate doing them, good material is scarce, and ultimately, they show absolutely nothing useful to directors. Cold readings are preferable but, at least for us, were almost always reserved for individual show callbacks unless there was some immediate need for an understudy.

Limiting auditionees' songs to 32 bars each of an uptempo and a ballad not only demonstrates vocal chops, but also an actor's ability to choose appropriate selections, which often translates to the actor's overall abilities to make good onstage choices.

And if you ever get your own Annie Garson, and you film it, put that tape or SD card in a bank lockbox! I promise you're going to want it later.

CHAPTER 27

The Haunted Lobby

FALL 2004

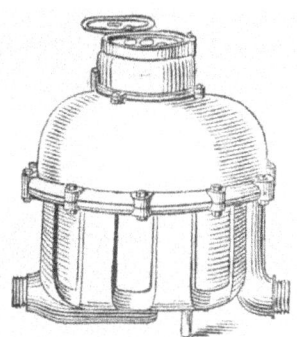

A funny thing happened as we began to construct the set for *Sweeney Todd*. I'd been in my degree program for a few months and my dream of maybe someday working for Disney had become a tangible, possibly achievable goal. I intended to create a show-stopping portfolio of design work to impress the red pants right off the Mouse.

My love of Disney's Haunted Mansion can be traced back to the life-changing visit I had to Disneyland at the age of 7. While my backyard, crawl-through haunted mansion was a flop, what I did to the Boiler Room's lobby in late September 2004 was a masterpiece.

I had a vision to create an immersive, right-out-of-Disneyland experience for guests from the moment they entered the boiler room building. It was the perfect time to create such an experience. With *Sweeney* about to be on stage, which is an intentionally creepy show, and

The Haunted Lobby

being in the Halloween slot, I intended the Haunted Lobby to be an attraction in and of itself. It also became the second of a dozen or so themed lobbies that had guests in awe remarking, "You should work for Disney!" One of the show's reviews even stated that the Haunted Lobby alone was worth the price of admission.

I went on a citywide, massive treasure hunt through every thrift and antique store in existence to gather a truckload of set dressing: Creepy thrift-store paintings; candlesticks and candelabras; dilapidated suitcases and birdcages; a variety of lighting devices; and an enormous bolt of semi-sheer black fabric for ten bucks that ended up draping the lobby, house, and stage.

Knowing it would force me to repaint the lobby before the Christmas show, I nevertheless glued and stapled Victorian-style wallpaper to the drywall, then tore and peeled it. The finishing touch was dry sponging black and green paint on it to emulate haunted-house mold. Then I added layers of torn drapes and, in the right setting with the right lighting, those paintings took on a different look. I hung our large chandelier over the middle of the lobby and applied cobwebs. An antique candelabra-style lamp flickered at the corner of the box-office counter, and a disembodied hand holding a flickering candle hung above the entrance to the house. And atop a stack of thrift-store Mediterranean end tables sat an enormous clear ball with a talking head inside.

Yes. A talking head. À la Madame Leota in Disney's Haunted Mansion. Finding the clear ball was difficult, but finally a lighting store had an industrial fixture, that, after cutting a large hole for "Leota II," became the iconic crystal ball. I found instructions online for building an animatronic, saying-whatever-you-want head by using a Douglas Fir Christmas decoration. After cutting the mechanical eyes, mouth, and motor out of the tree—which was not an easy task—I inserted them in a foam wig head. Then, a rubber Halloween mask of a witch was glued and pinned to the head. The motor wires ran through the foam to the back where the motor was inserted. A wig and a neck scarf were added and the whole thing was placed in the ball. And because I found the model tree with an audio input, I was able to play anything and the head would react and speak or sing along.

Beth Eakin O'Neill, who was the Official Voice of the Boiler Room, went into the studio to record Leota II's dialogue. I committed to running the box office on all show nights (except Thursdays due to school), and from behind the counter I would trigger her audio. When a guest would approach Leota II, I'd play a wisecracking line that more than once caused the guest to jump back. My command center for audio, lighting, and effects was tucked under the counter between the popcorn oil and will-call tickets.

The big, open area above the restrooms became my playground for creating elaborate displays. For the Haunted Lobby, it was the attic with open windows in front of a scrim where lightning flashed. There were props, lights, and a self-rocking rocking chair courtesy of a windshield-wiper motor my Dad rigged. There was even a Pepper's Ghost effect in which lighting and mirrors projected a ghostly image. Independent audio sources throughout the lobby provided a true surround-sound experience.

It was a challenge to not flood the lobby with waning daylight before Daylight Saving Time kicked in, and I always hoped guests would arrive after it was dark outside. When I brought back the Haunted Lobby for 2005's *The Secret Garden* (which had ghost characters in the show), I constructed a mini-entry to block outside light. Cobbled together with two folding screens, some scrap lumber, and a lot of fabric, it certainly broke every possible City code.

From that point forward, I created a themed lobby for every show until my swan song at BRT, 2006's *Angel Street*. For *That '60s Christmas*

Show, I made an aluminum Christmas tree forest above the restrooms. Down below, it was Christmas morning 1963 with vintage gift items around another aluminum tree. There were at least eight of those trees I found on eBay and charged to my personal credit cards.

For *Grease,* the lobby was the entrance to my "living yearbook" set concept with 24-inch by 36-inch vintage yearbook photos covering the walls.

For *Godspell,* it was an elaborate prelude to the abandoned theme park set on stage. Above the restrooms was an animatronic fun-house laughing lady along with actual amusement-park décor from a defunct park in Alabama from which I sourced four vintage ride vehicles, three of which were on stage.

For *On Golden Pond,* the lobby became a bait shop. I built a rowboat atop the restrooms and surrounded it with water effects and artificial plants. Fishing nets were fashioned into a canopy over the lower lobby. And at the concessions counter, guests could buy baggies of gummy worm edible bait.

For *Epic Proportions,* I built a 1920s-era Hollywoodland sign for the attic. Down below, palms, a vintage floor radio, and a display of old movie projectors and reels of film enthralled guests.

For *How to Succeed in Business Without Really Trying,* it was all 1960s office machines and dressing including a mimeograph machine that weighed as much as a Chevy Cavalier.

For *Disney's Beauty and the Beast,* the lobby became the Beast's library.

Anything Goes, the 2006 season opener, had a totally nautical theme.

And finally for *Angel Street,* I brought back select elements from the Haunted Lobby to create a small Victorian parlor.

Along the way, I had Rick Malkin photographically document all my work which became part of the self-promo kit I sent to Disney. Between the lobbies and the elaborate sets I created and/or dressed, I was well on my way to total exhaustion.

CHAPTER 28

Cutting Edge

FALL 2004

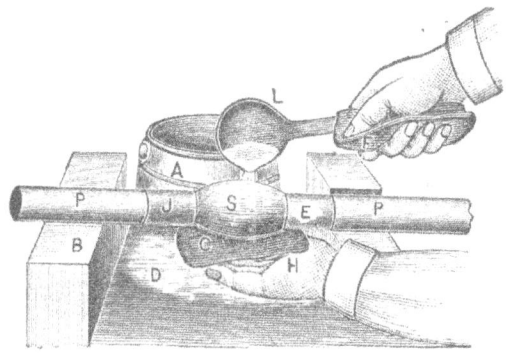

We survived the near-demise of the Boiler Room, reveled in its triumphant comeback, suffered through another mind-numbing round of season auditions, and arrived at our next do-or-die moment.

Sweeney Todd is a beloved, albeit niche, Stephen Sondheim show. Its premise of a barber and a baker working in tandem to murder customers and bake them into pies risked being too edgy. I mean, Franklin couldn't handle the sexual satisfaction commercial in *I Love You, You're Perfect, Now Change*. As it turned out, apparently, murder and cannibalism are acceptable. Go figure. This was one of Jamey's bucket-list shows he longed to direct. I wasn't sold on it when we dropped it into the 2004 season, but after listening to the cast album, I fell in love with its—forgive me—razor-sharp wit and delightful songs.

Of all of Sondheim's shows, *Sweeney Todd* has perhaps the most fiercely loyal fan base. It was a show that could have put the final nail in BRT's coffin if it failed. But if it succeeded, as it did, it could and did further cement BRT's reputation as the best musical theater in Nashville, an honor we'd already received in 2002. It required a large cast of top-flight singers and actors, a collection of difficult props and set pieces, a hoard of period costumes, and a multi-functional set. It was an all-hands-on-deck venture.

First, the casting. We had a large turnout at a cattle call followed by a long night of callbacks. Some roles were easy to fill such as Scott Rice playing Beadle Bamford, a first-rate fop; and Shauntina Phillips as the Beggarwoman. Joe Truman, a newcomer who was pursuing country-music stardom, had a lovely legit tenor voice and was a shoo-in for Anthony Hope, a young sailor who rescues Sweeney Todd (formerly known as Benjamin Barker) at sea.

From there, casting was a massive undertaking for Jamey. Although she was up against several actresses, Lisa Gillespie and her at-times husky chest voice and impeccable comic timing emerged as *the* Mrs. Lovett. I think she was the quintessential Lovett, even topping Angela Lansbury who originated the role.

Not only did she receive glowing reviews, but she was also immortalized in a tattoo on some guy's calf. No one was looking for the image, but one day Google coughed up a photo of the tattoo that exactly matched Lisa's pose and expression in our publicity photo. Yes, *Sweeney Todd* was one of those shows that had achieved a cult-like following.

At callbacks, reading and singing dragged on for hours. Two or three finalists for the title role kept us at the theater until at least midnight. After all auditionees were released and Jamey, Corbin, Lauri, and I laid out headshots across the stage, Jamey was no closer to choosing an actor for Sweeney than he had been five hours prior. He wasn't even sure there was an actor at callbacks who could play the role.

Jamey held a second callback for only the title role and after much consideration, newcomer Alan Lee was cast as Sweeney Todd. And together with Lisa's Mrs. Lovett, they were the embodiment of theater magic. With a cast that included Daniel as Adolfo Pirelli, John Warren as Judge Turpin, and Rachel Latremore as Johanna along with a versatile and talented ensemble, it was practically a who's-who of Nashville theater.

Working with Anthony, who had worked for BRT in various technical roles, I designed a scaled-down version of the Broadway revolving pie shop that serves as the primary set unit. The lower level was Mrs. Lovett's kitchen on one side and her back parlor on the other. The second level was Sweeney's "tonsorial parlor" aka barbershop.

But that wasn't all.

The principal gag required a custom, mechanical barber chair that, when a special handle was pulled, would transform from a mere chair to a 45-degree-angle slide. Anthony built the tricky piece and I upholstered it. The interior of the revolving unit was a continuation of the slide from the top level, where, via a trap door, the murdered customers would drop onto a thick foam pad, then exit upstage.

The upstage platform (or bridge as we called it) from *Chicago* that ran the full width of the stage was brought back. Two rolling stair units were built to access the top of the pie shop and the bridge depending on the scene. Additional set pieces included an "oven" for Act Two that stowed under the bridge; a plank used as a tabletop with sawhorses as supports and two benches; a large meat grinder (it was actually an antique corn grinder found in a Franklin antique store); a portable scrim attached to two poles; a coffin; and the overdressing and furniture for the back parlor.

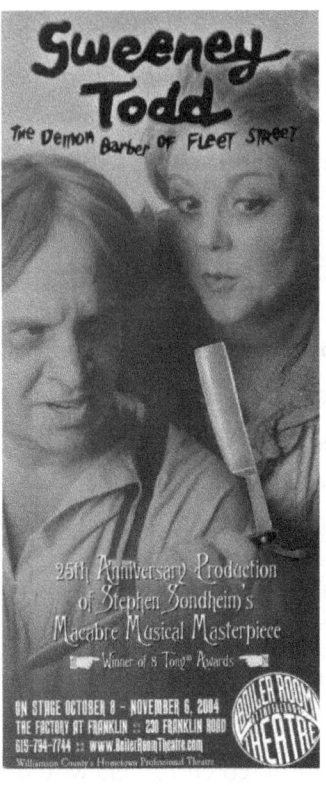

Rack card for *Sweeney Todd*, 2004.

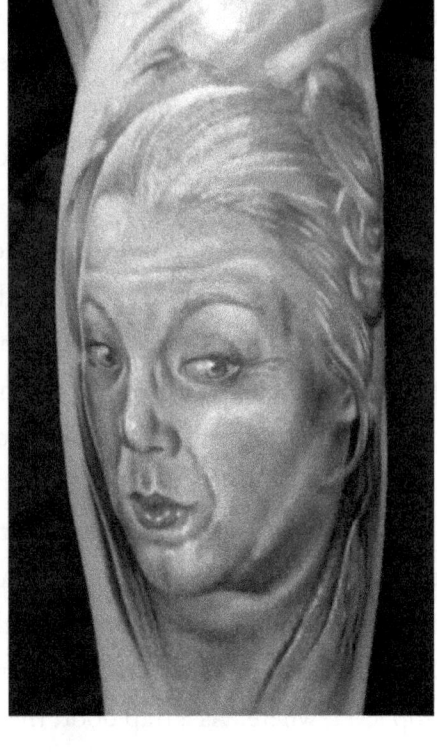

Lisa Gillespie as Mrs. Lovett immortalized in a tattoo on some random guy's leg.

Props for the show were a challenge for me, but one I dove into with my Disney dreams front of mind.

The most important props were Sweeney's razors. I exhausted online stores for prop razors and found nothing but plastic ones for Halloween use. The razors in the show needed to be metal, glimmer in stage light, yet be so dull that they could safely slide across an actor's throat. As previously mentioned, I enlisted my Dad, an engineer who could fix and build anything. He fashioned the set of three razors complete with handles into which the blades were housed. They were truly works of art. I kept the set when I left BRT and often thought of selling them on eBay. But I finally did what felt was best and right: I sent one razor to Alan, one to Jamey, and kept one for the Boiler Room archives.

If that wasn't enough, Alan would also have to apply stage blood as he slashed actors' throats with the dull instruments. Again, an online search produced nothing. A visit to a medical supply store yielded clear plastic tubing, but I still needed a bladder or bulb for the stage blood. And I needed a dozen of these blood delivery tubes per show. One night it came to me as I was pulling other props from my little prop shop above the dressing rooms. A bunch of rubber grapes fell to the floor and upon retrieving them, I realized that a single rubber grape could hold the right amount of stage blood for each throat slash. Alan and the actor who played Tobias were instructed to hold the grape with the attached medical tubing in the palm of their hand and to place the end of the tube between two fingers. As they dragged the prop razor across a throat, they would squeeze the grape-bulb to deliver a line of blood. The trick worked most of the time, and when it did, it had a frightening effect.

For the back parlor in Act Two, that is redecorated thanks to Mrs. Lovett's new-found source of income, I used two sheets of luan plywood pre-dressed with wallpaper and attached artwork that hung on a set of hooks. During intermission, the panels were placed, the plain parlor curtain was swapped for an ornate one, and two pieces of custom furniture were added, a settee and a harmonium which was a type of small organ.

I combed the antique stores for a small, Victorian settee and something that could look like the harmonium Mrs. Lovett acquires from a burned-down chapel. There was nothing to be found. So I got creative and built a settee out of a sturdy, Colonial-style coffee table from a thrift store for the base, custom-cut plywood for the back, then upholstered it. *Presto!* One miniature, yet practical settee.

I found a similar Colonial coffee table with rails around three sides, stripped it and re-stained it, added tall legs and a music holder, painted a keyboard on it, and *voila!* One harmonium. I have only rudimentary construction skills and the piece proved to be a bit wobbly. It had to stay put for several revolutions of the pie shop, so the legs inserted into holes on the parlor floor.

Even seemingly simple props weren't easy. In Act One, Anthony courts Johanna, who has been looking at birds in cages on a bird vendor's pole, and buys her the one she's been admiring. He then sings "Johanna," and after a hostile encounter mid-song with Judge Turpin and the Beadle, who reaches in and snaps the bird's neck, Anthony sings a final verse and breaks the cage in half. Perhaps on Broadway they broke a different cage for each performance. But we didn't have the budget for that, so I had yet another prop challenge.

I was in a habit of listening to Disney music and having Disney films playing as much as possible to keep my focus on my dream of working one day for the Mouse. One night I watched *The Parent Trap* as I built the furniture and was reminded that one of the identical twins had built at camp a rickety birdcage out of popsicle sticks.

Eureka!

My birdcage dilemma was solved. With wooden dowels, I built two halves of a realistic cage that connected with hook-and-eye latches painted to blend with the wood. The latches were on the upstage side of the cage, and in advance of the cage destruction, Joe would unlatch the hooks, then pull the halves apart, creating the illusion he was actually breaking the cage in two. The fake bird hung lifeless from a little swing.

Then there were the meat pies.

During Mrs. Lovett's first number in Act One, she rolls out dough (beating it in time to the music), and makes seemingly edible pies. For each show, I provided her with dough from two large tubes of Pillsbury Crescent Rolls, a fresh bowl of flour, and Gaines-Burgers dog food as meat. Then there were the already-baked prop pies which I made in my kitchen and shellacked in my basement. Finally, there were the edible pies for the cast in the Act Two opening number "God, That's Good!" during which the ensemble snarfs down a dozen or so pies. The solution: Hostess apple pies. Or chocolate. Or the really nasty raisin pies. The cast cursed me on raisin-pie nights, but I was at the mercy of grocery-store stock. They probably tasted worse than human pies.

Sets and props aside, everyone was at the top of their game for *Sweeney Todd.* Jamey's casting and direction was flawless. Mark Beall's music direction was perfect. Billy Ditty's costumes, particularly those for Mrs. Lovett, were fantastic.

And Corbin's lighting was incredible. He placed brown gels over all the general stage-wash fixtures giving the show an antique, dirty glow. The specialty lights above the pie shop coupled with stage fog made the stage depth appear twice its actual size. And when Alan was carried out in a plain coffin at the top of the show, then emerged in red light and fog, it was highly effective and creepy. The antique, exposed brick surrounding the stage and the rusty, painted-over windows all worked to create a vintage industrial look. It wasn't the antique iron set used on

Broadway, nor did it need to be. As with *Sweeney*, and for other shows, our crumbling brick walls actually enhanced set designs, particularly for *Little Shop of Horrors, A Chorus Line, Chicago, Cabaret, Urinetown,* and *Rent*. Amy Stumpfl of *Nashville City Paper* had nice remarks:

. . .

"*Sweeney Todd is* particularly challenging for the Boiler Room's small space. But the theater's dark industrial features fit right in with the show's gritty feel. Kempfer's set is amazing, capturing Fleet Street in all its dingy glory."

. . .

Peggy Shaw of *The Tennessean* published a feature about the show:

. . .

"*Sweeney Todd* marks BRT's 25th production at the same time that the musical thriller is celebrating its silver anniversary. And The Factory theater, with its industrial features, is a fitting venue for the Industrial Age story…"

. . .

Even Martin Brady had trouble finding fault with the show in his review titled "A Finger in Every Pie: Inspired production of creepy Sondheim classic may be Boiler Room's best work yet":

. . .

"Director Jamey Green has done a superlative job, somehow managing to turn the intimacy of the BRT space to his advantage. His actors may have some logistical hurdles, the cast of 17 having not only to conjure 1840s London but also to endure some set challenges that require technical collaboration from all. Yet the Sondheim material, with all its lyrical complexities and deliberately discordant musical textures, comes through with the impact of a fine piece of chamber opera. Yes, the sets could be grander; but scenic designer Lewis Kempfer, with minimal resources, provides all we really need. And yes, this show has been played by 70-piece orchestras; yet musical director Mark Beall makes the most out of a four-piece combo, including two keyboards…

"… This production represents a high-water mark for this overachieving company, which has courageously worked through its limitations, and now, at the end of its fourth season, is staging one of the modern musical theater's most challenging works in grand style…

"… The lead players are terrific, but the foundation here is a strong ensemble…. Lisa Gillespie, who plays the manipulative pie shop proprietor Mrs. Lovett, is alone worth the price of admission. She's very funny and sings up a highly professional storm until her fated end…"

...

Brady's review was one of the best we'd received since the inaugural production in 2001. There were a couple of other glowing reviews, but they've since disappeared from online. In any case, the show was celebrated by audiences and critics alike, and it was a welcome validation of our work after surviving our near collapse just months earlier.

Boiler Room Voices

ALAN LEE

Lightning in a Bottle

Between 2004 and 2011, the Boiler Room Theatre was the closest thing to a theatrical home I have ever known. Thanks to the theater founded by Lewis Kempfer and the Brothers Green—Jamey and Corbin—I was able to perform with a group of gifted actors, singers, musicians, and artists who, time and again, created magic for those who saw the lightning in a bottle that took place on our little stage in front of our small but loyal audiences.

I first became aware of the Boiler Room when I went to see a dear friend, Lane Wright, in a production of *Six Degrees of Separation*, and was impressed by the level of craft displayed by the production. Later, another dear friend, Phil Perry, got me out to the Boiler Room to see his outstanding work in a production of *Sylvia*, so when a few months after that when I saw that they were having auditions for *Sweeney Todd*, I jumped at the chance.

A few words about me. At the time of the audition, I had not stepped on a stage in seven years. It was not for lack of desire, but those past seven years had been a dark and trying time of multiple catastrophes that did not kill me nor make me stronger. I have been a performer for my entire life and have worked in every kind of small-time, show-business endeavor in which it is not possible to make a living. For short amounts of time, I had even made a living at it, whether it was in regional theater in my native Louisiana or in Los Angeles as an NBC page in Burbank or on the road as a New Christy Minstrel. My efforts at getting into the Big Time were greeted largely in the same way that a fly is greeted by a speeding car's windshield, and after a couple of decades of this, I had a hard time making yet another try.

But *Sweeney Todd*. A role that sat at the top of my bucket list. Dare I try it?

I dared, and to my amazement and gratitude, Jamey Green, the director of that production, cast me as the Demon Barber for what turned out to be one of the greatest experiences of my performing life.

Sweeney is a challenge for the best of theaters and I soon found out that doing a musical with such a challenging score was catnip to Nashville musicians and singing actors who rose joyfully to that challenge. Nashville musicians are some of the best in the world and they are infinitely more versatile than their country-music label. Same for singing actors. The talent and craft displayed throughout my time with the Boiler Room was always of a level far above any small-time theater work I had been involved in before.

Sweeney became the first of many great experiences on that stage. I only have the memories now, but they remain vivid. Lisa Gillespie's Mrs. Lovett was a joy and her command of the character was impressive. I had seen Angela Lansbury and George Hearn in the first national tour and Lisa did not suffer in comparison. The entire ensemble was not only up to the challenge, but unfailingly supportive of each other and the show, an experience which was repeated in every Boiler Room show I was involved in after that. I would work many times with these members of the Boiler Room family, not only Lisa, but many others, like Patrick Kramer, the bird seller in *Sweeney*, who came offstage one night with a separated shoulder (things happen), got it popped back in place, and didn't even miss his next entrance. I would later play in the ensemble in support of his J. Pierpont Finch in *How to Succeed In Business Without Really Trying*, a show that also featured Melinda Doolittle, who raised the roof in "Brotherhood of Man" and would go on to fame on *American Idol*. These were quality people.

Time and again, I was invited to take part in the fun, and high-level fun it was. From *Sweeney*, I went on to play everything from leads to ensemble in show after show and had the time of my life. Some of the high points, in addition to *Sweeney*, were playing Will Rogers in *The Will Rogers Follies*, Tevye in *Fiddler on the Roof* (both Will and Tevye were bucket-list roles), Pilate in *Jesus Christ Superstar*, Cladwell in *Urinetown*, Doolittle in *My Fair Lady* (where I learned the joy of playing a character who doesn't have to carry the show, but gets the 11 o'clock-number and carte blanche to steal everything that's not nailed down whenever he's on stage), as well as nonmusical roles like Manningham in *Angel Street*, and parts in shows including *On Golden Pond*, *Epic Proportions* (a full ensemble hoot of a show), and many others.

Among my happiest memories are those of working together with my Boiler Room family to rise to the challenges, both artistic and logistic, of putting great theater on that small stage. From the musical challenge of Sondheim's *Assassins* to the engineering challenge of mounting *Disney's Beauty and the Beast* (25 of us on stage for "Be Our Guest" tested the limits of stage space). I can't talk about the space limits of that wingless little stage without praising the amazing set design of Lewis Kempfer and Anthony Popolo who, time and again, overcame those limits to produce impressive sets that revolved, opened, or transformed to provide shows with absolutely beautiful settings in which to play.

The Boiler Room experience showed me that work of professional excellence could be done by gifted theater artists who banded together to overcome the limitations of "small-time" theater. The main thing that kept this magic happening was the positivity and mutual support that is a vital part of the Nashville way. This is an attitude that comes from the Nashville music industry, but extends to all performing arts. It consists of the recognition that you must not only be good at what you do, but nice to your fellow artists to make something that brings the spotlight to the work and not just the individual ego. It also helps that we had, like the Nashville recording scene, enough world-class artists available that we could choose not to work with toxic, selfish performers. Those that found themselves in a Boiler Room show would either leave that at the door or not be cast in another. I was spoiled by working, time and again, with ensembles who all showed up on time, worked hard, and supported the show and each other. All too often, particularly in the small-time, every show has that one actor who makes an otherwise good experience a bad one. I have never had less of that behavior than in my time with the Boiler Room.

My last show with the Boiler Room was *The Rocky Horror Show* around Halloween of 2011. I was honored to play the Criminologist in a production that exemplified every quality of my Boiler Room experience. In 2012, I followed my path away from Nashville and by the time it led me back, the Boiler Room Theatre was no more. I miss it terribly and were it still here, I would be working in every show they would let me, being paid too little to live and having more fun than is usually legal. I am forever grateful.

CHAPTER 29

The Most Wonderful Gift of the Year

CHRISTMAS 2004

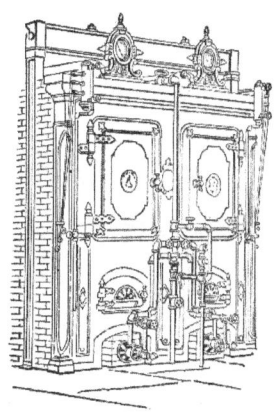

During season planning for 2004, the Brothers Green and I were having a typical LLC meeting outside the backstage door during a 2003 *Smoky Mountain Mist* matinee. Although we'd become a 401(c)(3) non-profit in 2002, we still called our frequent, informal discussions "LLC meetings," during which some business was conducted, and full packs of cigarettes were often consumed by each person.

Season planning went the way it usually had in the past.

I'd pitch a show, say *West Side Story*, that I thought would be a draw for season tickets, but was usually deemed too large for the stage or too frequently done and I'd be reminded of our mission. As a matter of record, I knew our mission statement quite well; hell, I wrote it.

Then, as expected, Corbin would pitch *Noises Off*. While it was a funny play, it had only marginal name recognition, and we would always remind him that the entire set had to turn 180 degrees at intermission.

Inevitably, we got to the Christmas slot. We used to joke that we could set a plate of steaming dog poop on stage and shows would sell out. Because it was Christmas. We'd done *1940s* twice (granted, the remount did not sell out) as well as the too-short *Dickens*. We tossed around some of the same show names we tossed around for every Christmas slot, shows such as *Oliver, Scrooge,* and *Meet Me in St. Louis*. Nothing felt right. Then Jamey suggested "maybe something original."

"What about a show concept similar to *1940s*, but set 20 years later in a TV studio?" I suggested.

"Ooh, that actually sounds great," Jamey said.

"What's the plot?" Corbin asked.

"I don't know. But we'd have a year to write the show. All I need right now for the season campaign is a title," I said. Then I blurted out *That '60s Christmas Show*.

More oohs.

The title, I explained, would look and sound familiar due to the popular TV series, *That '70s Show*. And you can't copyright a title. "So gents, do we have a Christmas show?"

"That definitely sounds worth pursuing," Jamey said. "When are we going to write the thing?"

"Well, I guess sometime next year," I said. "I'll start a draft as soon as possible." It would be my first original show to write, produce, and direct.

But once we were into 2004, time slipped by and all that existed were chicken-scratch notes I'd made on my commute to the theater. But no real work had begun, especially once we hit the financial crisis.

I was vaguely aware of a show set in the same time period with perhaps a slightly similar premise, but from my extensive study of musical theater, it still seemed a mostly untapped show setup. Admittedly, the plot was wafer-thin, just barely enough of one to string together arrangements of the songs I grew up with from two Christmas albums: The RCA Living Voices' *The Little Drummer Boy* and Brenda Lee's *Merry Christmas from Brenda Lee*.

The bulk of the writing was done frantically during the run of *Sweeney Todd*, which is why in the original script there are lines such as "There's no place like London" in the comedy sketch. The entire show was written in approximately two weeks, not a far cry from how Jamey's Avante Garage! shows were written.

Although I was loath to use a setup similar to the one in *The 1940s Radio Hour*, I finally understood why those writers had included it. But I wouldn't allow it to be a pantomime as I'd already learned that the one in *1940s* was confusing to audiences. Still, it was the same idea—we had to get all the TV show's characters on stage and reveal bits about each of them. Although it was done with dialogue, it always felt clunky to me and the show never really took off until the musical downbeat of the fictional 1963 *Jack Clurman Christmas Kaleidoscope*.

Jamey and I handpicked the cast; no auditions were held. We needed the best and most talented members of the BRT family. For the table read, I brought in a vintage record player and those albums that inspired the vast majority of the show's soundtrack as well as one of my vintage Hoover upright vacuums that would be used in the show. I got the usual "what the hell is this all about" looks from a couple of the cast members, but I always tried to make things fun and memorable.

The show's characters include a Dean Martinesque host, Jack Clurman, who was played by Alan Lee; a bumbling show announcer named Dick Flowers played by the late Wesley Fox; Annette Bodicelli, a busty, bawdy vocal knockout played by Megan; Doris Jeffries, an airhead in an enormous blonde beehive wig, played by Melodie; Candi Bradenton, the show's female featured dancer played by Lauri; Robby Burgess, a handsome young tenor and Candi's dance partner played by Joe Truman; Marty Lowenstein, the show's resident comic, played by Patrick Kramer; and the Key Grip, played by L.T. Kirk, who serves as the TV show's entire technical staff the night of the Christmas show and storm. It wasn't clear if our guests understood the Key Grip joke (just read the credits after any movie) and I should have called him the Floor Manager as that was his chief role and correct title. He would herd actors on and offstage, always be timing things, and taking the show to commercial breaks.

The characters perform seemingly endless medleys because that was the popular fare in all the early 1960s television specials (Andy Williams, Lawrence Welk, and the like). We peppered in an occasional solo and took commercial breaks every ten minutes or so when we switched from colorful show lighting to harsh white work light. Some of the breaks were an opportunity to reveal more about the characters or to further the one-note plot, which is that the popular TV show's Christmas special gets up-ended by a terrific snowstorm in New York City and the guest stars (that incredulously include Brenda Lee, Zero Mostel, Gypsy Rose Lee, the Singing Nun, and Elvis) are all stranded in the Holland Tunnel and unable to get to the studio. As such, the cast in the second act impersonates the guest stars with the hopes that home audiences won't know the difference. It was a stupid, stupid plot and I take full responsibility.

I've been a collector of odd stuff all my life and in 2003, one of my largest collections was vintage Hoover vacuums and corresponding advertising. It came in handy. Scrawled in a small spiral notebook while driving, the Hoover commercial was the first content written for the show.

On a few of the commercial breaks, live spots are performed as they were back in the 1950s and early 1960s. The Hoover spot proved to be a moment during which audiences howled and women of a certain age cackled with delight. Jack Clurman says, "And gentlemen, if you're still looking for that perfect gift for your sweetie, pay special attention to this message by Candi, Annette, and Doris." At that moment, our three actresses clad in identical house dresses in different colors would wheel a vintage Hoover upright vacuum in a coordinating color onstage. That alone had women in the audience guffawing. But then came my lyrics:

"GIVE HER THE GIFT THAT WILL MOVE HER TO TEARS
A GIFT THAT WILL LAST HER THE REST OF HER YEARS
WON'T SHE BE SURPRISED
JUST WATCH AS SHE CRIES
'CAUSE NOTHING SUCKS…
… LIKE A HOOVER!"

The female audience members, who were probably about to pee their pants from laughing so hard, could relate—they likely had received a vacuum as a Christmas gift at some point. But it was actually a cherished gift back in the day, and my old Hoover magazine ads showing a dashing husbands and too-delighted-for-words wives receiving a vacuum were my inspiration. Back then, if a guy gave his gal a vacuum, he'd be covered in grateful kisses. Do it in present day, and the guy would be clobbered by an upright. That live promo spot was a highlight of every performance.

The medleys include "The Joys of Winter Frolic" (songs about snow), "The Colors of Christmas" ("Silver Bells," "White Christmas," etc.), "The Brenda Lee Medley," "Christmas Around the World" ("Mele

Kalikimaka," "Christmas in Killarney," etc.), and "The Religious Melody," which includes the hymn "Away in a Manger." Melodie, without direction to do so, performed faux sign language that was brilliant. We got complaints about it because some guests felt we were being disrespectful or blasphemous. Truth is, it was perfect for the goody-two-shoes Doris who was always over the top yet always sincere.

The convoluted plot twist rears its contrived head at the top of Act Two. The characters are informed that none of the guest stars can make it to the studio. (We already had Brenda Lee missing in action in Act One requiring Megan's character to reluctantly cover three of Ms. Lee's Christmas tunes due to a talent-show rivalry from several years prior.) The stars' luggage and costumes had made it to the studio earlier in the day. The Singing Nun and Elvis have identical luggage (what are the odds?) and the bags are swapped by Annette forcing Robby to play the Singing Nun. Joe's performance as well as Megan's as Elvis in a gold lamé jumpsuit five times too large worked beautifully and elicited hearty laughs. When Joe sat on a stool center stage, in a nun's habit, with a guitar, and adjusted his tunic to bare a hairy leg and sock garter, it was genuinely funny. Later, Megan flopping about in shiny fabric messing up the colors in the iconic Elvis arrangement of "Blue Christmas" was comedy gold. The other guest-star spots just seemed forced. Because they were.

Then there was the infamous comedy sketch.

During the show's setup in Act One, the characters refer to two sketches, one from *It's a Wonderful Life* and another from *A Christmas Carol*. During the commercial break before the Act Two sketch, Jack Clurman learns from the Key Grip that the show is running too long and "will run over into the John Gary special." As such, Jack cuts the *Wonderful Life* sketch because "it's not really a Christmas movie anyway." News of the cut sketch is miscommunicated and as the "curtain rises" on the comedic highlight of the evening, audiences soon realize that the confused characters are combining sketches.

Before things get too mixed up in the sketch, there's the classic scene between Scrooge and Bob Cratchit when he asks for time off. We also had him asking for money because of his disabled son. It may have been opening-night jitters, but the most perfect flub exited Joe Truman's mouth as Bob: "You see, my Tiny Tim is limp." Huge, uproarious, piss-your-pants laughter that had to have gone on for at least a solid minute. And a minute in theater time can be an eternity. Realizing his mistake, Joe as Bob corrects himself: "My Tiny Tim has a limp… HAS a limp." Immediately after the show I told Joe, "Cut, print, keep that line in permanently."

Alan played Scrooge who is visited by Patrick's Clarence Oddbody, Angel Second Class. Before the final visitation, the one by the Ghost of Christmas Future (technically the Ghost of Christmas Yet to Come), audiences find Scrooge and George Bailey in bed together as the third ghost—rather, Annette in the Elvis costume—knocking on the bedroom door. The two guys exchange glances with George Bailey telling Scrooge, "You take this one." The ensuing comedy, thanks to Megan, was right out of a Carol Burnett show.

Elvis picks up a *Wonderful Life* line stating that, "When someone's not around it leaves a terrible hole. Speaking of holes, you ever play Toledo?" punctuated by a rim shot. I was working as house manager and got to repeatedly observe one of the heartiest laughs I could remember, that is, until an exasperated Scrooge asks Elvis, "What do you want from me?"

Elvis replies, "Well, I'm kinda *hon-gry*. I'll take a peanut butter and banana *sam-ich* if you got one. No? Got some bacon? Cheese log?" It was pure Megan improv gold. Audience laughter went off the Richter scale and Megan fought hard to suppress a laugh by running her tongue

The Most Wonderful Gift of the Year

around inside her mouth. Alan simply threw the blanket over his head. The gag never failed.

But the comedy sketch was nearly cut from the show. I believed in it, but the cast did not. We had a few invited guests at final dress, and they told us they were lost.

"Let's see how it plays in front of an audience, then we can cut it if necessary," I said.

I'm glad we gave it a shot because on opening night, one might have thought it was the best comedy ever written (it wasn't). The laughter shook the little brick building so hard I feared an old pipe might become detached.

"I guess it needed an audience," Jamey said.

For all the delicious comedy that we either created or which happened by happy accident, there was always one glorious moment in every performance that brought the audience to their feet. On a network commercial break, show host Jack Clurman chokes on one of Doris's tea cake cookies. The cookie is dislodged (usually at some poor first-row guest) but—thin plot alert—Jack can't sing the big "Jesu Bambino" number. The Key Grip is quickly recruited and after some pretty intense (and obviously fake) first-verse jitters, L.T. in his trained operatic voice brought down the house with a glorious rendition of the song. It was our way to feature L.T. and I think all agreed it was damned awesome. He frequently received a standing ovation after the number.

That '60s Christmas Show was scheduled for a typical five-week run, but all performances sold out almost overnight as word quickly spread that some fabulous holiday hilarity was happening in the cozy Boiler Room. We shoehorned in additional performances wherever possible, and by the final week, we played 11 shows in a row, including one on a Monday night, two on a Sunday, and three on the final Saturday.

120 SEATS IN A BOILER ROOM

Mercifully, we received a glowing review by Peggy Shaw at *The Tennessean:*

. . .

"Hoofers 'Robbie' [SIC] and 'Candi' tap dance to 'Winter Wonderland' in a routine patterned after Bobby and Cissy from *The Lawrence Welk Show*... The glitziest part of the show isn't the period costumes, but the aluminum trees... 'You'll never see more aluminum Christmas trees in the same place anywhere, anytime!' said Kempfer whose mom, a 1962 high-school graduate, consulted on the show."

. . .

Martin's review was as fluffy as a first snow:

. . .

"Jamey Green and Lewis Kempfer are the creators of this intentionally cornball salute to '60s entertainment culture, which has some good-natured retro fun while covering the range of time-honored Christmas music...

"... The performances are mixed but generally energetic and infused with mirth. Lee seems tentative, and he doesn't fully conjure the insincere savoir faire of Rat Pack Vegas. But Patrick Kramer is hilarious doing an Irish jig; Joe Truman sings with heartfelt spirit as easily as he works the spoofs; and L.T. Kirk, as the TV show's key grip, emerges late in the evening to offer a gorgeous rendition of 'Jesu Bambino.' Meanwhile, [Megan] Murphy holds

The Most Wonderful Gift of the Year

the whole thing together with her first-rate vocal power and giddy acting."

. . .

He also called out the lack of a plot and got us on a technicality for using music that didn't exist in 1963 such as "Feliz Navidad." Geez, we weren't trying to win the Pulitzer for Drama.

The show was further skewered in reviews for the 2006 remount due to the lack of a live TV show setup. My original concept was to use at least one vintage TV camera and a black-and-white monitor above the stage. But there was no room for a camera and definitely no money for the system, although I'm confident Anthony could have pulled it off.

Making another attempt at rolling out a remount of a Christmas show, we placed *'60s* in the 2006 season. I was already in California by that time and Megan ended up at the helm as director. She wanted to make some script revisions and I agreed only if I could work with her and have final approval.

Well, that didn't go quite as planned.

While we did replace a horrible sequence I had originally placed in the beginning of Act Two called the "Fashion Flash Forward," prefaced by Jack announcing a look at the latest Paris fashions, and featured the cast dressed in Woodstock-meets-*Hair* insane getups with a "Santa Medley" (again turning to the arrangements on my beloved childhood album), there were revisions I would not have approved. And I didn't find out about them until a couple years after receiving the archive DVD and finally mustered the courage to watch.

A live commercial spot for some brand of lipstick had the Robby replacement, Mike Baum, coming out to do the spot (in yet another mix-up) and generously applying the lip color. He started in typical Robby horror/panic/embarrassment until he surveyed his finished work in a compact mirror and was overly pleased with the results. I got a sort of

WTF-chuckle out of it and imagined it getting more laughs had Joe Truman done the bit.

Dan McGeachy replaced Wesley Fox as show announcer and brought improvements to the role. The dance sequences between Candi and Robby were bland due to a difference in dance skills. The cast also included Daniel Vincent replacing L.T.

But I was most horrified by the band curtains, a set of 36-inch high vintage drapes that in 2004 had neatly masked the onstage band from waist down hiding music stands and cords. They were originally installed on a curved metal pipe mounted on wooden uprights. For some reason, in 2006, the drapes were strung on a clothesline that sagged and drooped all around the band. It was an enormous sore thumb. And although my original mid-century backdrop pieces had been safely stored in the prop shop, they weren't used, but sloppily recreated.

Ticket sales were not a happy reprise of 2004's blockbuster windfall. The show didn't play to full houses and while still entertaining, it was clear from the DVD, audience reaction, and interviews with cast members that the show had lost its "oomph."

It had been a helluva wild ride in 2004, starting off with a lukewarm *Gypsy*, followed by the financial crisis, and finally going out in a huge bang that saved our butts. Between ticket sales for the Christmas show and blockbuster sales of season tickets for the 2005 Classic Tales season, it felt like the closing scene of *It's a Wonderful Life*. But in our case, we didn't even have time to count the money in the laundry basket. It didn't get us totally out of debt, but we were able to pay a large chunk of past-due rent, some other moldy bills, and were well poised for the ambitious 2005 season.

HOT TIPS

The Christmas Dilemma

If you are considering repeating shows in the holiday slot, be sure you're giving your guests what they want. Because a theater that Jamey knew of performed *The 1940s Radio Hour* every Christmas without fail, that was his original plan. But because the first year's audience response was mixed, we waited a year to bring it back, only to achieve similar results. The original run of *That '60s Christmas Show* was ticket-sale manna from Heaven, but the remount left the box office hungry. Later, after the Boiler Room's demise, Nashville Repertory Theatre had tremendous success with an annual mounting of the stage version of *A Christmas Story*, coincidentally headlined by Megan. That's no big surprise considering how beloved the movie is. I've always wondered if a musical version of *Christmas Vacation* would work. The takeaway is to know your audience. Better yet, *ask* your audience. Would they be interested in an annual tradition of the same Christmas show? Our intent was to avoid—at all costs—doing *A Christmas Carol* every damn year. Know thy audience.

2005 SEASON

Classic Tales

Grease
Godspell
On Golden Pond
Epic Proportions
How to Succeed in Business Without Really Trying
The Secret Garden
Disney's Beauty and the Beast

CHAPTER 30

The One That They Wanted

SEASON OPENER 2005

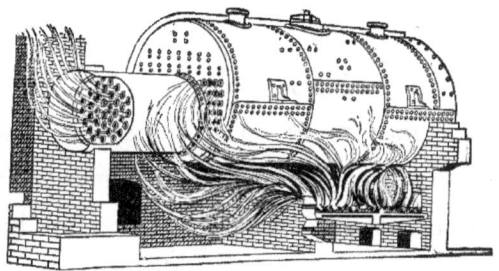

On a chilly October afternoon in 2004, my friend Greg and I attended the Nashville Swap Meet at the [Tennessee] Fairgrounds in search of props with the scant hope of finding something to use as Greased Lightnin' (the car) in *Grease*. Many productions blessed with larger stages often employ overdressed golf carts which, of course, is an ideal solution. Even larger stages use actual cars. That morning, neither of us expected to be shoving a 500-pound carnival car into the back of Greg's brand new, mid-sized SUV.

I'd found a few small items for set dressing, but as we were heading to his car, I saw it: A red, metallic carnival ride vehicle that appeared big enough to hold two actors. The seller wanted $800; I talked him down to $500.

And so it was that two gay guys and four straight, sweaty swap-meet dudes were lifting and shoving the thing into the back of Greg's SUV. I saw the first big scratch appear on one of the car's plastic panels. Greg said he wasn't worried. So, like a woman in her 14th hour of labor, we all continued to push. Hard. And finally, without grease, the thing went in.

The timing of finding Greased Lightnin' wasn't ideal. There was no room in the theater or the backstage building for the car, so I believe it was dumped at Anthony's. He would be, after all, the guy who transformed the car to have an elevated seat, practical headlights and sidelights, and a working horn. It was a hernia-inducing experience the day in early January 2005 when a team of eight guys lifted the impossibly heavy car over the house-left railing and onto the stage, where we essentially built a set around it.

It had been a slightly tough sell to Jamey for him to agree to do *Grease*, but I reminded him that the 2005 season needed to be the biggest blowout of season ticket sales ever to start crawling back to solvency. I briefly described my vision. He grumbled at first, mumbling about "never going to do *Sound of Music* or *Annie*," then suddenly gave in and said "sure." I think he was relieved that for the second year in a row, he didn't have to direct the season opener. That slot was always difficult because by the time you got the cast and crew back from holidays and got their head in the game, you had at best three weeks to mount a large show. And season-opening shows were always big.

Still stinging from Martin's previous reviews of my shows not being "definitive productions" (meaning the production had no unique characteristics to make it anything more than run-of-the-mill), I intended to mount the best possible *Grease*.

I assembled a dream cast with Laura Thomas as Sandy, newcomer Dan Whorton as Danny, Daniel, Dietz, Megan, Lori, Megan, Melodie,

Lauri, Billy Ditty, Patrick Kramer, Douglas Goodman, Laurel Baker, Jack E. Chambers, Adele Akin, newcomer Nick DeNuzio, and others.

The next part of that endeavor was obtaining the rights to the film songs ("Grease," "Hopelessly Devoted to You," and "You're the One That I Want") and permission to use them with the stage show's forgettable ones ("It's Raining on Prom Night" and "All Choked Up"). I threw the extra fees on a personal credit card so we wouldn't have to start digging into our season-ticket funds.

I brought back my double-decker set. The malt shop and bedroom units we built for *Nunsense* became pull-outs from the main set that included the band platform up top, a second-story jut-out for "Those Magic Changes" and "Beauty School Dropout," two moveable stair units at stage left and right (holdovers from *Sweeney Todd),* and a set of double doors that hid a rollout platform on which Greased Lightnin' lived.

The doors were expertly painted by Joe Truman to look like the interior of a 1950s high school. It never failed to elicit audible gasps when, following a blast of the car horn, the doors burst open, and Greased Lightnin' "drove" downstage with Kenickie (Dietz) at the wheel and headlights blaring. A simple but truly awesome bit.

The stage-right wall pulled out and spun 180 degrees to become the bed and wall in Marty's bedroom for the slumber-party scene. Additional dressing, including a vanity table and chair, was carried out by the cast. After the scene, the wall unit spun around and tucked neatly back into the set.

The soda-fountain counter and its three authentic stools that were also used in *Nunsense* were affixed to a new base on wheels and pulled out from the stage-left wall. The unit was sturdy enough for Danny and Sandy to dance upon. After that scene—*whoosh!*—the unit returned to its storage position in mere seconds.

The One That They Wanted

The underside of the second-story jut-out was equipped with hooks and Velcro to accommodate scenic elements such as a Rydell High banner, pink curtains for Marty's bedroom, and Mylar drapes for the prom. And within the stage appendage was hidden a fog machine for Teen Angel's entrance and exit. High upstage were three "45 RPM" records; the two smaller ones at either side of the stage had circular cupboard doors that opened to reveal Vince Fontaine at various times during the first act. I couldn't resist making one of the records an Annette Funicello hit, "First Name Initial."

While it may not have been perceived by audiences, my concept was a living yearbook that began in the lobby with enormous blow-ups of actual period yearbook photos. Inside the theater, the faux proscenium arch was covered with more of the huge photos, each one carefully selected to resemble one of the Grease characters, all pulled from random yearbooks purchased at an antique mall. The only non-random photo was one of my Mom, circa 1962. Her photo appeared third up on stage left and, to me, represented Frenchy due to her glamorous look. When my Mom came to Nashville to see the show, she squealed with delight when she saw her photo as I'd left it as a surprise. I also made Rydell's school colors the same as her high school's: orange and black. Yes, a strange color combination, quite the departure from the well known red and white used in the film.

But the colors were just one of many Easter eggs I'd placed in the show to honor Mom. After all, she instilled in me my love of the 1950s. And here's a note of trivia: while Rydell's colors in the films are red and white, in the original Broadway show and script for licensing, the colors were and are green and brown. Yuck! I think those colors were selected to make a lyric rhyme work. Or they were *someone else's* mother's school colors. I did break a cardinal rule by rewriting the fight song to make the rhymes work with orange and black.

120 SEATS IN A BOILER ROOM

After the opening overture of the tune "Grease," dim lights picked up the main cast posed, yearbook style, on the two stair units holding up hinged frames affixed to the outer railings. From there, they sang the *a cappella*, madrigal version of "We Go Together." If you squinted hard enough, between the cast, the wooden frames, and the proscenium photos, you *might* have got the yearbook concept. No one ever did. It was a waste of wood and hardware, however, when the lead guitar (played by Sloan Yarborough) blasted the opening riffs of the "Alma Mater Parody" and the cast dropped the frames and charged the main stage level, it did add something. Not exactly sure what. But something.

At every opportunity, I did whatever I could to plus up what is generally considered a less-than-stellar script without stepping into hot water. I asked Jamey to add a *Stomp*-like section to "Greased Lightnin'" in which the guys grabbed wrenches and beat the hell out of the metal on our carnival car. It was an exciting moment for the audience, although I think it lasted 16 measures too long. Then, the guys went into an extended dance break with matching hubcaps. Sonny, played by Nick DeNuzio, who was a great dancer despite his large frame and became a BRT regular for many shows, badly sliced one of his hands on his hubcap during the dance one night. Being the trooper he was, he wrapped his hand in his red shop rag and didn't miss a beat.

As I had done with *Chicago,* I tried to combine the best of the Broadway version and the movie in my production. In the script, during Act One, the scene prompting Rizzo to sing "Look at Me, I'm Sandra Dee" occurs as the Burger Palace Boys (it was only the T-Birds in the films) and Pink Ladies are hanging out in a park, not in the slumber party. Contractually, that can't be changed. Lori Ellis née Eisenhauer was my Rizzo and the show's choreographer. We added some fun bits to the song to honor my love of Annette and Disney after the lyrics mention the famous Mouseketeer. In the stage show, the scene and act culminate with

"We Go Together." But before that happened, in my version, instead of Sandy running offstage, she would run up the stage-right stairs and from below the oversized record, sing "Hopelessly Devoted to You." Typically, the movie song is swapped out for the Act Two prom song. But I've always liked "It's Raining on Prom Night" with clever lyrics such as "It's wilting, the quilting, on my Maidenform [bra]" and retained it as written in the script. So I fudged it a bit.

I was frequently asked why we didn't do the John Travolta "Sandy" number in the drive-in scene since we were doing the movie songs. First, it's not (or at least it wasn't in 2005) available for licensing to be used in the stage show. Second, I've always thought it was far inferior to the original "Alone at a Drive-In Movie" which has some clever lines, particularly one comparing speaker knobs to female, well, you-know-whats. And third, had we been able and had chosen to do the movie song, audiences would have expected to hear the overdone Travolta licks and turns. As a director, I always wanted to give the audience what they hoped to hear but also throw them some curves. Which is why in "Sandra Dee" there wasn't the Stockard Channing "cough-cough-cough" bit after a lyric about smoking, and it's the reason why in "There Are Worse Things I Could Do," I forbid Lori to do the long-since-cliché "MIS—TER righ—ight" trademark Stockard take.

But my favorite trick on my audiences occurred in the diner (not the movie's school carnival) when Sandy makes her appearance in the trademark skintight black pants and black pumps. We simply added a curly fall to Laura Thomas' pulled-back blonde hair rather than going full Olivia bad-perm wig. In the stage show, Danny and Sandy sing "All Choked Up," a song I've always liked a lot. From the house—when I was working house—I would inevitably hear an anxious rustle of programs when the iconic "bah dah dum dum, bah dah dum dum" opening riff wasn't played and Danny didn't start wailing about being cold. We did at least half of "All Choked Up," then after a hard stop, the band played that oh-so-familiar riff leading into "You're the One That I Want." Frequently, I heard a chorus of relieved "yays" and cheers from the audience. I loved the tease. I loved that guests had been afraid we wouldn't do their beloved song. But we didn't let them down. Jamey wrote backup vocals for the cast and it worked beautifully. We honored the stage show while ultimately giving guests what *they* wanted. A bonus is that a humble little video of our mash-up on YouTube has, as of this writing, received nearly 14,000 views. That's a lot for a humble little video.

On a personal note, *Grease* marked the last time (as of this writing) that I appeared on stage, at least as a performer. Due to schedules, Daniel and I shared the cameo role of Teen Angel, again, with my own touch for the character. Due to my love of James Dean, I had our Teen Angel dressed in Dean's iconic *Rebel Without a Cause* look, that is, red jacket, white t-shirt, and motorcycle boots. We topped him off with a party-store Elvis wig with a pompadour that extended nearly a foot and spray-painted it blonde-gold. Daniel's Teen Angel vocal performance was an exciting whirlwind through period falsettos and non-period boy-band riffs while mine was strictly Broadway and not very exciting. I didn't even want to be on stage anymore; I'd come to hate it. I spent the run sick, but when my Mom visited, I stumbled vocally through one show for her. The show was a loving tribute to her anyway. I had to. As a true tenor, I've never had a falsetto and could belt to a high D-flat (at least in *Hair* anyway). But I could barely hit any of the high notes and I let Daniel finish the run. I was done performing. Especially after reading the glowing review below from *Nashville City Paper*.

. . .

"As many theater companies can tell you, presenting a play that's also known as a blockbuster movie can be dangerous. Yes, you're sure to fill up some seats based on name recognition alone. But most audience members will be armed with powerful pre-conceived notions of what the show should be. And when the inevitable comparisons are made, most theater troupes simply don't stand up.

"... Fortunately, nothing could be further from the truth as the Boiler Room kicks off its fifth season...

"... Dan Whorton shines in his BRT debut as Danny Zuko... offers a nice blend of comedy and cool, with a Travoltaesque swagger and a killer voice. He puts his talents to good use in 'Alone at a Drive-In Movie,' working the audience for extra laughs...

"... Daniel Vincent nearly steals the show as Teen Angel, singing 'Beauty School Dropout' with a vocal range that would make even Frankie Valli jealous..."

. . .

Martin Brady was seemingly loath to review *Grease*, and it was probably to our benefit that he did not. I imagine a review in which he would have spent the majority comparing the original Broadway script's flaws to a hatred of the 1978 film, adding just an "it was OK" remark regarding our production and making an accusation that Sandy was played by a guy in drag.

Although *Grease* is done *ad nauseum* by high schools and community theaters, it isn't a staple of professional theater. Perhaps that's why my publicity angle worked so well. We had been doing live promotional in-studio television appearances since BRT's beginning, but *Grease* marked our first on-location live spot. I assembled the cast at 3:30 in the morning. After they guzzled coffee and noshed on breakfast goodies I'd supplied, they stumbled through the numbers we would do as the band wandered in, also mostly asleep. But no Jamey. No matter. No one ever got to early-morning things on time, although really, there aren't many in live theater.

By the time channel-whatever showed up for the live hits—there would be three times the station would cut live to BRT—I still didn't have a piano player or conductor. Megan kept trying to call him. No answer. No one assumed anything worse than a missed alarm clock buzz. Even so, it was a problem. Without alerting the TV station, I talked to the band, and they decided to have Doug Bright, the bass player, serve as conductor. Fortunately, we had an electric guitar in the mix and Sloan expertly covered key entrance riffs.

We pulled it off.

As the last of the cast and band was leaving the theater around seven, Jamey wandered in, dressed in his customary trench coat with coffee mug in hand, to prep for early voice lessons.

"Hey."

"We missed you this morning," I said.

"What was this morning?"

"The live hits for *Grease*."

"Oh, crap."

HOT TIPS

Not So Magic Changes

Remember, never make changes to a show's script without permission from the publisher/licensing company. I broke the rules numerous times putting our productions at risk as I'd heard of shows that were forced to shut down. The opposite of the adage is true here: "It's easier to ask for permission and eliminate the need to apologize later."

And sometimes in live theater, all you can do is say, "Oh, crap."

And that's OK.

AND A COOL THING

It's rare to learn of the whereabouts of a donated, discarded, or lost prop or set piece. You're not actively tracking it nor is it looking for you. So it was pure awesome-sauce to learn in 2020 that part of Greased Lightnin' lives on. Its candy apple, sparkly red fiberglass shell hangs on an old industrial brick wall at The Mill at Lebanon, a sprawling complex repurposed much the same way The Factory at Franklin was. I even did their website (in addition to The Factory's) back in the day. Not much remains of the car—we beat the metal parts to Kingdom Come during the stomp sequence over six weeks of shows, so most of that is gone. The practical lighting and horn were removed and ostensibly went back to Anthony. But I think there's a plaque commemorating it.

And that's cool as hell.

Greased Lightnin' lives on in The Mill at Lebanon, Lebanon, Tennessee.

CHAPTER 31

Rocket Man

SECOND SLOT 2005

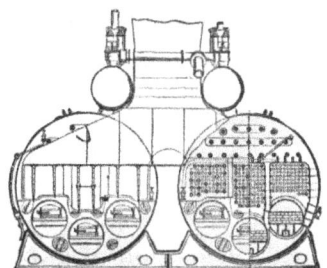

For the last 17 years, Corbin and I have had a friendly disagreement about who came up with the set concept for *Godspell*. My memory is that Corbin wanted the setting to be a run-down playground. (*Godspell* is one of those shows that can take place in a wide variety of settings.) Here's how I remember it playing out.

I said, "Let's do one better than that. How about an abandoned amusement park?" For me, it married two of my loves: creepy things and theme parks. I also had the rundown amusement-park setting from the film version of *The Wiz* in my head. "We already have a ten-ton carnival car on stage. Let's build a set around it and delay a dozen hernias removing the thing."

"I'll have to give that some thought," Corbin drawled in his soft, Southern accent. "I was imagining a slide and one of those merry-go-round things."

"I've seen that done before," I bluffed. "We can do better."

"Gotta think about it."

No matter who had the theme park idea, it's no longer important. What does matter is that Corbin and I always made a great design team. We'd often have our differences of opinion, but could usually arrive at a compromise that leaned in my direction. I was hoping that would be the case because I'd imagined and sketched a totally immersive experience, akin to the Haunted Lobby for *Sweeney Todd*, an experience that would begin the moment guests entered the lobby.

A day or two later, Corbin stopped by the box office. "So, that amusement park idea. Do you know where we could get more ride vehicles?"

"Yep, I sure do." I had talked months prior with an eBay seller in Alabama who had lots of parts of an abandoned theme park.

I finally found the scrap of paper on which I'd written the name of the seller. We made contact and he sent me photos and prices for all the pieces and parts he was selling. I explained my vision and my budget cap of $500. For the money, he put together a package that included a kiddie roller-coaster cart, part of a boat-ride boat, a fantastic turquoise rocket ride vehicle, and some assorted signage and amusement-park wreckage, and even included bringing the stuff up from Alabama to the theater.

For *Grease,* we still had the "bridge" from *Sweeney,* that is, the second-story platform that bolted through the upstage brick wall and was supported by plenty of four-by-four wooden posts. For the *Godspell* set, it became the remnants of a roller coaster with the ride vehicle hanging perilously off the track. The band was partially obscured behind the wooden structure painted distressed white. Against the stage-level part of the roller coaster was a spinning wooden wheel, the kind one might have seen a showgirl attached to in a knife-throwing act in a Vaudeville show.

We moved Greased Lightnin' to stage left and built a circular ride platform around it. I created a mid-century style sign complete with missing letters out of luan and Tyvek foam and added broken light bulbs.

At stage right we constructed a dart-toss game booth with decrepit prizes still hanging inside next to long-since deflated balloons. It also served as a storage area for props used in the show.

But the *pièce de résistance* was the rocket that Corbin rigged with thick aircraft cable to the theater's rafters. Below it, I created a section of a rocket ride launchpad with painted vacuum hoses and PVC tubes serving as remnants of space-age décor.

Nick, who had been in *Grease*, was a *Godspell* cast member and Corbin blocked him to climb into the hanging rocket for some bit in the show. It might have made more sense for a smaller-framed actor to inhabit the rocket, but Nick was the most eager. During a mid-run performance, one of the scariest onstage moments in BRT's history occurred when one of the four cables failed and the rocket with Nick inside dropped three feet toward the stage. There was an audible gasp uttered by audience and cast alike, and I think it scared the bejesus out of Nick. Fortunately, the remaining cables held and Nick safely climbed down. The rocket's rigging was reinforced, but I don't remember any cast member being inside it for the remainder of the show's run.

Daniel Vincent, who played Jesus, had an odd track record with a common theme in the roles that he played. In 1999, in *Hair*, he played Claude, who dies. In 2001, in *A Chorus Line*, he played Paul, who injures his knee and loses the chorus job. In *Man of La Mancha*, his character is beaten to a pulp. In 2003's *Musical Comedy Murders of 1940*, his character is murdered. Likewise in *Chicago*. And murdered again in 2004's *Sweeney Todd*—twice actually: first as Adolfo Pirelli and then again as a random barbershop patron. As Teen Angel in *Grease*, he was already dead, as was the case in *Forever Plaid*. Later in 2005, he played a character who has died from cholera in *The Secret Garden*, and in 2007's *Urinetown*, his lead character is thrown off a building.

But playing Jesus in *Godspell* might have been the most challenging. While crucifying him onstage might have been too much for audiences, he was placed on the big wooden wheel, bracing his feet and grabbing pegs for dear life as the cast spun him like it was *The Price is Right*. Oh, and he had to sing while being spun. And sometimes he was left upside down. Yes, Daniel Vincent had developed a reputation for playing characters who were maimed or met unlikely endings. But he consistently garnered great reviews. Amy Stumpfl of *Nashville City Paper* said:

...

"From the moment you step into the theater, your senses are hit with unusual sights and sounds—from cheesy carousel music to the smell of freshly popped popcorn. The lobby and stage are set as an abandoned amusement park, with faded signs, a rusted-out bumper car, and other debris.... With... a strong supporting cast, Daniel Vincent is free to explore a full range of emotions with his quiet, yet commanding portrayal of Jesus. His voice is truly lovely, and he manages to expose Jesus' human side without seeming preachy or condescending."

...

Godspell wasn't quite the blockbuster that *Grease* was. It was, after all, the Gospel story in the Easter slot in Williamson County, when guests were busy with church activities. Still, the show drew enthusiastic audiences and that was worth a minor miracle at the box office.

CHAPTER 32

Something Gold, Something New

SPRING & FIRST SUMMER SLOT 2005

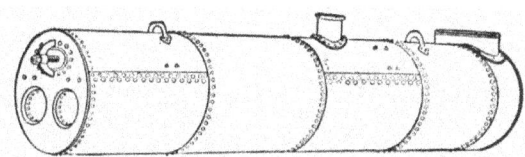

Perhaps to prepare us for three major musicals back to back, we scheduled two straight plays in a row. Our M.O. was to do six musicals per year, with one straight play thrown in to save a few bucks and to give the musical performers and musicians a break.

On Golden Pond is overdone, pedestrian fare for community theaters. But in the interest of the 2005 Classic Tales do-or-die season, it seemed to fit. It was in its own way a classic story, and it was, after all, the season in which we had to make major bankroll to ensure survival.

Our production wasn't a definitive one. But it was rock-solid under Jamey's skillful direction. It stayed true to the script and original setting, not some wacky version in which the cabin is actually an outpost on an uncharted planet in another galaxy. It wasn't color-blind in its casting nor did it have a woman playing Norman. Just the classic version.

The late Marianne Clark was a brilliant Ethel and the late BRT newcomer Douglas Davis was a respectable Norman. The leads were supported by a supporting cast that included Laura Skaug, Alan Lee, and Phil Perry.

I put in approximately 150 hours creating a realistic lakeside cabin interior. After Corbin had the walls up, I went to work applying a rough plaster coating to all the flats (which ruined them for future use depending on the show) and painted them a burnt orange color aged with sponged-on brown.

While I'm not a painter, and although I'd painted a purposely cheesy backdrop for *Hamlet!*, I embraced the challenge of painting a realistic drop of Golden Pond and its surrounding flora. I had no idea what I was doing and used multiple cans of latex paint from previous shows. Printed photos of lakes guided my work. I had plenty of Bob Ross-like "happy little accidents" and was actually thrilled with my work.

Furnishing the set was great fun, loading the cabin interior with a large assortment of thrift-store finds.

But my biggest challenge was creating the stone fireplace. Online searches for guidance produced nothing useful so I experimented with half-inch-thick Tyvek foam insulation sheets. I screwed them to the wooden fireplace structure, then with a wide flat-head screwdriver, carved random grout channels between stones. I painted those channels dark gray, then built up the stonework with plaster. Faux-finish painting using a variety of sponges and brushes achieved the look I wanted. I surprised myself again and had figured out how I would later create the stone walls in the Beast's castle.

Unfortunately, the show either wasn't reviewed, or printed copies didn't make it into my archives. Nonetheless, audiences were exuberant and enjoyed what they said was the best version of *On Golden Pond* they'd ever seen. For a straight play, ticket sales were robust.

120 SEATS IN A BOILER ROOM

The second straight play of the 2005 season was the then-recent Off-Broadway comedy *Epic Proportions*. It was the riskiest show of the season being completely unknown to the vast majority of guests.

Written by Larry Coen and David Crane (co-creator of *Friends*), the play is set in the 1930s and tells the story of two brothers, Phil (played by Jack E. Chambers) and Benny (played by Douglas Goodman) who go to the Arizona desert to work as extras in a Biblical epic film, *Exeunt Omnes*, directed by a famous recluse by the name of D.W. DeWitt.

All 3,400 extras are supervised by Louise Goldman, played by Megan, who divides them into four groups. Phil is a "three" and gets to appear in pleasant scenes of feasts and parades, while Benny has the misfortune of being a "four" meaning he appears in scenes of all the Ten Plagues. Romance and a brotherly rivalry, as well as hilarity, ensues.

The all-star cast also included Lisa, Alan, Thomas, and Sloan. The set entailed an enormous staircase, on which many scenes were played and a desert backdrop I had painted. I took a cue from the Joe Correll "school of backdrop painting" and placed a lone camel on one of the sand dunes. Joe often hid a figure on his Avante Garage! backdrops such as an out-of-place leprechaun on the Scotland drop for *McBeth!* The show became the sleeper hit of the 2005 season and made more at the box office than we projected. *The Nashville Scene* even gave the show a great review:

. . .

> "... while the comedy's limited scope might be ill-suited for a big Broadway house, a more intimate venue can make for a more forgiving theatrical experience. That's exactly what's happening in the new production at Boiler Room Theatre. Director Laura Skaug takes eight of the better Boiler Room regulars and whips them into a comic

frenzy, and much of the evening... is side-splittingly good."

...

CHAPTER 33

A Glorious Success and a Well-Kept Secret

SECOND SUMMER SLOT & FALL 2005

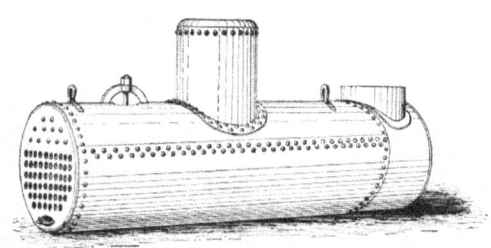

It was once said that if Frank Loesser could get gamblers to sing and dance, he could successfully do the same with businessmen. And in 1961, that's exactly what he did with the musical *How to Succeed Without Really Trying*. It ran on Broadway for more than 1,400 performances, won seven Tony Awards, and won the Pulitzer Prize for Drama. It's a big show with big musical numbers and a big infectious score.

We had mixed results with Loesser's *Guys and Dolls* in 2003, but although *How to Succeed* was lesser (no pun intended) known, I thought its music was superior in that it was a delightful combination of lively production numbers and lush ballads. It was one of the shows I pitched during 2005 season planning, and it didn't need much discourse.

Our challenge, as was our challenge with most shows, was making the show work on a unit set with a few smaller set pieces that could come and go. I designed a set that had, upstage of the second-level bridge, a simple New York City skyline backdrop with a wall of open window frames on the front of the walkway. Below was a wall inside a period office building with a bank of two elevators. A great deal of the show's action involves characters making quick entrances and exits via the elevators, essentially a modern version of a British farce. The elevator-door action was simple yet mesmerizing. It required two dedicated stagehands to work each elevator's door—we just used standard sliding closet doors—and they looked so damn real.

I went big and bold with the color scheme—all lime green and turquoise—and it worked perfectly as the mid-century backdrop for Billy Ditty's delightful period costumes.

The small set pieces were many and included three, two-drawer "filing cabinets" that served as the bases for several different-sized desktops; nine rolling stenographer desks with matching chairs; and nine matching vintage typewriters. Thank goodness for eBay. I needed uniformity and I found it. Also included were six men's restroom sink-and-mirror frame units that attached to six of the stenographer bases; two artificial floor plants; and the "Treasure Hunt" pirate unit.

The cast comprised a variety of BRT's stalwarts with Patrick and Megan in the leading roles, backed by a large cast that included Melodie, Lauri, Nick, Laura Thomas, Melinda Doolittle, Mike Baum, Lane Wright, Scott Rice, Thomas DeMarcus, and the late John Wilson who had been with us in Euphoria's *God Bless You, Mr. Rosewater*.

The story is of an eager window washer, J. Pierrepont Finch (Patrick) who reads the book *How to Succeed in Business Without Really Trying* as he works. The book instructs him via a voiceover, that was performed by Jack E. Chambers, and upon being inspired exclaims, "I can!" before the opening number's downbeat. He lands a job in the mailroom at the World Wide Wicket Company and through a combination of lucky coincidences and fortunate mishaps, quickly works his way to a vice president position. Along the way he finds romance with Rosemary Pilkington (Megan) and constantly butts heads with the arrogant and nepotism-minded president's nephew Bud Frump, who was played by comedy extraordinaire Thomas DeMarcus.

Alan Lee recounts the story of perhaps the most memorable moment of the show's run. He explains the infamous "I hate this" incident. "What raised this to the level of lexicon was that we were all (Patrick and male chorus) facing the fourth wall singing straight out through the frames of the 'Executive Washroom mirrors.' During the quietest moment of the song, this kid's voice, set on maximum whine, rings out in the theater 'I HATE THIS!' Nowhere to hide. We were all looking out at the audience, trying desperately not to crack, especially Patrick. I just remember coming off after the song and sharing one of the greatest offstage laughs of all time."

Thomas DeMarcus explains further. "To add to this H2S story, at the end when Bud, me, becomes a window washer, the company sings 'though for the departed we shed a mournful tear' and the whole cast looks upstage at me on the second-level cleaning windows. Normally I would say 'I can' calling back to how Finch opens the show. But on this particular glorious night I said, 'I hate this' in a loud voice. It got some hearty laughs from the audience. Not my most professional [moment], but still, I was happy to crack up the cast."

We received a glowing review from Amy Stumpfl with *Nashville City Paper*:

...

"Established in 2000 as Williamson County's first resident professional theater… [BRT] has made a name for itself presenting a healthy mix of dramatic and musical classics, as well as some original works. But with its current production of *How to Succeed in Business without Really Trying*, BRT appears to be perfecting its own formula for success...

"... But Thomas DeMarcus nearly steals the show as the delightfully smarmy Bud Frump. DeMarcus makes the most of every scene, shamelessly mugging it up... complete with horn-rimmed glasses and rust-colored leisure suit. Speaking of which, Billy Ditty deserves high marks for his '60s inspired couture... Ditty's costume design delivers a delicious slice of nostalgia. Likewise, Lewis Kempfer's inventive set and retro scenic design makes the most of BRT's limited space."

...

Then there was the Martin Brady review in the *Nashville Scene*. In his inimitable way, he devoted half the review lamenting the outdated premise of the show and why it wasn't relevant. But he did have a few nice things to say:

...

"Patrick Kramer is splendidly cast in the role that made a career for impish Broadway and film actor Robert Morse. Kramer finds his own distinctive rhythms, gets his laughs and proves an able-voiced match for [Megan] Murphy in the beautiful 'Rosemary' and the usually overlooked but infinitely clever 'Been a Long Day'... Kramer also handles the tuneful 'I Believe in You' with equal amounts of smarm and charm, and carries 'The Company Way' and 'Grand Old Ivy,' two of the show's better duets…

"… The rousing closer, 'Brotherhood of Man,' is a hugely impressive full-cast affair featuring the tabletop performance of Melinda Doolittle as a reserved executive secretary who breaks out in full-blown gospel/blues voice."

…

It's true that Melinda roused copious amounts of applause and even an occasional mid-show standing ovation. Her next show would be *American Idol* in 2007 when she made it to third place amongst the finalists. Most would agree she should have won the entire season. Yes, she was *that* good.

Martin did point out that the instrumentation could have been better. Because of the second story on stage being needed for the window-washer moments, the band was back in the tech booth. And as such, it was two keyboards, bass, and drums. *How to Succeed* has a bold and brassy score that would have sounded amazing with our seven to eight-piece onstage band that we had for *Chicago, Anything Goes,* and countless other shows. It was the usual dilemma of sacrificing band size for set necessities.

Despite any shortcomings, *How to Succeed* was the summer blockbuster we needed.

In between the summer blockbuster and the winter *Beast*, there was *The Secret Garden*. It remains a secret, or rather, a mystery. No production photos were taken of the show. No critic reviewed the show. No one remembers much about the production.

Here's what's known. The show sold well enough, but it had a large cast and didn't make money. We'd banked on kids knowing the story, but by 2005, it seems the book may have fallen out of fashion. The set was sparse and used the second-level bridge for the comings and goings of ghostly characters. Because the show had numerous characters who were ghosts, it inspired me to bring back the Haunted Lobby.

Cast member Daniel Vincent shared his memories. "The band was in the booth. We used the second [onstage] level for a lot of the flashbacks and ghostly things. The guy playing Dickon was super f-cking weird and the callback audition went on until I finally told Corbin to cast him instead of me. Malcolm and his German mother were amazing. The actress playing my wife was a batshit-crazy nightmare. She wanted us to very inappropriately make out at one point. I had to sing the vocals offstage for the guy that was playing the Indian/African character. Above all, Neely [O'Brien Green] was gorgeous with outstanding vocals."

In large productions of the musical, there's typically a glorious reveal of the secret garden. Corbin, who directed and designed the set, had a great plan for the reveal to be done with projection effects. Either due to lack of equipment, equipment failure, or the effect simply not working, the full, magical garden didn't materialize.

A collective panic ensued.

Lattice panels that may have been part of the original design were repurposed. So I, along with a few others, spent two days stapling every artificial flower and palm branch from my prop inventory to a set of lattice arches. When that still wasn't enough, I cleaned out every floral clearance bin in town. Whatever Plan B garden-reveal effect Corbin had in mind, it still didn't work. But we did our best, which is sometimes all you can do.

HOT TIPS

All Hail the Costumer

The hardest-to-find theater craftsperson is the costumer. Without a good one, you're sunk. We were able to stumble through our first season without one with mixed results. You'll recall how earlier in this book we had a totally inept costumer for *Ruthless!* who ultimately delivered a partial lot of costumes, most of which were unusable. For *A Chorus Line*, we were able to rent the iconic finale costumes. The remaining shows in the inaugural season were relatively easy, pulling from actors' own wardrobes and finds from thrift stores.

We were mightily blessed when Erin Parker became our Resident Costumer in 2002 and expertly costumed big shows including *Guys and Dolls*, *Chicago*, and the Avante Garage! remounts. As Managing Director, I was terrified when Erin gave her notice; she was going on tour with a show. I costumed *Nunsense*, and we were lucky to get Billy Ditty—the best costumer in Nashville—to tackle *Sweeney Todd* while I interviewed and hired our next Resident Costumer, Cat Eberwine. I hired her largely because of her Disney experience and our being one year out from *Disney's Beauty and the Beast*. She started building costumes a full year in advance.

All Hail the Costumer

And for *How to Succeed...* Billy Ditty stepped in to costume an enormous show filled with period costumes and the musical number "Paris Original" that had at least nine women onstage in identical evening gowns.

As a theater owner or manager, your team might be able to, as we did, stumble through some smaller, non-costume-centric productions, but it's imperative to have an expert costumer on your team, or you'll be limited with the shows you can pull off.

Find that costumer and treat him or her like gold.

CHAPTER 34

Wrangling the Beast

CHRISTMAS 2005

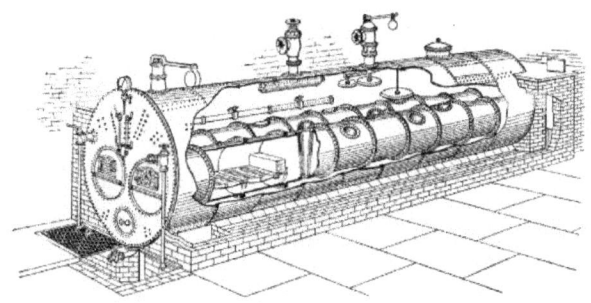

By the eighth gallon of purple paint for the Beast's castle, I'd easily put 200 hours in on the set. I'd enlisted my friend Jonathan Bryant, Devin Clevenger, and his mom, Mary Numinem. By and large, the four of us comprised the scenic painting team for the monstrous set. Well, not counting Brian, a friend of Daniel's who was fantastically talented and painted the three full-size backdrops. And Daniel, to whom I would assign painting tasks to complete while working the box office. Ultimately, the Beast's castle set required 13 gallons of purple paint.

We were still two weeks from opening and my exhaustion was bad. Those multiple-sclerosis-like symptoms were back with a vengeance. I was constantly losing my balance which was dangerous as I worked on the top rungs of eight- or fourteen-foot ladders. I didn't think I could go on.

But I had to.

It was my show. I pitched it, sold it, was directing it, and was creating the single-most detailed set I'd ever attempted. But you know by now that I had ulterior, Mouse-sized motives. I needed portfolio photos of a set so impressive they would make Disney take notice.

The show had more than its share of problems, the first of which was my casting, which wasn't really a problem, but was perceived as one. I didn't plan it, nor could I have foreseen such an outcome. But at the callback audition, that stretched until one in the morning, a clear choice for Belle and Beast had emerged: Laura Thomas and Dan Whorton, respectively, who had been my Sandy and Danny in the season's opener. I was as shocked as everyone else, but their chemistry was *that* good. Blame it on being an onstage couple at the beginning of the season, but they were perfect together. The rejected auditionees for the roles said I was biased. I wasn't.

My design was aggressive for the small stage and Anthony took the lead on technical direction and set construction. The set included two main revolving structures, one side of each serving as buildings in Belle's village, the other sides being parts of the interior of the Beast's castle. My design intention was for the rotating units to have even more functions. Thankfully, Anthony, who engineered and built the intricate pie shop for *Sweeney Todd,* understood my vision and had the time and interest in bringing it to life.

Three stage-width backdrops helped provide the required settings. A proscenium-line backdrop was the enchanted forest leaving 18 inches of playing space for the show's introduction when the Prince is turned into the Beast at the top of the show and for the two fights with the pack of wolves. The second drop was squeezed between the rotating units and the staircase inside the Beast's castle. Because we had no wing space and little usable fly space, the first two drops were essentially huge shower curtains and were pulled from side to side. The third drop covered the brick wall upstage of the infamous "bridge" and was painted to look like an elevated walkway inside the castle.

Two miniature side stages were built below the faux proscenium arch. Stage right was a hint of an interior of Belle's cottage with two walls, set dressing, and a stool. At stage left was a suggestion of Gaston's village pub with a wall covered with faux fur and actual antlers I'd found on eBay and in tiny Tennessee towns such as Leiper's Fork.

Cast and crew member Devin Clevenger, who had grown up with the theater via the Act Too program, shared his memories with me. "BRT was a very special place in my life. You may not know this, but my wife and I were engaged on opening night of a Boiler Room show. We still have the photos from backstage," Devin said. "I also want to thank you. You played such a role in my life as an artist. I loved learning from you. Specifically, the unforgettable odor of drilling screws through actual antlers for Gaston's lodge. You can put together a show better than anyone I know. Thank you for taking your time with me and being such a bright spot in my life."

The stage right unit spun 180 degrees to become the tall fireplace in the castle with a Halloween flame decoration hidden behind real logs. But when the unit split open, the fireplace flipped to one side as a rounded bed dropped into place and became Belle's bedroom. Several layers of thick, ornate fabric were unfurled and became the partial canopy for the bed. When those scenes were done, the two sides closed, the bed was automatically returned to its storage position, and the fireplace dropped back into place. Then, it would spin around, and the audience was back in the village.

The stage left unit, when rotated into castle position, became a practical dungeon with a small alcove behind an ornate iron door into which Maurice (Belle's father) would crawl. That unit "unfolded" into three panels that created the Beast's library. Mary spent dozens of hours painting faux book spines on the inside flats. For that set, real books would have been prohibitively heavy for the rotating unit. But there was one actual book camouflaged to blend with the other painted spines. Belle would pull the book to read to the Beast. It was a tiny detail, but looked amazing and magical.

Further upstage, just beyond the two multipurpose units, was the landing of an ornate staircase inside the castle that appeared to climb to dizzying heights on either side. It had three steps on both sides of the landing, one step above the stage floor, with a taller set of steps behind the stage-left dungeon that led to the Beast's "west-wing" lair. A set of newel posts crowned with large, intricate finials flanked the landing.

For several weeks, my days were mostly sleepless. I did the bare minimum of my Managing Director tasks such as bookkeeping and marketing, then went back to the set from hell. I would cut thin foam strips and glue them on the village sides of the two rotating units creating the detail that made them appear to be authentic pieces of English Tudor architecture. I'd glue straw and cardboard shingles to forced-perspective rooftops, and paint nooks and crannies no audience member would ever see. But I did it anyway on the odd chance that they might. That was the Disney method and I followed it to the gothic capital-D letter.

Trying to pull off an enormous show—arguably the largest ever mounted on BRT's tiny stage—was a constant challenge. Despite three tech rehearsals with the full cast in full costumes, there were times after we opened when things just fell apart. There was the night when the village backdrop was pulled in full light before the two units turned to the castle sides. My rule was that the revolves had to move before backdrops opened or closed, lest they get stuck, which happened. The crude method of opening and closing the drops, as if they were monstrous shower curtains, was noisy, and the grommets I had placed in the tops of the drops frequently tore loose due to the cast pulling incorrectly. To save money for the show's run, I ran lights where I could also take notes for the cast. On several occasions, I watched in helpless horror when a scene change didn't go as planned.

BRT had never done a show with a recorded track before. It was no one's first choice to do *Beast* that way—certainly not Jamey's—but we had no other option. The less-than-impressive band configuration of two keyboards, bass, and drums in the booth that we'd used before just wasn't going to work with a majestic orchestral score. Even with Jamey playing live keyboard in the booth each night and operating the soundtrack, there were myriad issues. He was able to cover painfully long scene changes when necessary in a way no recorded track could. Despite audio monitors placed in many places on stage, the cast still had trouble hearing the track during parts of some tunes, especially "The Mob Song," and I'm thankful for the vocal technicians (Megan, Nick, Melodie, and Scott Rice) who helped steer the cast back "on track" as needed. One of the iconic statements that made it into BRT lexicon was Sondra saying, "Just push play and go." I took it as a negative statement and from the way the cast was always disgruntled about, well, everything, I'd say I was right.

Two views of the set for *Disney's Beauty and the Beast*, 2005. Photos by Rick Malkin.

There was one humiliating show when our outdated and barely-functioning-on-a-good-day lighting system failed during the iconic "Be Our Guest" number. Corbin had purchased four "moving" lighting instruments for the show which were programmed to do a variety of things in conjunction with lighting cues for static fixtures and my work with the spotlight. To make the show work, we had wires and cables everywhere on stage, hidden up the brick walls, up through the rotating units, and across the backstage floor under thick layers of gaff tape. The cast did yeoman's work navigating impossibly tight offstage corridors in enormous costumes. But they were often vocal about how we never should have attempted the show in the Boiler Room.

The constant foot traffic over the taped-down XLR lighting cables had done a number on their functionality, and during that performance, during that gigantic production number, I lost control of the lighting board. This had happened before going back to *I Love You, You're Perfect, Now Change* with Teressa stuck in the booth with a dead board when she had to call on-off cues via cell phone to Corbin at the breaker box. It was clunky then, but not the end of the world.

This felt like the end of the world.

One general wash setting remained operational, so between turning the full stage lights on and off and swinging the spotlight wildly to create some semblance of excitement, I did what I could. We took an early intermission as Corbin frantically rushed to the theater. Thirty awkward minutes later, the lighting was restored by way of some technical hocus-pocus he managed to spin.

Finally, there was the show when the Beast's magical transformation back to human form didn't work. It had happened on final dress, so we at least had a plan to cover the moment. We had six foggers installed under the mid-upstage stairs and landing. The Beast, who had been played by a stunt double during the end of the chase sequence to accommodate Dan getting out of makeup and prosthetics and was swapped out at the end of the fight, is supposed to rise above the stage and spin around, then lowered to be revealed as the handsome Prince. Flying an actor in the BRT space was impossible, unless one counts Nick in the rocket. So, Cat built a transformation cloak with a shoulder structure that allowed Dan to lift the costume high over his head. Under the right light and in plenty of fog, it looked like the Beast was rising and morphing until the cloak was dropped and the Prince was revealed.

When it had become clear to the three of us in the booth (me, Jamey, and audio tech Chelsea Brannon who would later play the title role in *Thoroughly Modern Millie*) that all the foggers had failed (thanks to the same foot-trodden XLR cables), Jamey vamped live while the tech crew desperately tried to get them going. Finally, the production stage manager said "just go." The result was seeing the clunky mechanics of the Beast's transformation.

I just hung my head and wanted to cry. I'd put us in this mess.

And I nearly killed, via overwork, Cat Eberwine, our then-Resident Costumer, who had built, with her own skeleton crew, the 125 costumes used in the show. Not only was she bound by the special rider in the show license that no costume from the Disney film nor stage show could be duplicated, she had to make costumes that would fit on our postage-stamp stage. Her work was stunning. Belle's iconic gold ball gown was a close, but not identical, work of art and engineering. The Lumiere (candelabra) and Cogsworth (mantle clock) costumes were intricate and had working parts, from the former's "flame hands" to the latter's swinging pendulum, clock front that opened, and the winding latch that was added on the back for the second act. Mrs. Potts' costume was awkward and a constant nuisance for Lisa Gillespie, who always had to pull a child actor inside a rolling tea cart. Even so, they looked good. The real *pièce de résistance* was the costume for Madame de la Grande Bouche (translation from French: "the big-mouthed lady"), better known as the wardrobe in Belle's bedroom in the enchanted castle. Sondra Morton was perfection in the role and a magician fitting the truly enormous costume through the narrowest of offstage passages. The doors opened as well as a drawer from which she would pull lingerie for one of the best sight gags in the show.

Add to those costumes Babette (the feather duster), Devin as a flower vase, a set of salt and pepper shakers, a cheese grater, a creamer and sugar bowl, three plates, three napkins, and probably the kitchen sink in "Be Our Guest," it was a near-impossible costume build.

But audiences were totally blown away and critics gushed as we added as many performances as we could possibly fit in the run.

Amy Stumpfl of *Nashville City Paper* wrote:

...

> "Any way you slice it, *Disney's Beauty and the Beast* is a big show. Big cast, big set, big costumes and big show-stopping numbers. So when I heard that the Boiler Room Theatre (BRT)—a decidedly intimate venue… was planning to close out its season with this whopper of a musical, I was a bit skeptical. Granted, the folks at BRT have worked wonders before, staging major productions such as *Sweeney Todd* and *Grease*. But… *Beast?* I had to see it for myself.
>
> "Director and production designer Lewis Kempfer has created a remarkably detailed set that succeeds in transporting the audience into Belle's (and the Beast's) magical world. Resident Costumer Cat Eberwine has outdone herself, constructing more than 125 costumes of her own design rather than simply renting them…"

Susan Leathers of the *Franklin Review Appeal* had this to say:

. . .

"'How in the world is Boiler Room going to pull it off?' I asked myself every time I sat through one of the theater's productions this season.

"... Well, Boiler Room Theatre does pull it off. Every inch of its small stage is maximized through creative backdrops and sets that change from French village to [the] Beast's castle in no time.

"... In each of the BRT productions I have attended this year, there has been at least a small gap between the main and supporting cast members. Not so in *Beauty and the Beast*. Director Lewis Kempfer has assembled an ensemble of 25 actors who are perfectly cast."

. . .

I was somewhat surprised that a certain critic didn't review the show. I knew he wasn't a fan, and couldn't believe he missed the opportunity to diss us. but, as I have surmised about previous shows,—and this is just my opinion—he likely would have used at least half the column inches belaboring the differences between the animated film and the Broadway show and why it should never have been mounted on stage, then toss a few comments in about BRT's production including "too big for their stage," "cast was mostly good" yet praising Lisa Gillespie, and something nasty about my direction. Glad he didn't bother to show up.

120 SEATS IN A BOILER ROOM

After a year that exhausted me to illness, 2005 was in the bag, and we had managed to sell season and general admission tickets exactly as I stated and hoped they would.

HOT TIPS

Production Budgets

Always do a production budget before the first person is cast, or the first prop purchased, or the first length of thread goes into a costume. At BRT, we rarely did a budget and went into nearly every show blindly, assuming everything would work out for the best or that a basket of cash would land inside our lobby doors.

It's humbling, eye-opening work that should provide a roadmap for each new production. The budget may force a low-dollar figure on costumes. Think, then, if there's another theater company from whose wardrobe department you could borrow or rent the costume plot.

Show rights are usually one of the most expensive line items, a close tie perhaps with payroll, if you pay your actors. Would a shorter run of the production make more sense? Fewer bucks towards royalties, but if you have limited seating, it might be quite hard to make money on a show.

In any case, buy a spare set of finials.

Boiler Room Voices

LANE WRIGHT

Upon a Strong Foundation

Between 2002 and 2013, I was fortunate to be cast in a dozen productions at the Boiler Room Theatre, as well as directing one show. Five of the shows I did were straight plays, as was the play I directed; even though I've never really thought of myself as a musical-theater performer, the remaining seven shows I was in at BRT were musicals, just a little less than half the number of musicals I've done in my life, not including high school and college. What's more, I sang in all but one of the BRT musicals I did, including a Sondheim musical. So my time at BRT stretched me when it came to musical theater.

My first show at BRT, though, was among the nonmusicals. In John Guare's *Six Degrees of Separation*, I played the role of Flan, who with his wife Ouisa, deal in art on a private basis, and who is among a number of people in their circle bamboozled by a young man, Paul, claiming to be the son of actor Sidney Poitier. Flan is a terrific role, and I was fortuitously cast alongside many actors I'd be working with numerous times in the future, both at BRT and elsewhere.

Upon a Strong Foundation

My favorite story connected to *Six Degrees* concerns a scene in which Paul cooks pasta for dinner for the main couple and an out-of-town guest. We had been using supermarket pasta salad for its relative ease, and apparently this one night the salad had been held onto just a little too far past its sell-by date. When the three of us took a big forkful into our mouths, we simultaneously looked at each other with horror at the taste. We managed to pick at the rest of what was on our plates without actually eating it, but it was all we could manage to keep from laughing when we had lines about how delicious the meal Paul had fixed was.

My first musical at BRT was Frank Loesser's *Guys and Dolls*, and due to my height (I am 6'7" tall), I was an obvious choice for Big Jule. *Guys and Dolls* is a large show, but somehow it was made to fit on the fairly small BRT stage. After the opening "Runyonland" number, I had quite a while before I appeared onstage again, so in rehearsal I was able to watch and be impressed by the musical talent I was working with. I was certainly glad I didn't have any solo singing with so many strong voices surrounding me.

I will say it is a good thing I have never tried to be a gambler, because the scene in which I had the most lines, the big crap game in Act Two, turned out to be my bugaboo. I couldn't keep the rules of craps straight in my head, which resulted in a couple of nights (or even more) during which I got a bit lost and had to rely on my fellow cast members to bail me out. Fortunately, I was also bailed out of most of the choreography in "The Crapshooters Ballet," when it became clear I simply couldn't keep up. Dietz Osborne, our choreographer, claimed it was because the stage was too crowded, which was nice of him.

My only directing credit at BRT, A.R. Gurney's *Sylvia*, is a comedy about a New York couple who owns the titular character—a dog—and what she does to their relationship. Sylvia is played by a human, and the actress who played her was asked to move out of her comfort zone in more ways than one. To begin with, she had almost only had experience appearing in musicals, and she had never done a straight play before. *Sylvia* is definitely not a musical. Even though three of the characters sing Cole Porter's "Ev'ry Time We Say Good-Bye" at one point, it's sung with each character sitting or standing in place, and Lauri's greatest strength was as a dancer and choreographer. So this was a challenge in that regard.

The other way it was out of her comfort zone is that Sylvia's language can be a bit rough (or ruff, if you will) with a healthy number of four-letter words. Lauri in real life has strong religious beliefs and doesn't tend to use those kinds of words, but as Sylvia she had to. Fortunately, Lauri is a trooper and said the lines the script required, and I think part of the fun of seeing the show, at least for those who knew her, was hearing her say words onstage they'd never heard her say in real life.

Of all the musicals I was in at BRT, the one of which I was the proudest was the one in which I, a character singer at best, got to sing Sondheim. The show was *Into the Woods*, which I had seen during its national tour, and I got to play the dual role of the Narrator/Mysterious Man. Fortunately for me, Tom Aldridge, the actor who played the part in its original Broadway run, also had a distinctly character voice, so I felt sure I could do it. I only sang in two songs (not counting the finale); the first, "Ever After" as the Narrator, and the second, "No More" as the Mysterious Man. But even easy Sondheim isn't all that easy. It helped that I sang the latter song with BRT's artistic and musical director Jamey Green, so I knew I was in good hands onstage at that point.

Into the Woods is a huge show, starting out with three houses onstage—houses that have to move out of the way once everyone enters the woods. Fortunately, the set, skillfully designed by technical director Corbin Green, made it all work, even if actors had to squeeze through some tight openings to get into place. I was busy through three-quarters of the show changing between the Narrator and Mysterious Man, and I only really got a chance to breathe midway through the second act after one of my characters got fed to the giant. Still, it was artistically one of the most satisfying shows I've ever done.

Steve Martin's *Picasso at the Lapin Agile*, in which I played the bartender Freddy, was my absolute favorite show at the Boiler Room. It was one of those "lightning in a bottle" casts that was a joy to work with, under the direction of the marvelous Laura Skaug. Although most productions that I am aware of have played the show without accents, we gave the French characters French (or at least pseudo-French) accents, Einstein had a German accent, and only the couple of American characters had American accents. I was afraid this wouldn't work, and maybe in some instances it wouldn't have, but in ours it worked beautifully. The script is so clever and the ideas in it so ingeniously manifested that there were always new things to find, and it was one of those productions that seemed to just get better with every performance. To me, the final performance was the best one of the run, and it was one of those rare shows I could happily have continued to do for many more weeks.

My next Boiler Room show was one of my bucket-list shows, Harvey Schmidt and Tom Jones's Off-Broadway record-breaker *The Fantasticks*. I had seen the show about a dozen years into its incredible 42-year original run, and then in numerous local productions, and I had thought I would have my best shot at the role of Henry, the old actor, who doesn't sing much. Instead, I was cast as Luisa's father, Bellomy, which allowed me to be part of several songs, most of which I knew from countless times listening to the original cast recording. As usual, I was surrounded by a top-notch cast, including our Matt, Ciarán McCarthy, who went on to star in the musical *Kinky Boots* on Broadway.

The following year, I was in one of several shows that had originally been created for the Avante Garage!, which was sort of a precursor to the

Boiler Room. They were supposedly shows from the fictional Rosencrantz Theatre, a family affair that recycled all sorts of inappropriate source material into musicals. This one was called *Les Miz 2: A Tale of Two Cities*, and it managed to spoof the original *Les Misérables* while still telling the actual story of Dickens' novel. Each actor was essentially playing two characters (at least): one, the actor who

was a part of the Rosencrantz Theatre, complete with some kind of character quirk, and the other, the character in the musical they were presenting. I was Gary Ross, an actor with absolutely no sense of direction—he didn't know his left from his right—who was playing lawyer Jarvis Lorry. The show was lots of spoofy fun, and the music was actually quite impressive, with some incredible voices surrounding me.

The set included a turntable, and it and I did not get along. One time the turntable began to revolve too fast while I was on it, and I ended up being flung off it, landing painfully on the stage floor (fortunately I was not hurt much). Another time I was trying to exit and ran right into the turntable, once again landing on my rear. For the first episode, I can blame those moving the turntable, but for the second I can only blame myself.

Each of the shows I was involved with at the Boiler Room Theatre was memorable, as were most of the productions I was able to watch from the audience. I appreciate the hard work, time, and effort that co-founders Jamey, Corbin, and Lewis, and others put into getting BRT off the ground. The consistently high quality of the work there throughout its existence was a testament to all that initial hard work. The productions I saw and was in, as well as all the ones I didn't get the chance to see, would never have happened if BRT's founders hadn't built a strong foundation. The quality of the shows I saw was remarkable. Some of the best theater in the Nashville area, particularly when it comes to musicals, happened on that small stage at The Factory at Franklin.

2006 SEASON

Your Ticket to Adventure

Anything Goes
Angel Street
Forever Plaid
Almost a Midsummer's Night Dream
Big River
Cabaret
That '60s Christmas Show

CHAPTER 35

What Goes?

SEASON OPENER 2006

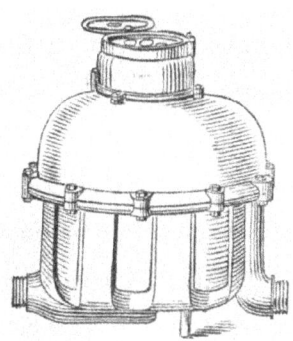

I'd hated *Anything Goes* since I first saw it at the illustrious Boulder's Dinner Theatre. It is basically a bunch of Cole Porter tunes slapped together around a razor-thin plot. But I knew it was beloved and would sell, which is why I suggested it as the season opener for 2006. Jamey had joyfully relinquished his post as director of each season-opening show when I took *Gypsy* in 2004. It was fine by me because I had no personal life and didn't mind working through the holidays on chores such as blocking. I also had a knack for pulling off the big shows in a big way.

But after *Beast*, I was so exhausted I almost searched for an outside director to take the show. Yet I knew that my remaining time with BRT was limited. Sure, I didn't know when I would leave, only that I would, and that it would be in 2006. There were too many things I could no

What Goes?

longer tolerate. So I stuck with the show with the intention of getting even more portfolio photos for my Disney pitch.

Erin Parker, who had departed BRT in 2004 for a national tour or some performance work out of town, was back, and it became immediately clear during the callbacks that she was Reno Sweeney with her huge voice and laser-sharp comic timing. Billy Ditty was the perfect Billy Crocker. I hadn't fully realized before then what a true triple threat (singer, actor, and dancer) he was. I am still blown away with his masculine, Gene Kellyesque dancing. Lauri was my Hope Harcourt for her dance ability and glorious pairing with Billy. Daron Bruce played Moonface Martin, and Corbin turned in a delightful take on Elisha J. Whitney. It took some convincing, but I got Sondra to play Evangeline Harcourt, Hope's mother, who brings her precious pooch, Cheeky (who was played by my beloved Buzz the pug), on board the SS *American*. Buzz was so well-behaved in *Gypsy* that I knew he would be the same again. He was unfazed having to wear costumes ranging from a life preserver to a sailor's cap.

I brought back the double-decker set, wondering if audiences were tiring of it. But each time I used the concept, I tweaked it just enough to do something new. This time, under the second level was a revolving platform. One side was generic, lending itself to a variety of on-board settings. The other side was, if I may boast a bit, a sumptuously decorated First Class, Art Deco style cabin with a decadently draped bed, stylish back wall with practical light fixtures, a period phone, a fur rug, and a Deco smoking stand. Each side of the stage had grand staircases and the side brick walls were covered with the black drapes.

Taking a cue from my *Beast* set, I kept the upstage brick wall covered with a backdrop painted as the open sea. Two smoke stacks flanked either side of the upper deck and the railing was made of silver pipe and aircraft-cable railings to suggest shipboard fittings. Somehow I convinced Jamey to convince the band to wear white dinner jackets and tux shirts since they were in full view.

The overall effect was thrilling to me. I'd finally conquered the exposed brick, and the set, painted mostly in a beautiful light blue with dark blue accents, really had the look of a period ocean liner.

The show sold extremely well and guests made the effort to share positive comments. Here's a snippet from a February 7, 2006 email from guest Caneta Hawkins:

...

> "To the cast and crew of *Anything Goes:* Kudos to all for another brilliant production… The great dancing and musical numbers we've come to expect from BRT were all in place. Superb costumes as well. We are so fortunate to have BRT in Franklin. I love professional theater that doesn't require that I head into Nashville. Thanks to everyone involved, but I must say Buzz (Kempfer's pug) gets my vote for 'best in show.' Give that dog another treat."

...

Amy Stumpfl of *Nashville City Paper* was quite impressed:

...

> "Director Lewis Kempfer has assembled a cracker-jack cast… Erin Parker is sensational as Reno, offering all the sass of a young Ethel Merman, with a much more refined voice. Billy Ditty is equally charming as Billy [Crocker] with solid vocals and fabulous dance moves…. Finally,

hats off to the entire production team for pulling off yet another big musical in BRT's intimate space. The set, costumes, lighting, and, of course, musical direction are all spot on."

. . .

And in its first review of a Boiler Room Theatre show, Chad Young of *Parent World* gushed:

. . .

"If the Boiler Room Theatre's 2006 opener… is an appetizer for the kind of entertainment that is yet to come this year, then be prepared for quite a magnificent feast… Lewis Kempfer did a top-notch job directing this must-see production… Patrick Kramer's side-splitting rendition of 'The Gypsy in Me' is a prime example of why he has become a favorite among BRT audiences…"

. . .

CHAPTER 36

Dying Swan Song

SECOND SLOT 2006

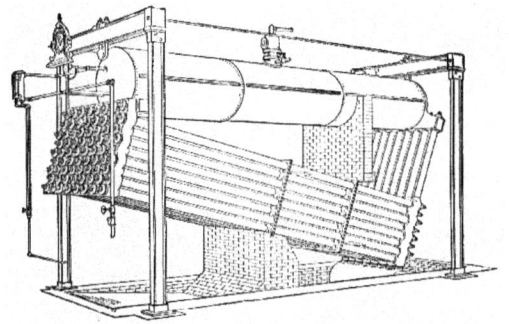

Now comes the part of the story
That gets a little bit down
On his way to the Golden State
Lewis made people frown

Cheesed off is more like it.

By the spring of 2006, I had pretty much cemented my position as Resident Martyr. I had few friends left—if ever I had any—from the Boiler Room casts. By that time, I was always in an argument with Jamey. Corbin was slow to return my incessant calls about set issues. I had resorted to painting and dressing sets overnight early in 2005 just to avoid everyone.

I just didn't know how deep the damage went.

That is, until the infamous "I Am Spartacus" missive that was sent by email to a select group of approximately 25 cast and crew members' email addresses on March 19, 2006, five years and three days from the day I'd put heart, soul, and savings into opening BRT's doors. No, I didn't do it alone. But if you've read this far, you know I've generously given credit where credit is due and largely left out the vast majority of unkindness that I easily could have included in this book, but chose not to.

The email was extremely hurtful. The author had some valid points, but the mature thing would have been to talk to me either one-on-one or together with Jamey and Corbin. In a way, it confirmed what I was already working towards: leaving BRT. It was clear from the email that I wasn't wanted nor welcome at the business I helped bring to life. And although I had yet to send my promo kits to Disney, I knew *Angel Street* would be my last BRT show. The *Spartacus* email cemented the decision.

I'd always understood—up until this writing in 2022—that Spartacus was some great film martyr. The website Culture Matters explained the true meaning. The site states, "A Roman general announces to a group of former slaves that unless they identify Spartacus they will all be crucified. Spartacus prepares to speak up but then all around him, others stand to declare: 'I am Spartacus!' It is perhaps the ultimate demonstration of human solidarity and heroism."

Wow.

So, I wasn't Spartacus, I was the evil Roman general, and the author of the email (who I will not be naming), was speaking for the BRT masses. Finally understanding the true meaning, the hurt is as fresh as of this writing as it was in 2006.

I wrestled with including this episode in the book, but the email cut me so deeply and influenced my leaving so greatly that I decided that it must. It was also collectively one of BRT's darkest moments.

Basically, it said BRT was filled with "talented people, the stalwarts who give so much of themselves to the theater, are bright, joyful, loving spirits who revel in not only their own good work, but the shared good work of putting something that they are proud of in front of an audience."

The author continued, "But there has always been the one constant negative. The one individual who continues to insult, belittle, undermine and bully every effort that these wonderful people make." (If you know me or have read my memoir, I've been on the receiving end of belittling and bullying my entire life and those are things I don't do to others.) I was called a miserable person, "a murderer of good times," and a martyr.

Finally, the author concluded with, "You can consider this an intervention by someone who wants your happiness, or you can consider this a 'Goodbye Asshole' from someone who tried to get through to your best self. It's up to you. I've said what I've got to say. If you're not changing your behavior then I've got nothing more to say to you."

It's true that I was a martyr of sorts for a business I loved, but, in my opinion, I was never cruel to people. I worked without pay so that others would receive a paycheck. I stopped going to cast parties when it was clear I wasn't welcome, hoping the fun wouldn't be spoiled.

Although I had been a major part of creating the Boiler Room Theatre, I had apparently become its biggest liability. So, in my self-deprecating way, I decided that every last person ever associated with the Boiler Room Theatre should share in the fun of publicly humiliating me. So I forwarded the email to every email address I had. And while I don't remember doing so, evidently, it was I who had made paper copies and plastered them all over backstage. If I were going to be tarred and feathered for doing all I could to keep a theater I co-founded alive, then everyone should get to observe.

An event that occurred backstage after the final dress rehearsal of *Angel Street*, with an unnamed cast or crew member, was the email writer's final straw and prompted him or her to write the vitriol. Jamey remembers the incident, but I do not. I told a cast member that his or her makeup looked "high school." I probably meant unprofessional. The actor took it hard and the email writer consoled and protected him or her. During the stress of theater "hell weeks," all sorts of comments fly as everyone is trying desperately to perfect a show before it opens to the public.

But the words were so barbed, so filled with hatred, that I nearly took my own life. Yes, you read that correctly. And at that time, I had no doubt the BRT masses would rejoice at my suicide.

Angel Street may have been the best nonmusical play BRT produced in its first five years. It had a talented cast led by Alan Lee, Jennifer Richmond, Kay Ayers-Sowell, Nick DeNuzio, and a policeman cameo role that was played by everyone from Jamey to drummer and photographer Rick Malkin to Anthony Popolo. It was the stage version that preceded the film *Gaslight*, a Victorian thriller of a husband trying to drive his wife crazy.

Corbin was at the helm as director, and it was exemplary direction. The whole production from Cat Eberwine's sumptuous period costumes to Jamey's musical soundtrack to the interesting, non-box unit set Corbin built that I got to decorate was a group effort with everyone putting their best work on display.

The production received solid reviews, and I received some of the best reviews of my career for my set decoration. Martin Brady was especially jubilant in his review:

120 SEATS IN A BOILER ROOM

...

"Thanks to some wary direction by Corbin Green, and even more to the efforts of a quality ensemble of players, the Boiler Room Theatre's production is a qualified success... the roguish Mr. Manningham, played with appropriate hubris by Alan Lee, lords his creepy paternalistic superiority over his pale-skinned delicate flower of a mate, enacted by Jennifer Richmond.... In her BRT debut, Richmond turns in an admirably controlled, subtly expressive performance, conjuring the sympathetic innocence of Grace Kelly in Alfred Hitchcock's well-known film *Dial*...

"... The action is played on an intimate yet marvelous period set by Lewis Kempfer, who works in some appealing details—a quietly elegant staircase, atmospheric window treatments, hanging portraits, various *objets d'art*, and the play's signature gaslights... An edgy piano score, designed by Jamey Green, ebbs and flows throughout the evening, adding to the tension without ever trying to do more..."

...

Evans Donnell had nice things to say about the set in particular. And since this chapter was largely devoted to lambasting me, I will end it on a high note. At least for me.

...

"Boiler Room Theatre's revival of *Angel Street* maintains the suspense of Patrick Hamilton's play while exuding a highly polished panache. The Victorian melodrama-meets-psychological thriller is played to the hilt by director Corbin Green's rock-solid ensemble, and their well-crafted performances are complemented by a richly detailed set...

"Set decorator Lewis Kempfer spent weeks sourcing all the furnishings, props, and set dressings, including finding doors and an antique mantel from salvage yards. The result is a sumptuous, beautifully detailed set that equals the hard work put in by the actors without overpowering their efforts...

"Boiler Room Theatre has done a good job of mixing popular shows with riskier fare in its six seasons. *Angel Street* is one of those riskier ventures, but strong preparation and artistic choices allow the gamble to pay off."

...

BOWS

I'm Leaving—I'm Gone

AUGUST 2006

After it had been made perfectly clear that I wasn't welcome at the Boiler Room Theatre, I devoted my time to crafting the most creative self-promotional kits possible to get delivered to each recipient's desk and hopefully wow my potential employers. I received several responses and went out for interviews. While no job offer was extended, Walt Disney Imagineering (WDI) told me, "Get out here!"

I spent my first months in California impossibly sick. I could only eat silly Donald Duck peppermints I bought at Disneyland and occasionally the number seven combo at Taco Bell: A cheese quesadilla, a taco that I would throw out, and a Sierra Mist to drink. I couldn't stomach cereal, Pop-Tarts, or even Diet Coke. I was still going through the seroconversion for a devastating immune disease. I found a primary care doctor in neighboring Altadena, but he had no idea what was wrong with me.

I would eventually cram an entire houseful of furniture and set dressing into a charming cottage in Pasadena with an alley backing up to my bedroom, a perfect location to be awakened numerous times by gunshots.

Still, I'd been in California for more than three weeks and nearly everything I owned was on that Russian moving truck held up in New Jersey. But I'd brought in my car my computer and peripherals. I set up my workstation on a flimsy folding table I'd bought at a Walmart somewhere off the 210. And between bouts of vicious nausea, I made follow-up calls to the Disney people who'd interviewed me, while still managing the books and marketing for the Boiler Room. The Disney folks went silent not returning my calls and Daniel was slow to get weekly sales data to me. So there was a lot of time to pace and panic and spin on making perhaps the worst decision of my life. Sometimes I'd go to the beach, or the Anaheim resort, if I had the energy.

I remained involved with some theater decisions, but I could feel the boot planting itself firmly on my butt—I'd left and quickly sensed the work-from-California arrangement wouldn't be tolerated for long. Once Daniel understood the accounting, I turned it over.

Because of my unemployed status, I insisted on doing the theater's marketing materials for a monthly fee I desperately needed but only sporadically received.

Thankfully, in late August, I was offered a major art director consulting job for new entertainment including a stage overdressing in New Orleans Square in Disneyland. It led to my being hired into a salaried role as a production manager. New Orleans Square had always been extra special to me and felt miraculous that it was the location for my first Disney job. It was even built in 1966, the same year I was born. It was magical and exhilarating.

I moved countless times and had major personal issues, yet insisted on continuing to design BRT's marketing materials, programs, and website. But I was being pushed out more with every passing month and my once-helpful show selection suggestions were largely "poo-poohed." Other agendas were in play now and mine wasn't relevant.

Last straws have been a recurring idiom in this book. The climactic final last straw was mine. I hadn't been paid in nearly two years, and in 2011, the marketing-from-afar arrangement finally ran out of steam. Sondra's wife was a graphic designer and I started noticing web homepages I'd designed were being rapidly replaced with new ones. This then, was the absolute last straw that dangled before me like a carrot on a stick in front of a cartoon character.

On November 11, 2011 (11/11/11) I told the Boiler Room Theatre to go to hell.

But in 2007, there would be one more show.

2007 SEASON

Unlock the Magic

The Will Rogers Follies
Lucky Stiff (remount)
The Miss Firecracker Contest
And a Nightingale Sang
Urinetown
Into the Woods
Billy Bob's Holiday Hoedown

CHAPTER 37

The Last Hurrah

CHRISTMAS 2007

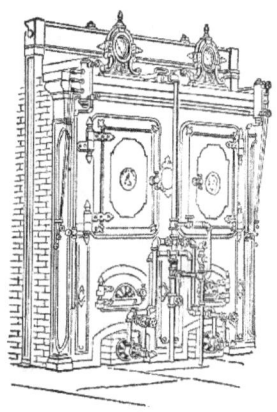

During the five years I worked for BRT from afar, I was still involved with season planning. I remained up-to-date on shows, although it was agony to play the CDs and I was loath to see any musical in person. I mostly suggested big name shows I knew could fit on the Boiler Room stage. At first, my show ideas were embraced and accepted. During the late summer of 2006, per usual, Jamey, Corbin, and I planned the 2007 season.

For 2007's "Unlock the Magic" seventh season, the shows had little to do with the season-brochure theme; I loosely riffed on the number seven and we slotted in seven shows we hoped would not only sell season tickets, but also perform well at the box office throughout the year.

The Last Hurrah

We found ourselves in the typical predicament for the Christmas slot. I threw out an idea for a show that was roughly based on Stephen Henry's role in Rosencrantz (Avante Garage!) shows in which he played Billy Bob, an awkward gas-station attendant who loved donning Shakespearean tights, a short tunic, and cowboy boots to play various characters.

"What if we gave Billy Bob his own Christmas show with members of his family or trailer-park neighbors trying to put on some kind of holiday production?" I suggested.

"That might work. We should probably steer clear from the Avante Garage! character, though," said Jamey. "I don't know how Michael and Joe would feel about it."

"So we change his last name and hometown," I said. "But we write the part for Stephen, because, be honest, no one else can really play Billy Bob. We lock him in early. And since this wouldn't be a Shakespeare parody, he never appears in his trademark tights and boots."

"What do we do for music?"

"We do more parody songs and write some original stuff."

"What's the story?" Corbin asked.

"Hell if I know, but I can be working on ideas during the next year," I said

"It's basically the model we used for *That '60s Christmas Show*. We stick it in the season and write the show a month before rehearsals start." I knew we really would need more than a month, but it was a way to sell the idea to Jamey so he wouldn't feel pressured or expected to work on the thing all year.

So, another unwritten show was sold to the season-ticket holders. By writing a long paragraph of copy for the brochure, I laid out that Billy Bob Judkins (using a different last name for the revised character), his extended family in Piney Grove, Alabama, and a few outsiders, would all come together to put on a show in the church basement as they readied their family band for a never-to-be shot at a recording deal in the Music City (Nashville) to make a Christmas album. I wrote he'd include a set of twin sisters called The Herbig Twins (played by holiday-show stalwarts Megan and Melodie) from Kentucky who'd "had their fill of playing theme parks and Hooters," and who also wore an extraordinary amount of makeup. There would be Memaw and Pepaw, played by Mary Bea Johnson and Jim Green respectively. Billy Bob's 8-year-old daughter, Billy Bobwina, played primarily by Hope Dyra—yet another Act Too alumna now performing in New York City—would add the essential "kid in the act" component.

As I began making notes during 2007, new characters were penned, including Cousin Moles (played by newcomer Shane Bridges); Thelma Louisa aka Miriam Montgomery Meyerhoff (played by Sondra); Nora Morgenstern, an undercover reporter embedded in Iraq (played by Lauri) where Moles was stationed with the Army; and some random locals.

The record deal plot point provided opportunities for forced laughs such as Billy Bob saying they could have a hit LP, just before producing an actual record album, "Why, just look at the success John Denver had with the Muppets." We pushed the Muppets gag twice too many times than the golden rule of "threes" in comedy dictates.

After renting a house just blocks from Disneyland that I couldn't afford, I moved to a cheaper place in Long Beach in early 2007, and once again had a commute during which I wrote perhaps the best number of the show, a naughty little duet for the twins called "Unwrap My Love (This Christmas Morning)" with plenty of sexual innuendo like "open up my box and look inside." A parody of "We Need a Little Christmas" from *Mame* became a rousing opening number called "A Good Ole-Fashioned Redneck Family Christmas" with a chunk of lyrics including:

The Last Hurrah

> "CAUSE WE'RE GONNA HAVE A
> GOOD OLE-FASHIONED REDNECK FAMILY CHRISTMAS
> A REAL RIP ROARIN' NOT TOO BORIN' HOLIDAY FEAST
> (YES MA'AM)
> WE'RE GONNA HAVE A
> GOOD OLE-FASHIONED REDNECK FAMILY CHRISTMAS
> KICK OFF YOUR BOOTS, ENJOY THE SHOW (YA HOO)
> PLEASE PICK UP YOUR TRASH BEFORE YOU GO"

But perhaps the best number was a solo, a parody of a famous tune from *My Fair Lady*. Shane was a master at over-the-top comedy. The Army has discharged Cousin Moles due to an infection in his foot and the character awkwardly hobbles around stage in Army fatigues with a single crutch wearing a surgical boot explaining how he met an "enchanting Arab doll," and despite her face being hidden under her hijab, he professes "But I love her, Billy Bob, I surely do." Upon the musical intro, he throws down the crutch and assumes perfect posture for the parody song, "I've Grown Accustomed to Not Seeing Her Face." Audiences always knew what was coming and the laughter was raucous. Here's one of the verses:

> "I KNOW YOU THINK THIS STRANGE OF ME
> JUST AS WEIRD AS IT CAN BE
> TO WANT A WOMAN WHO'S EXOTIC
> AND I FIND HIGHLY EROTIC
> I'VE GROWN ACCUSTOMED TO NOT SEEING HER FACE"

But there was more. Jamey and I had a blast writing a Sondheimesque bridge that was pure gold:

> "I DON'T KNOW WHAT HAPPENS NOW
> I AM HERE AND SHE IS THERE
> IF I AM HERE AND SHE IS THERE
> AND CAN'T AFFORD COSTLY AIRFARE
> WHERE SHE IS WHERE
> AND I'M NOT HERE
> WHERE SHE IS WHERE
> THAT LEAVES ME TOTALLY NOWHERE
> I CANNOT TAKE THIS WEAR AND TEAR
> I'VE GROWN ACCUSTOMED TO NOT SEEING HER FACE"

The show attempted to lampoon everything from *Christmas Vacation* to the Peanuts' Christmas special to *A Christmas Story*. A twist on the famous leg lamp was my idea because, despite being a gay man, I've always been fascinated with boobs. A large wooden crate marked "fragile" (pronounced frag-JEE-lay by Pepaw) is delivered at the top of Act Two, and after the requisite lighting special and angelic chorus, the men remove something they call a "booby lamp." Designed to be the next body section up from the leg lamp, a woman's mannequin torso was dressed in a bustier matching that of the leg's lingerie in the film, and a hat with foot-long black fringe served as a shade and a suggestion that the lamp, when properly displayed in the trailer's "front winder," would look like a dame. The men then embark on an original tune that's equal parts beautiful ballad in four-part harmony and a foot-stomping chorus all under the song title "Ode to a Lamp" in which the refrain featured the lyric, "Oh, Booby Lamp."

We managed to poke fun at real-life situations such as a complaint Sondra got from an angry parent after one of her children's summer-camp shows in which the girls had to shimmy. Thelma Louise is admonished by Pepaw for always being a rebel, "ever since they had to pull you out of that school show for shaking your upper region." Pepaw's

The Last Hurrah

line is nearly a direct quote yelled by the parent. We always secretly hoped the parent would attend a performance and get her comeuppance, but if she did, we never knew.

In a rare turnabout of events, a Disney senior art director, Bradley Kaye, designed the set and even drew a complete set of blueprints from which Corbin would build the authentic single-wide trailer with an enormous television antenna on the roof, a porch cluttered with trashy set dressing and thrift-store Christmas decorations, and a tire swing at stage left. We repurposed the trees from *Into the Woods* which preceded the show, and they added great depth.

I made three trips to Nashville to visit my old thrift-store haunts for set dressing, to finish writing the script, to dress the set, and direct the show for two non-contiguous weeks. The show did gangbuster business. For all its redneck cheesiness, I'm proud of the show, even though there are plenty of things to be reworked. I still imagine publishing the show one day.

Martin destroyed the show in his review:

. . .

"Boiler Room Theatre got an early start on the holidays, opening its new, seasonally inspired production a week before Thanksgiving. But it seems that the creators of this original show didn't leave this turkey in the oven long enough.

"… For all its mirthful intentions, *Billy Bob's Holiday Hoedown* suffers substantially from undercooked comic material, and from broadly played performances that are often commensurately overdone. The latter might well be the byproduct of the energetic players' desperate attempt to compensate for the script's lack of meat…

120 SEATS IN A BOILER ROOM

"... [the] musical selections... are primarily a collection of song parodies and comedy numbers from co-authors Jamey Green and Lewis Kempfer. There are a few tunes that manage to impress with some combination of wacko humor or spirited musicality. These include... a duet by the tarty Herbig sisters called 'Unwrap My Love (This Christmas Morning)'—which includes the line, 'open up my box and look inside'—and also 'Ode to a Lamp,' in which interesting and elaborate vocal harmonies regale a novelty song that couldn't be less pertinent to the story.

"... Discerning theatergoers looking for live seasonal entertainment can do better than *Billy Bob's Holiday Hoedown*, but if irreverence is what you want, there's a little of it herein."

...

EXIT MUSIC
Because We Knew You
2008 TO 2014

The Boiler Room Theatre would soldier on for nine more years, ultimately producing a total of 96 full Mainstage productions and seven benefit shows, not including the countless children's shows that Act Too Players mounted. Thirteen full seasons and one partial. Really, not too shabby for a business naysayers warned wouldn't survive a year.

From Day One, things were never easy at BRT. Some shows blew off the proverbial roof. Shows such as *I Love You, You're Perfect, Now Change; A Chorus Line; Lucky Stiff* (2002); *McBeth! The Musical Comedy!; Chicago; Nunsense; Sweeney Todd; That '60s Christmas Show* (2004)*; Grease; How to Succeed in Business Without Really Trying; Disney's Beauty and the Beast; Anything Goes; Forever Plaid; Urinetown; Into the Woods; Thoroughly Modern Millie; Jesus Christ Superstar; Fiddler on the Roof; Rent; Annie Get Your Gun; The Rocky Horror Show;* and *Next to Normal* all had spectacular sales, additional performances were shoehorned in, and in some cases, guests clamored for a show's run to be extended, especially with *Chicago*.

Most other shows fell somewhere between boon and bust doing quite respectively and often garnering glowing critical reviews, even if they didn't always attract large audiences. To my knowledge, BRT never mounted a true stinker of a show although some shows fared poorly with critics and others offended guests.

Each of the benefit shows drew packed houses, even if they ultimately didn't bring in the much-needed cash infusion. The 2007 benefit concert, *Melinda Doolittle and Friends*, staged at Liberty Hall inside The Factory's main building, was perfectly timed with Melinda's stellar run on the sixth *American Idol* television season. Viewers nationwide felt strongly that she should have won, but alas, things rarely go as hoped. It was actually an accident that Melinda even ended up at the auditions; she went with a group of friends and auditioned for fun. She was cast and history was made.

But there were also shows that fell flat and failed to find an audience. During those productions, BRT struggled to make payroll. In the case of *Sunday in the Park with George,* the show was forced to end the run early by nearly a week. Those were heartbreaking times to be sure, especially when so much was put into rehearsal, costumes, and sets.

Another flop was 2004's *The Last Five Years*. The seeds of future destruction were planted during that show with an actor making his BRT debut who, with a friend, offered to take over the Boiler Room. Tempting as it may have been, we weren't ready to give up. No, we continued to march courageously forward.

Something happened in 2010 to fire up the rumor mill regarding the theater's future. Carole Robinson with the *Williamson Herald* interviewed Corbin in late June 2010:

. . .

> "Celebrating its 10th anniversary as Franklin's only resident professional theater company, officials at the Boiler Room Theatre said they are planning on celebrating many more anniversaries. Rumors have been

circulating about the theater closing, however, 'We are NOT closing,' Corbin Green, [managing] director and one of the founders, said numerous times during the interview. 'We would close kicking and screaming.'"

. . .

But the winds truly changed in 2012 when original owner Calvin LeHew sold The Factory at Franklin. Even going back to 2006 when I left, we were operating without the protection of a lease. It was perhaps around 2004 that Rod Pewitt, then-general-manager, stopped doing written leases for us and business was essentially conducted with a Southern handshake.

"Once the new owner bought The Factory, there was an ominous, palpable change in the air," said Jamey Green. "Ultimately they gutted the space and turned it into what someone along the way had suggested: A small venue for acoustic concerts and new-artist showcases."

The timing couldn't have been worse. For the first time ever, the Boiler Room Theatre was completely, totally out of debt and in the best financial shape it had ever been, with the road ahead looking rosy. Then Corbin was informed of The Factory's plan to bring Building 6 up to code due to the building being reclassified. Improvements would include new lighting and sound systems. Beefed-up electrical. Better dressing rooms. Increased seating capacity, perhaps with the addition of a balcony that we always wanted. And the behemoth asbestos-filled boiler taking up half the back building? Gone. It all seemed a dream come true. But it required BRT to completely move out of the building—costumes, props, backstage and box-office stuff—all had to be gone by a date in early January 2014. The renovation work would only take a few months, six tops.

But there was something else.

Whatever the impetus, it seemed that BRT's longstanding arrangement with occupying the building full time ran out of steam. Of course, it's the prerogative of commercial property owners to utilize, renovate, and lease space as they see fit. It just so happened that the new owners had a vision for the boiler room building that differed from ours and, to an extent, Calvin's.

That was the day of reckoning—the theater company learned it had lost its namesake space. Not totally lost, but under a new arrangement that had taken aback Boiler Room Theatre management. The Factory would create a new performance venue that could be rented by any party, the same as with any of its event halls and spaces. BRT could lease the building as scheduling permitted. It was a jarring revelation that completely changed the business model by which BRT had operated for 13 years.

Of course, the rumor mill boiled over. I can only imagine the wild stories that might have circulated.

The Factory planned to demolish the building to put in a Ferris wheel.

Or a troupe of mimes wanted the venue to perform a year-round show called *Stuck in a Brick Box*.

Or even that a clothing designer named Jane Mancini wanted to turn the space into a showcase boutique for her risqué line of beachwear called Steamy Bikinis.

The actor community, notorious for being perhaps the worst gossip mongers, believed there was a nefarious plan afoot to quash the Boiler Room Theatre because another theater company didn't want competition.

Not one of any of the plausible or nonsensical (or my creatively inventive) rumors proved to have an ounce of truth.

BRT didn't announce a 2014 season nor sell season tickets based on renovation timeline uncertainties, but forged ahead best it could. They mounted the new musical *Bonnie and Clyde* in Liberty Hall at The Factory. Then, unknowingly, mounted its last production ever, *Legally Blonde*, at the then-recently renovated Franklin Theatre (once a 1920s-era movie house) on Main Street.

Then came the agonizing months of the unknown. As the months dragged into 2015, the ominous feeling of which Jamey spoke had grown: Things weren't looking good as BRT had, by that time, lost all momentum. The projected timeline for renovation took much longer than expected due to the revised building codes and approvals.

It had now been a year with BRT having no influx of revenue. The incredible blessing of finally being in the black reverted to being in the familiar red. BRT was down to a skeleton staff, and had burned through everything remaining in the coffers renting storage space for sets and costumes and retaining its phone number and website. At that point, mounting a show in another venue was virtually impossible. Its core actors and craftspeople had moved on to new projects. BRT management repeatedly reached out to The Factory, but calls often weren't returned and there were scant updates.

From former BRT folks who'd peeked inside or attended music events in the new Building 6, details and photos of the new space began to emerge.

The original 120 burgundy seats had been ripped out and replaced with blue movie theater stadium seating going up to where the tech booth was. It's unknown what the seating capacity had become, but judging from photos, my guess is 60 at best.

The box office/concessions counter was removed and the "seating capacity" of each of the one-at-a-time restrooms doubled. The main entrance moved to the opposite side of the building and a box office and small bar were built under the stadium seating. Sounded a lot like our original plan.

At least nine feet of depth was chopped off the stage, rendering it useless for theatrical productions with the possible exception of *Waiting for Godot* (which only requires two actors and a bench). A drum alcove had been inserted in the upstage wall. A new lighting system had been installed and was operated from beneath the seating bank.

While beautiful and modern, the completed renovations were so impactful that the venue could no longer accommodate the full theatrical shows that BRT had produced since 2001. The building's character had also largely been stripped away.

The Boiler Room Theatre was no more.

Online searches and photos revealed that, for a brief time, Building 6 was called The Little Brick Theater. Then, as it is today, named the Mockingbird Theater.

Sure, the building still stands, but it's a cold shell of its former life when it was filled with laughter, tears, and love.

Even today, changes are happening at The Factory under its third owner who purchased the sprawling complex for $56 million in late 2021. In a review for a resident theater (although never in the boiler room building), Studio Tenn, plans have been announced for Jamison Hall, previously a multipurpose event space adjacent to Building 6, to build out the space to become a permanent theater with balcony seating and rehearsal space.

In a way, all the changes honor Calvin's admiration of Walt Disney and reflect a famous quote spoken by Walt on Disneyland's opening day in 1955: That Disneyland would never be complete as long as there is imagination left in the world. So it seems for The Factory at Franklin. And that's OK. Life goes on until it doesn't.

Starting a theater company is not an uncommon endeavor. Much like restaurants, albeit with less frequency, theaters come and go, sometimes never making much of a splash, and sometimes never making it past one production. The pandemic certainly has changed the landscape of the Nashville theater community—some longtime stalwart companies such as Chaffin's Barn Dinner Theatre folded from the literal overnight shutdown of the world, while others have since re-emerged and seemingly picked up where they left off after a 21-month hiatus. Some new players have joined the landscape. But COVID-19 flares have caused theaters nationwide to halt or close shows early. Even in 2022, Broadway is still struggling due to COVID. The Boiler Room Theatre may or may not have survived the pandemic. Had BRT returned to using its former space, albeit as an outside entity, it might have squeezed in another four seasons filled with tiny shows before the world fell apart in March 2020. But it probably would not have celebrated its 20th anniversary.

But, damn, the Boiler Room Theatre had one hell of a run.

Boiler Room Voices

DAVID WARFLE

Where I Grew Up

It was 2002, and I was a fairly innocent 15-year-old who had just moved to Tennessee when I reached out to the Boiler Room Theatre to see if they needed any audio or lighting people. They wrote back pretty promptly and said that they were getting ready for tech rehearsals for *McBeth! The Musical Comedy!* and could use a sound person. I was excited to get involved and a couple of days later, headed down to BRT to meet everyone and get started. I was immediately greeted by a couple of guys on stage cursing at each other while blaring "The Distance" by Cake, and a drag queen (Blanche, played by co-founder Lewis Kempfer) who just would not break character. I was very confused but intrigued. I spent the next few weeks confused, but loving every moment of running sound for the show.

The next show was *Man of La Mancha*, and that's where I began to see the real beauty and talent that BRT had to offer. It was certainly there during *McBeth!*, but I don't think I could see it as well when I was still trying to figure everything and everyone out. I also ran lights for *Man of La Mancha*, because it wasn't as demanding as sound, which was great because I could really let everything sink in. Each night, as I watched the great Dan McGeachy sing his heart out, I knew this is where I belonged and I was glad I'd found a new place to call home.

In all, I worked on around 50 productions at BRT, while mainly running sound, but also did some lighting design and stage-managed a couple of shows. One of my favorite things at BRT was that your job was never your only job. From helping build sets, to running the box office, to tearing tickets, to seating disgruntled Engineers Club members, taking out the trash, serving popcorn, and my favorite, walking Lewis's Buzz the pug, every day was just a little different.

We spent many nights of rehearsals until one or two in the morning, and a couple of times had to be back by five or six for a morning TV promo live shot, and while these times could be stressful and frustrating, we always found a way to make it fun. One of my favorite things looking back was our efforts in the tech booth to mildly distract the actors. We'd create illuminated signs, do ridiculous things, and my all-time favorite was during Jamey and Lewis's original, *That '60s Christmas Show,* when we tied lights around a vacuum and sent it riding across the tech booth during the unofficially named "Jesus Medley." Alan Lee handled it like a champ, but later acknowledged he had a bit of trouble keeping it together.

From an audience perspective, I don't think many of our guests knew the amount of work and challenges that went into these shows. The major shows we pulled off like *Disney's Beauty and the Beast* and *Chicago,* to the shows with crazy effects like *Sweeney Todd* and *Assassins,* were only possible because of our amazing team who could figure out how to take a stage as small as the one we had and make it feel like a massive Broadway stage. The heart and the energy that our little space had was truly inspiring. There was always the struggle to stay afloat, but we always found a way. We had some of the absolute best patrons that anyone could ask for, and they supported us by buying season tickets every single year, even if they didn't love all the shows, and when we had fundraisers, people showed up.

The Boiler Room Theatre became a second home to me and it's where I truly feel like I grew up. Even on nights when there wasn't rehearsal or a show, you could usually find at least a couple of us sitting there chatting and spending time together. Together, we went through health issues, marriages, divorces, births, deaths, and absolutely everything in between. We fought with each other, probably even more than we showed the love, but at the end of the day, through all of it, we were a giant messy family that would do anything for any one of us who needed anything at all. It taught me patience, it taught me how to fight back when I saw something I knew was wrong, and most of all, it taught me a new level of caring for people, no matter their circumstances. When I look back at my high school and college days, I won't think about school, I'll think about the hours that I spent at the Boiler Room Theatre.

ENCORE

There's Only This

2022

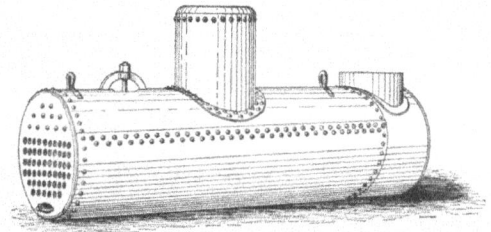

Yes, anyone can open a theater.

The thing is, not even the original Factory owner ever imagined the little building being used as a performance venue. No, that took the vision and ingenuity of the BRT founders. No one, upon walking into that pile of rubble and pigeon poop, could imagine big-name musicals being performed in a charming space akin to an Off-Broadway theater. In some photos, the interior looks eerily like the New York Theatre Workshop where *Rent* debuted.

It takes a special breed of person who can see beyond a dilapidated mess and envision something quite different, something quite wonderful. BRT's four co-founders stood in the middle of a building that looked like a condemned tenement on New York's Lower East Side and saw a stage populated by talented actors and artisans and 100 or more seats filled with happy guests whose spirits had been lightened and hearts and minds opened.

We didn't know how to take a building that was literally falling apart and turn it into something special. We didn't know whether we could raise the money to build out the venue and open the doors, let alone survive for 13 full seasons. It was the hardest work any of us had ever done. But we knew it had to be done, and we were the ones to do it. We all felt it.

We disagreed. We argued. We stressed out. We broke things and almost went broke numerous times. We hated each other for brief moments until our hearts were awash with admiration and forgiveness. But more than anything, we loved. We loved the art we were so blessed to make. And we loved each other, warts and all. So when it was all, once again, stripped bare, what remained was love.

It's what we did out of sheer love.

Thank you my friends and friends unknown.

APPENDIX A

Bibliography

Joe DiPietro and Jimmy Roberts. *I Love You, You're Perfect, Now Change.* Music Theatre International. Copyright 1996, 1997. Page 1-1-1.

Martin Brady. (2001). 'Room For More.' *Nashville Scene.* March 29, 2001. Available at: https://www.nashvillescene.com/arts-culture/article/13005562/room-for-more. (Accessed: March 14, 2021).

Martin Brady. (2001). 'Simmering Satire.' *Nashville Scene.* June 21, 2001. Available at: https://www.nashvillescene.com/arts-culture/article/13005891/simmering-satire. (Accessed: March 14, 2021)

Martin Brady. (2001). 'Musical Pair.' *Nashville Scene.* August 2, 2001. Available at: https://www.nashvillescene.com/arts-culture/article/13006030/musical-pair (Accessed: March 22, 2021)

Mitchell Kline. (2002). 'Tried-and-true trio: Boiler Room Theatre owners ready for second season at The Factory.' *The Review Appeal.* February 1, 2002. From the Boiler Room Theatre's archives.

Martin Brady. (2002). 'Out of Tune.' *Nashville Scene.* February 14, 2002. Available at https://www.nashvillescene.com/arts-culture/article/13006763/out-of-tune (Accessed: March 25, 2021)

Martin Brady. (2002). 'Dead On.' *Nashville Scene.* March 28, 2002. Available at https://www.nashvillescene.com/arts-culture/article/13006932/dead-on. (Accessed on March 29, 2021.

APPENDIX A

Leo Sochocki. (2002). 'The Boiler Room's *Little Shop* Grows on You.' *The City Paper*. June 6, 2002. From the Boiler Room Theatre's archives.

Martin Brady. (2002). 'A Question of Degree.' *Nashville Scene*. June 27, 2002. Available at https://www.nashvillescene.com/arts-culture/article/13007332/a-question-of-degree. (Accessed on March 30, 2021).

John Guare. "Six Degrees of Separation." Dramatists Play Service. 1992. Page 50. Available at: http://www.custommade.org/wp-content/uploads/2015/10/six.pdf. (Accessed on March 30, 2021).

Kazu Hishida. (2002). 'Love/Hate Mail: One More Chance, Please?' *Nashville Scene*. July 4, 2002. Available at: https://www.nashvillescene.com/news/article/13007366/lovehate-mail. (Accessed March 31, 2021).

Martin Brady. (2002). 'Scots in Song.' *Nashville Scene*. August 29, 2002. Available at: https://www.nashvillescene.com/arts-culture/article/13007598/scots-in-song. (Accessed April 8, 2021).

Martin Brady. (2002). 'A Playful Christmas.' *Nashville Scene*. December 5, 2002. Available at: https://www.nashvillescene.com/arts-culture/article/13007993/a-playful-christmas. (Accessed April 10, 2021).

Evans Donnell. (2019). 'NCT's *Auntie Claus* is a Glittering Gift.' December 1, 2019. Stagecritic.com. Available at: http://stagecritic.com/articles. (Accessed April 10, 2021).

Martin Brady. (2003). 'Mixed Reviews.' February 6, 2003. *Nashville Scene*. Available at: https://www.nashvillescene.com/arts-culture/article/13008203/mixed-reviews. (Accessed April 10, 2021).

F. Daniel Kent. (2003). '*Chicago* Razzle Dazzles at the Boiler Room.' June 2003. *Out & About Nashville*. From the Boiler Room Theatre's archives.

Martin Brady. (2003). 'A Clarification on *Chicago*.' May 22, 2003. *Nashville Scene*. From the Boiler Room Theatre's archives.

Martin Brady. (2003). 'Arts & Music.' October 2, 2003. *Nashville Scene*. Available at: https://www.nashvillescene.com/arts-culture/article/13009045/arts-music. (Accessed April 10, 2021).

Evans Donnell. (2003). '*Cat* Leads Skillfully Reveal Anger, Pain Beneath Poetry of Williams' Dialogue.' August 12, 2003. *The Tennessean*. From the Boiler Room Theatre's archives.

Martin Brady. (2003). 'Tennessee Pride.' August 21, 2003. *Nashville Scene*. Available at: https://www.nashvillescene.com/arts culture/article/13008913/tennessee-pride. (Accessed June 1, 2021).

Martin Brady. (2004). 'A Durable *Gypsy*.' February 12, 2004. *Nashville Scene*. Available at https://www.nashvillescene.com/arts_culture/a-durable-gypsy/article_34c768b6-04c9-511a-977e-5614e5123db1.html, (Accessed June 19, 2021).

Michael Bouson, Joe Correll, Jamey Green, Kathy Shepard. *Hamlet! The Melancholy Dane!* Originally produced at the Avante Garage! in Nashville, Tennessee, 1993.

Amy Stumpfl. (2004). 'This sister act really shines.' *Nashville City Paper*. Date unavailable. From the Boiler Room Theatre's archives.

Amy Stumpfl. (2004). '*Sweeney Todd* Returns: Stage set for chills, laughs.' October 14, 2004. *Nashville City Paper*. From the Boiler Room Theatre's archives.

Peggy Shaw. (2004). 'Horrors! *Sweeney Todd* Opens at Boiler Room Theatre.' The October 8, 2004. *Tennessean: Williamson A.M*. From the Boiler Room Theatre's archives.

Martin Brady. (2004). 'A Finger in Every Pie.' October 21, 2004. *Nashville Scene*. Available at https://www.nashvillescene.com/arts_culture/a-finger-in-every-pie. (Accessed February 15, 2022).

Peggy Shaw. (2004). 'Ghost of TV Christmas past visits Boiler Room Theatre; Aluminum Christmas trees, beehives bring '60s TV specials back to life.' November 19, 2004. *The Tennessean, Williamson A.M*. From the Boiler Room Theatre's archives.

APPENDIX A

Martin Brady (2004). 'It's That Time of Year.' November 25, 2004. *Nashville Scene*. Available at https://www.nashvillescene.com/arts_culture/its-that-time-of-year/article_d799014b-50f3-558a-b23e-3b08d1f50971.html. (Accessed March 24, 2022).

Amy Stumpfl. (2005). '*Grease* is the word.' February 17, 2005. *Nashville City Paper*. From the Boiler Room Theater's archives.

Amy Stumpfl. (2005). 'Sights and smells: *Godspell* makes old new again.' March 31, 2005. *Nashville City Paper*. From the Boiler Room Theatre's archives.

Martin Brady. (2005). 'Holey Moses: Boiler Room's hilarious staging of a questionable script just might be miraculous.' *Nashville Scene*. June 23, 2005. From the Boiler Room Theatre's archives.

Amy Stumpfl. (2005). 'The sweet smell of success: BRT presents classic musical comedy.' *Nashville City Paper*. August 4, 2005. From the Boiler Room Theatre's archives.

Martin Brady. (2005). 'A Qualified Success: Despite some slow moments and a dated milieu, BRT's staging of a classic Broadway musical comedy entertains.' *Nashville Scene*. August 11, 2005. https://www.nashvillescene.com/arts_culture/a-qualified-success/article. (Accessed April 17, 2022).

Amy Stumpfl. (2005). 'BRT tames a Beast of a show.' *Nashville City Paper*. November 16, 2005. From the Boiler Room Theatre's archives.

Susan Leathers. (2005). 'Boiler Room does masterful job with *Beauty and the Beast*.' *Franklin Review Appeal*. November 23, 2005. From the Boiler Room Theatre's archives.

Ashley Northington. (2005). 'Local theater's latest show is quite THE BEAST.' *Franklin Review Appeal*. November 23, 2005. From the Boiler Room Theatre's archives.

Email from Caneta Hawkins to Lewis Kempfer. Subject: *Anything Goes*. February 7, 2006.

Amy Stumpfl. (2006). 'BRT opens sixth season with *Anything Goes*.' *Nashville City Paper*. February 8, 2006. From the Boiler Room Theatre's archives.

Chad Young. (2006). 'It's the Colosseum… The Louvre Museum… Baby, BRT's *Anything Goes* is the Top.' *Parent World.* January 31, 2006. From the Boiler Room Theatre's archives.

Peter Frost. (2015). 'I Am Spartacus.' *Culture Matters.* December 23, 2015. https://www.culturematters.org.uk/index.php/arts/films/item/2185-i-am-spartacus-by-peter-frost. (Accessed April 26, 2022).

Martin Brady. (2006). "A Fine Madness.' *Nashville Scene.* March 30, 2006. https://www.nashvillescene.com/arts_culture/a-fine-madness. (Accessed May 5, 2006).

Evans Donnell. (2006). 'Review: *Angel Street.'* *Backstage.* April 6, 2006. From the Boiler Room Theatre's archives.

Jamey Green, Lewis Kempfer. *Billy Bob's Holiday Hoedown.* Originally produced at the Boiler Room Theatre. 2007.

Martin Brady. (2007). 'Snowed Under: Boiler Room Theatre's holiday musical leaves much to be desired.' *Nashville Scene.* November 29, 2007. From the Boiler Room Theatre's archives.

Carole Robinson. (2010). 'Start spreading the news, Boiler Room Theatre is NOT closing.' *Williamson Herald.* June 30, 2010. Available at https://www.williamsonherald.com/features/business/start-spreading-the-news-boiler-room-theatre-is-not-closing. (Accessed May 29, 2022).

APPENDIX B

Season Schedules, Benefits, Grants, Awards

SEASON SCHEDULES

...

THE INAUGURAL 2001 SEASON

One Sensational Season

I Love You, You're Perfect, Now Change
Ruthless! The Musical
A Chorus Line
A Girl's Guide to Chaos
The 1940s Radio Hour

APPENDIX B

2002 SEASON

Around the World in Seven Plays

Baby, The Musical
Lucky Stiff
Little Shop of Horrors
Six Degrees of Separation
McBeth! The Musical Comedy!
Man of La Mancha
A Dickens of a Christmas Carol

. . .

2003 SEASON

Sentimental Journey

Guys and Dolls
The Musical Comedy Murders of 1940
Chicago
You're a Good Man, Charlie Brown
Cat on a Hot Tin Roof
Smoky Mountain Mist
The 1940s Radio Hour (remount)

. . .

2004 SEASON

Ignite Your Imagination

Gypsy
The Last Five Years
Hamlet! The Melancholy Dane! The Musical!
Sylvia
Nunsense
Sweeney Todd
That '60s Christmas Show

. . .

2005 SEASON

Classic Tales

Grease
Godspell
On Golden Pond
Epic Proportions
How to Succeed in Business Without Really Trying
The Secret Garden
Disney's Beauty and the Beast

. . .

APPENDIX B

2006 SEASON

Your Ticket to Adventure

Anything Goes
Angel Street
Forever Plaid
Almost a Midsummer's Night Dream
Big River
Cabaret
That '60s Christmas Show (remount)

. . .

2007 SEASON

Unlock the Magic

The Will Rogers Follies
Lucky Stiff (remount)
The Miss Firecracker Contest
And a Nightingale Sang
Urinetown
Into the Woods
Billy Bob's Holiday Hoedown

. . .

2008 SEASON

Thoroughly American (originally American Treasures)

Thoroughly Modern Millie (originally *Annie*)
Five Women Wearing the Same Dress
Assassins
The Complete History of America (Abridged)
Working: The Musical
Nuncrackers
Forever Plaid: Plaid Tidings

. . .

2009 SEASON

Season for the Senses

My Fair Lady
The Miracle Worker
Sunday in the Park with George
Picasso at Lapin Agile
Jesus Christ Superstar
Clue: The Musical
The Last Night of Ballyhoo / A Hard-Boiled Christmas

. . .

APPENDIX B

2010 SEASON

Tenth Anniversary

Fiddler on the Roof
The Fantasticks
Brighton Beach Memoirs
Nine: The Musical
Les Miz Two: A Tale of Two Cities
Rent
Christmas Belles

. . .

2011 SEASON

Be Entertained (originally Time Warp)

Annie Get Your Gun
Crimes of the Heart
I Do! I Do!
A Streetcar Named Desire
The 25th Annual Putnam County Spelling Bee
The Rocky Horror Show
Oliver! (originally *Annie*)

. . .

2012 SEASON

Magic to Do

Xanadu
Of Mice and Men
Next to Normal
Pippin
Steel Magnolias
Parade
A Year with Frog and Toad / Mrs. Cratchit's Wild Christmas Binge

. . .

2013 SEASON

Lucky Thirteen

Noises Off
Floyd Collins
Escanaba in da Moonlight
Promises, Promises
Who's Afraid of Virginia Woolf
The Producers
The Rocky Horror Show (remount; not part of season lineup)
Scrooge: The Musical

. . .

APPENDIX B

2014 SEASON (FINAL)

(no season schedule was announced)

Bonnie and Clyde (in Liberty Hall)
Legally Blonde (at the Franklin Theatre)

BENEFIT SHOWS/CONCERTS

The Boiler Room Bash (September 20, 2003; inside BRT)
Boiler Room Bash 2 (November 8, 2006; in Jamison Hall)
Melinda Doolittle and Friends (November 9, 2007; in Liberty Hall)
Boiler Room Broadway Blast (June 7, 2009; inside BRT)
Melinda Doolittle and Point of Grace (April 12, 2010; in Liberty Hall)
Nuns vs Plaids (year unknown; inside BRT)
Les Miserables (2013; in Liberty Hall)

GRANTS

Arts Builds Communities Grant (for *The Miracle Worker*, 2009)

Discretionary Grant through the Community Foundation of Middle Tennessee (2011, 2012)

AWARDS

2003 *Tennessean* Theater Awards
Best Supporting Actor—Tadd Himelrick in *You're a Good Man, Charlie Brown*
Best Supporting Actor—Dan McGeachy in *Cat on a Hot Tin Roof*
Best Supporting Actress—Lori Ellis née Eisenhauer in *Chicago*
Best Costume Design—Erin Parker for *Guys and Dolls* and *You're a Good Man, Charlie Brown*

2003 *Nashville Scene* "Best of 2003" Awards
Best Performance in a Musical—Lauri Dismuke née Bright

2004 *Nashville Scene* "Best of 2004" Awards
Best Director of a Musical—Jamey Green

2009 Sizzle Award—Best Live Theatre in Williamson County

2009 *Nashville Scene* "Best of 2009" Awards
Best Theatrical Impersonation of Jesus—Ben Van Diepen

2010 Sizzle Award—Best Live Theatre in Williamson County

2011 BroadwayWorld.com
Best Professional Theater; Best Musical; Best Director

2011 BroadwayWorld.com Nashville Awards
The Rocky Horror Show

Best Musical

Best Director of a Musical—Megan Murphy Chambers

Best Musical Direction—Jamey Green

Best Ensemble Performance in a Musical

Best Lighting Design

Best Set Design

Best Costume Design

First Night's Top 10 of 2012: Outstanding Theatrical Experiences
BRT Pressure Cooker

Special Note: The Boiler Room Theatre won several additional awards between 2010 and 2014, however, those web pages with award details have been removed or are no longer accessible. BRT received Best Play for 2011's *Of Mice and Men*; Best Music Director and Best Play for 2011's *The Rocky Horror Show*; Best Director for 2011's *Crimes of the Heart*; and Best Musical for 2013's *The Producers*.

APPENDIX C
Acknowledgements

Thank you to Lane Wright for his invaluable help with research.

Huge "thank-yous" go to the multitude of BRT cast and crew members who came forward with anecdotes and tales of how their involvement at the Boiler Room changed their careers and lives for the better. And my deepest gratitude goes to those folks who bravely turned their story into what I've called guest chapters. Many of these contributors had never written anything for publication before, but with loving encouragement, came through with heartfelt testimonials to BRT's influence.

Thank you to my beta readers Jake Cannon, Connie Landeck, Phil Perry, Daniel Vincent, Mancia Walker, David Warfle, and Lane Wright. And an extra thank you to Phil for helping craft the book's subtitle.

Thank you to my editor Paul Blane, who did such amazing work fine-tuning this book.

All my love to my parents who encouraged me to finish this book.

And thank you to all the friends who urged me to keep going with the creation of this book, echoing my own feeling that the story of the Boiler Room Theatre was not only worth telling, but necessary.

APPENDIX D
All the BRT People Ever

This is not intended to be a fully comprehensive list of all the people—casts, crews, theater staff, volunteers, and media partners. It was culled from 14 years' of programs and reviews, but to be sure, there are people who were missed. Often we enjoyed the help of volunteers painting sets or working as house managers, whose names never made it into a program. While the list includes the names of then-child actors in Mainstage shows, and there is likely a lot of crossover, it does not include the hundreds of children and teens who were enrolled in the Act Too children's theater program.

Adams, Jeffrey
Adams, Kate
Adams, Matty
Adams, Rob
Adams, Robert
Adams, Tyler Jeffrey
Adcock, Michael
Akin, Adele
Allen, Dennis
Allen, Kelly
Allen, Mark
Allen, Nancy

Allison, Greer
Amond, Laura
Anderson, Christopher
Anderson, Elaine
Anderson, Marie
Anthony, Cee
Ard, Elizabeth
Argo, Heather
Armstrong, Robert
Arnold, David
Atha, Pam

Austin, Brandy
Ayers-Sowell, Kay
Baker, Brooke
Baker, Doug
Baker, Laurel
Ballenger, Bethany
Banfield, Nina
Bank, Justin
Bargas, Lori
Basso, Chris
Bates, David
Baugher, Matt

APPENDIX D

Baum, Mike
Beall, Mark
Beam, Ashley
Beck, Allison
Bennett, Bruce
Bennett, Jordan
Berbee, Donna
Berk, Francine
Bernard, Karen
Bernard, Rachael
Berra, Nikki
Berryhill, Sandy
Best, Anna
Best, Morganne
Beurlein, Joseph
Bickel, Collier
Bielawski, David
Birdsong, Catherine
Bishop, Kelly
Bissell, Daniel
Blenharn, Lindsay
Blumanhourst, Aja
Blystone, Janet
Bodin, Brennan
Bolen, Ross
Bomar, Anne
Bond, Joshua
Bond, Tyler
Boone, Trish
Borderon, Marie-Vanel
Bourdet, Justin
Bouson, Michael
Bowen, Jama
Boyd, Justin
Boysen, Steve
Bradbury, Ellen
Bradley, Tevy
Brady, Martin
Brady, Phil
Brannon, Chelsea
Brazil, Travis Scott
Breland, Jennifer
Bridges, Pat
Bridges, Shane
Bridgette, Amanda
Bright, Doug
Broholm, Travis
Brooks, Stephanie
Brouillette, Paige
Brown, Jeremy
Bruce, Daron
Bryant, Jonathan
Bullard, Greg
Bupp, Corinne
Burke, Don
Burns, Colleen
Burns, Erin
Burns, Phillip
Burrus, Margaret
Busteed Singer, Keely
Buzz Kempfer, the dog
Byrd, Britt
Caldwell, Corey
Cameron-Bayer, Lynda
Candilora, Christina
Cannon, Jake
Cannon, Melissa
Carey, Bryttni
Carroll, Ann
Carrozziere, Rachel
Carson, Jefferson
Carswell, Colin
Carver, Lilly
Cavender, David O.
Chaffin, John
Chambers, Jack E.
Chambers, Trey
Cheney, Caley
Clark, Marianne
Clark, Maryanna
Cleveland, Joshua
Clevenger, Devin
Clubb, Kathryn
Coffer, Abi
Coffer, Katy
Coffer, Sadie
Coffer, Sue
Coleman, Joann
Conner, Bryce Nolan
Contreras, Billy
Cook, Paul J.
Cordes, Doug

Correia Stamps, Cathie
Correll, Joe
Cox, Allen
Cox, Gregg
Cox, Paul
Crabtree, Adam
Creech, Amanda
Crider, Lydia
Crist, Trish
Crockarell, Laura
Culberson, Josh
Cullum, Emily
Cunningham, Deanna
Currie, Kristin
Cyrus, Miley
D'Arco, Gina
Daddario, Victoria
Davidson, Bob
Davidson, John
Davin, Geoff
Davis, Douglas
Davis, Jeff
Day, Thomas
De la Torre, Annette
Dean, Olivia
Dean, Spencer
Delaney, Caroline
Delaney, Katie
DeMarcus, Thomas
Demerich, David
DeNuzio, Nick
Derminio, Andrew
Dewitt, Caleb
Diggs, Joel
DiGiorgi, Ashley
DiGiorgi, Mary
Dillard, Stephanie
Dismuke née Bright, Lauri
Ditty, Billy
Dobbins III, Van
Donnell, Evans
Doolittle, Melinda
Dorsey, Jaz
Doyel, Kymberly
Draggoo, Kelly
Drumheller, Andrew L.
Ducaj, Scott
Dunn, Bridget
Dunn, Chris
Dunn, Raven
Dyra, Hope
Dyra, Laura
Dyra, Luke
Dyra, Matthew
Eakin O'Neill, Elizabeth
Eberwine, Cat
Eberwine, Charlene
Eidam, Hope
Elkin, Leslie
Ellis née Eisenhauer, Lori
Ellis, Jef
Ellzy, Rena
Emerson, Deidre
Eppler, Nate
Ethridge, Emily
Evans, Jeremy John
Evans, Regina
Everitt, Ivan
Evick, Tyler
Fagley, Patrica
Fernandez, Sonia
Fields, Kashawn
Figueroa, Humberto
Fitzhugh, Tiger
Flautt, Anna
Flowers, Shelby
Fly, Aaron
Fly, Jordan
Ford, Kendra
Fortney, Alex
Fosse, Rosemary
Foster, Flynt
Fowler, Shea
Fox, Wesley
Frank-Gambill, Jennie Lee "Chicken"
Frank, Gus
Frazier-Maskiell, Scott

APPENDIX D

Freeman, Connie
French, Rose
Gahagan, Cameron
Gant, Katie
Gant, Paul
Gant, Sherry
Garcia, Erik
Gaspin, David
Gaspin, Heidi
Gatrell, Paul
German, Carolyn
Gibbs, Curtis
Gibbs, Lynda
Gill, Hayden
Gill, Lauren
Gillespie, Lisa
Glasgow, Ella
Godman, Lacee
Goeller, Heidi
Golden, Andrew
Goldsmith, Justin
Good, Kailey
Goodman, Douglas
Goodrich, Chris
Gottlieb, Jillian
Goude, Sarah
Graddy, Katherine
Green née Loibner, Letitia
Green, Barbara
Green, Corbin
Green, David Anthony
Green, Jamey
Green, Jim
Green, Joey
Green, Taylor
Greene, Teresa
Gregg, Jonathan
Guice, Abram
Gwinn, Brandon James
Haggard, Abigail
Haines Cantrell, Erica
Hall, Paige
Hamblin, Christopher
Hamilton, Cassie
Hamilton, Nathan
Hancock, Nathan
Hankins, Kyle
Harris, Jackson
Harton, Thomas
Hatfull Brooks, Reneé
Hayes, Dan
Hayes, Elizabeth
Heilman Runyon, Cristen
Heim, Jessica
Henderson, Jerry
Henry, Don O.
Henry, Stephen
Herr, Dale
Hess, Lindsay Terrizzi
Hicks, Madeleine
Hill, Brian
Hill, Rod
Hillaker, Don
Hillwig, Suzanne
Hilly, Charlie
Himelrick, Tadd
Hinchey, John
Hines, Holly
Hishida, Kazu
Hitchcock, Bryce Logan
Holden, Rebecca
Holder, Catherine Mai
Holder, Michael
Hollander, Stevie
Holloway, Stanley
Holman, Ford
Holman, Wanda
Holt, Kayla
Hood, Shivonne
Hosse, Wendy
Houston-Campbell, Anne
Howat, Andrea
Howell-Southworth, Teressa
Huber, Bill
Huff, Sarah Margaret

Hughes, Rozelle
Hunt, Ryan
Hutts, Sandra
Ingram, Ray
Ivey, Janet
Jacoway, Delaney
Janiszewski, Jaime
Jenkins, Christopher Thomas
Jennings, Carrie
Jennings, John
Jewel, Laura
Johnson, Jaclyn
Johnson, James Russell
Johnson, Mary Bea
Johnston, Hannah
Jones, Amy-Beth
Jones, Bill
Jones, Buck
Jones, Cassidy
Jones, Mia
Jones, Micky Scottbey
Jones, Penny
Jones, Piper
Jones, Stephen
Jordan, Emma
Jordan, Nick
Just, C. Anthony
Kaladimos, Demetria

Kalota, Liz
Kammerud, Jessica
Kaye, Bradley
Kearney, Isaiah
Keen, Bonnie
Keiningham, Titus
Kemp, D.D.S, David H
Kempfer, Lewis
Kennedy, Melody Dawn
Kilgore, Lee Beth
Kimbrough, Macon
Kincaid, Bill
King, Bakari
King, Wesley
Kircher Miller, Katie
Kirk, L.T.
Kitson, John
Kleine, Jennifer
Kloostra, Tara
Knott, Amy
Knowles, Anita
Knowles, JR
Kramer, Alex
Kramer, Patrick
Kraski, Debbie
Krikac, Kory
Kuxhause, Laura
Lacey, Nathan
Laemel, Corrie
Lahrman, Lyndsy

Landeck, Connie
Landeck, Jim
Langlois, Sabrina
Lasley, Will
Latremore, Rachek
Laughrey, Jason
Lawrence, Tyler
Layne, Sydney
Leavitt, Joe
Lebo, Megan
Lee, Alan
Lee, Olivia
LeHew, Calvin
Leonard, Addie
Leonard, Evelyn
Leopard, Bailey
Leopard, Becky
Levit, Joe
Levy, Abigail
Lewis, Jason-Edward
Lewis, Yoshie
Leyhue, Ryan
Lilly, Katrina
Lindley, Rebecca
Lipp, Carolyn S.
Lodholz, Virginia
Logsdon, Scott
Lohora, Emily
Lowery, Josh
Lynch, Austin
Lynn, Mark
Mackrell, Cana

APPENDIX D

Madden Adams, Melodie
Maddox, Alex
Malkin, Rick
Manka, Cara
Mann, Ella
Mann, Maarika
Manning, Martha
Marsh, Laura
Marshall, Blake
Matula, Laura
Mauldin, John
Maxwell (formerly Miller) née Westerman, Corrie
Maxwell, Jeremy
May, David
Mayo, Jesse
Mazzone, Marc
McCabe, Brabdon
McCall, Patricia
McCann, Colin
McCann, Zack
McCarthy, Ashley
McCarthy, Ciarán
McClain, Markus
McClendon, Devin
McCluskey, Molly
McConnell, Rachel
McCuiston, Angela
McDonough, Erin
McFarlin, Addison
McGeachy, Alice
McGeachy, Dan
McGinley, Tom
McHugh, Cari
McKendree, Allen
McKrell, Charis
McLemore, Terry
McNamara, Alexandra
McNeely, Carly
Meacham, Kate
Mead, Kevin
Meldrum, Landon
Mercer, Jess
Meyer, Jeremy
Meyerowitz, Daniel
Mihalek, Brooke
Miller, Chase
Miller, Jim
Miller, Kayte
Miller, Khan
Miller, Tom
Mire, Tyler
Missirian-Dill, Ohan
Mitchell, Kellye
Monday, Doyle
Moreale, Maggie
Morgan, Sarah
Morrison, Lark
Morse, Robin
Morton-Chaffin, Alexondra
Morton, Chris
Morton, Sondra
Moss, Stephen
Mothershead, Kyle
Motley-Fitch, Cathy
Mullen, Fred
Murphy Chambers, Megan
Murphy, Craig
Murray, Dante J. L.
Nappo, Antonio P.
Navarre, Valerie
Nelson, Cheyenne
Nettles, Julia Marie
Numinen, Don
Numinen, Mary
Nygren, Kim Thornton
O'Brien Green, Neely
O'Neal Brush, Evelyn
Oakley, Hannah
Occhiogrosso, Terry
Ochoa, José
Osborne, J. Dietz
Owen, Kristen
Oxnam, Brad
Parker, Erin
Partin, Grace
Peach, Art
Person, Jeff
Peters, Wilhelm

120 SEATS IN A BOILER ROOM

Pettit, Jeff
Pewitt, Rod
Peyton, Caroline
Phillips, Kacie
Phillips, Lucas
Phillips, Luke
Phillips, Shauntina
Phillips, Tracey
Picken, Tyson
Pippenger, Megan
Pisapia, Keri
Pizzi-Cage, Anna
Polk, Ashlie
Pope, Ashley
Pope, Micah
Pope, Noah
Popolo, Anthony
Porayko, Caitlyn
Porco, Luke
Presley, April
Proffitt, Lane
Pruitt née Whitney, Jessica Cristen
Pryor, Johnathan
Qualls, Russell
Raines Battle, Mary
Rajotte, Fran
Ramos, Luis
Ravelette, Jordan
Reilly, Pat
Reyland, Jim
Reynolds, Caleb
Reynolds, Madelyn

Rice, Scott
Richmond, Jennifer
Riggs, Andy
Roark, Michael
Roberts, Bob
Roberts, Brian
Roberts, James
Robinson, Joe
Robinson, Joseph
Roddick, Megan
Rogers, Brandy A.
Rogers, Lauren
Ropelewski, Deborah
Ropelewski, Frances
Ross, Tim
Rowlett, Erica
Roxy, the dog
Rudolph, James
Rudolph, Jay
Rushmore, Anna
Rychman, David
Sadler, Chesley
Sanchez, Tiffany
Sandoval Taylor, Katherine
Sasser, Layne
Schmidt, Tosha
Schoch, Sara
Scholes, Claire
Schwagel, Curtis
Scott, Aaron
Scott, Cela

Seage, Todd
Seaman, Chris
Seger, Harley
Sells, John
Sevier, Will
Shankle, Robby
Shaw, Peggy
Shepard, Kathy
Shepherd, Holly
Sheret Newman, Sylvia
Shipps, David
Shockley, Zach
Shuff, Ron
Shuff, Ron Jr.
Silengo, Melissa
Silvestro, John
Simmons, Michael
Simpson, Caroline
Skaug, Laura
Skinner, Jena
Smith, Alan
Smith, Deborah
Smith, Hailey
Smith, Jay
Smith, Jayme
Smith, Maggie
Smith, Robin Y.
Smith, Ryan
Smythe, Joe
Snodgrass, Daniel
Soltes, Fiona
Sparks, Linda

APPENDIX D

Speir, Linda
Spengler, Allie
Stamps, Cathie Correia
Stamps, Steve
Stanley, Ruth
Stapp, Annie
Stegall, Jen
Stemmler, Julie
Stepnieski, Doli
Stevenson, Alan
Steward, Scott
Stewart, Kirby
Stewart, Scott
Stonerock, Andrew
Stoub, Hane
Street Foust, Cary
Street, Pat
Strong, Memory
Stuart, Emilia Paige
Stumpfl, Amy
Suggs, David
Suico, Gabe
Suico, Terri
Sullivan, Jay
Sumner, Joshua
Tamble, Judy
Tant, Michael
Tant, William
Taylor, Matthew
Taylor, Thad
Thomas, Laura L.
Tines, Karrah
Todd, Cindy
Trabucco, Heather
Troutt, Jim
Truman, Joe
Tucker, Cate
Tucker, Joshua Jonas
Tudor, Jordan
Turner, Andrew
Van Diepen, Benjamin
Van Hook, Kenny
VanDyke, Jason
Vanlandingham, Mark
Vanosdall, Grant
Vaughn, Geri
Veglio, Katie
Vincent, Daniel
Vito, Ara
Wade, Tyler
Waldrop, Joshua
Wallace, Alex
Wallace, Alexandra
Wantiez, Darci
Ware, Taylor
Warfle, David
Warpinski, Joe
Warren, John
Warren, Lily
Weaver, Liam
Weaver, Seth
Webb, Chad
Webb, Isabel
Webber, Blair
Webber, Heather
Wells, David
West, Steve
Westbrook, Harry
White, Jennifer
White, Vicki
Whitehead Brown, Nancy
Whitehead, Anna
Whiting, Morgan
Whitlow, Emily
Whorton, Dan
Williams, David
Williams, Jan
Williams, Jeffrey
Williams, Melissa
Wilson, Alis
Wilson, Ashley
Wilson, John
Wilson, Kristin
Wilson, Scott
Winfield Sibrel, Bart
Wise, Tracy
Wlas, Bryan
Woelber, Bethany
Wofford, Reagan
Woodruff, Matthew
Woods, Kree
Worden, Tyler
Wright, Brian

120 SEATS IN A BOILER ROOM

Wright, Lane
Wright, Lisa Marie
Wyatt, Kim
Wyckoff, Bobby
Yamishita, Sage
Yarborough, Sloan
Yates, Lynn
Young, Amelia
Zappacosta née McNealy, Kara
Zeigler, Dan
Zeringue Pettet, Emily
Zimmerman, Brian

APPENDIX E

Corporate Sponsors and Advertisers

The Boiler Room Theatre was blessed with a multitude of corporate sponsors, donors, advertisers, media partners, and in-kind sponsors. This is not intended to be a comprehensive list. Undoubtedly, many other organizations lent a hand to BRT.

Allegra Design - Print - Mail
Allegra Print & Imaging
American Home Mortgage
American Tuxedo
An Original New Design Company
Andrews Cadillac
Aromatherapy Solutions
Arte Imports
Artisan Guitars
Arts.gov
B's Plants
BaRolo Catering
Baskin Robbins 31 Ice Cream & Yogurt
Bellevue Dance Center

Belmont University Little Theatre
Bluewind Art Bar
Bob Parks Realty
Bob Parks Realty
Bongo Java
Boxwood Bistro
Canton Chinese Restaurant
Carpet Den Interiors
Christopher & Banks/cj banks
Circa Antiques & Interiors
Community Foundation
Cook's Pest Control
Cookie Parcel
Cool Springs Galleria
Cool Springs Limousine

APPENDIX E

Cool Springs Paint and Decorating
Crye-Leike Realtors Leiper's Fork
Crystal Springs
Discount Plumbing and Electric Supply
Dr. Kellye N. Rice
DunzWorks
e+h Architects (Official Architects of the Boiler Room Theatre)
Enterprise Rent-a-Car
Establishment Jazz Orchestra, The
Examiner, The
Fairy Grotto
Fashion Cleaners
Fins of Franklin
Flashback Vintage Clothing
Flying Horse Restaurant
Foundations Recovery Network
Franklin Bone & Joint Clinic
Franklin Historic Presbyterian Church
Franklin Marriott Cool Springs
Franklin Review-Appeal
Franklin School District
Franklin Urological Consultants
FranklinIs…
FranklinLife
Gant Nation
Georgia Boot
Grace Cumberland Presbyterian Church
Green's Cabinets
Happy Tales Humane
Harpeth True Value Home Center
Hewitt Garden & Design Center
Hilliard Lyons—Nelson, Cavender & Graham
Holly Hines Photography
Home Depot
Hume-Fogg High School
Images by Heath
Jan Williams School of Music
JKelley Studios
John Cannon Fine Art
Judson Baptist Church
Juel Salon and Spa
Kemp Orthodontics
Lakewood Community Theater
Lee Company
Leipers Fork Cabinet Design
Lightning 100/Tuned In Broadcasting
Lithographics

Little Cottage, The
Lowe's
Main Street Antique Mall & Deli
Mallory Station Storage
Marble Design Concepts, Inc.
Mark English Gallery of Fine Art
Matteo's Pizzeria
Mercedes-Benz of Nashville
Mére Bulles Restaurant
Ming's Chinese Buffet
Moody's Tire & Auto Service
Nashville Public Library
Nashville Scene
NationLink Wireless
Nelson Mazda
Off Broadway Shoe Warehouse
OneHope Wine
OneSource Printing
Oxford Real Estate Company, The
Pam Lewis Foundation, The
Pargo's American Food & Sprits
Peniruth Ingram, CPA
People's Church, The
Performance Studios
Pinnacle Financial Partners
Pinnacle National Bank
Premier Fitness
Princeton's Grille
ProServ of Brentwood
Residential Services
Ptowtow.com
Pull-Tight Players
Query, The
RCC Western Stores
Reliant Bank
Rena C. Ellzy, Weichert Realtors, The Andrews Group
Robinson Taekwondo
Rodney Mitchell Salon
Rolling Hills Hospital
Saffire Restaurant
Shuff's Music & Piano Showroom
Shure Microphones
Silver Screen Productions
Simple Spaces Consulting
Sleeping Dog Productions
SmartDM
SmartReminders.com
Southgate Studio and Fine Art
Spectrum Antiques & Interiors
Spring Tree Media
St. Cecilia Academy
Stoveworks Restaurant
Stuttgart South
Sunnyside Entertainment

APPENDIX E

Sweet Shoppe, The
T.G.I. Friday's
Tell Me I'm Pretty
Tennessean, The
Tennessee Repertory Theatre
Third Coast Clay
Times Past & Present Antiques & Gifts
ToeToaster Technology
Treasure Trove
Triad Hospitals/Quorum Health Resources
Vecta Creative
Viction Media
WAMB Radio
Williamson A.M.
Williamson County Schools
Williamson Medical Center
Williamson Memorial Funeral Home & Gardens
Williamson Parent
WSMV
Yeoman's in the Fork

ABOUT THE AUTHOR

Photo © 2016 Martin Bentsen, NYC

Lewis Kempfer is an award-winning author and performing arts jack of all trades from Denver, Colorado. After completing his studies in print journalism at Arizona State University, he earned a development deal to be a country recording artist and relocated to Nashville. He co-founded the Boiler Room Theatre in 2000, where his design work eventually landed him a dream job with the Walt Disney Company in L.A. His 2019 literary debut of *Don't Mind Me, I'm Just Having a Bad Life: A Memoir* earned seven awards, including First Place for LGBTQ Biographies in the 2022 BookFest Awards; the 2021 Independent Author Network Book of the Year Award for LGBTQ; and the 2021 Indie Reader Discovery Category Award for LGBTQ Non-Fiction, among others. After three roller-coaster decades of fulfilling his dreams, Lewis returned to Denver, where he and his best canine mate, Marty McPug, make a dynamic duo.

Please visit LewisKempfer.com and BoilerRoomTheatreBook.com Reviews on Amazon and Goodreads greatly appreciated!

www.ingramcontent.com/pod-product-compliance
Lightning Source LLC
Chambersburg PA
CBHW070525090426
42735CB00013B/2866